Heinz-Dietrich Fischer

Touching Images of Delight and Sorrow

Pulitzer Prize Panorama

edited by

Prof. Dr. Heinz-Dietrich Fischer
(Bochum)

Volume 26

LIT

Heinz-Dietrich Fischer

Touching Images of Delight and Sorrow

Pulitzer Prize Winning Feature Photos

LIT

On the front cover, the upper photo, by Pulitzer Prize winners Ken Geiger and William Snyder, was published in the 'Dallas Morning News' on July 8, 1992.
The picture below, by Pulitzer Prize winner Anthony Suau of the 'Denver Post', was published on June 1, 1983.
The photo on the back-cover, by Pulitzer Prize winner Donald C. Turnley of the 'Detroit Free Press', was published on December 29, 1989.

Gefördert durch Mittel der Pressestiftung RWV, Essen

Bibliographic information published by the Deutsche Nationalbibliothek
The Deutsche Nationalbibliothek lists this publication in the Deutsche Nationalbibliografie; detailed bibliographic data are available in the Internet at http://dnb.dnb.de.

ISBN 978-3-643-91455-2 (pb)
ISBN 978-3-643-96455-7 (PDF)

A catalogue record for this book is available from the British Library.

Flössergasse 10
CH-8001 Zürich
Tel. +41 (0) 76-632 84 35
E-Mail: zuerich@lit-verlag.ch https://www.lit-verlag.ch

Distribution:

In the UK: Global Book Marketing, e-mail: mo@centralbooks.com
In North America: Independent Publishers Group, e-mail: orders@ipgbook.com
In Germany: LIT Verlag Fresnostr. 2, D-48159 Münster
Tel. +49 (0) 2 51-620 32 22, Fax +49 (0) 2 51-922 60 99, e-mail: vertrieb@lit-verlag.de

Preface

When Joseph Pulitzer (1847-1911) in his testament created the basis for the prizes named after him, he mentioned several awards groups in journalism and letters, but there was no Pulitzer Prize for newspaper pictures. It lasted until 1942, in the midst of World War II, that an award called „Photography“ was established for all kinds of press pictures. This general photo award was split into two separate groups in 1968, one of them named „Spot News Photography“, later renamed to „Breaking News Photography.“ The other new award group from 1968 on got the headline „Feature Photography.“

It was thought „for an outstanding example of feature photography in black and white or color, which may consist of a photograph or photographs, a sequence or an album.“ Today the award's title is shortened to this version: „For a distinguished example of feature photography in black and white or color, which may consist of a photograph or photographs.“ Unfortunately, there does not exist a precise definition that could help the jurors to determine the character of a feature photo. According to the Open Pen Photographic Society, „a feature photograph might be described as a news image that supplements the headline stories.“

The book at hand documents the Pulitzer Prizes for Feature Photography during the fifty two years of existence, located in the Pulitzer Prize Collection at Columbia University in New York City. In addition, Pulitzer Prize Administrator Edward M. Kliment made available the Feature Photography Jury reports from all the years, documenting the selection criteria by the committee members. The pictures are reproduced with reference to the „Doctrine of Fair Use“ as embodied in the United States Copyright Act. According to this doctrine, excerpts of copyrighted works may be reprinted when their use does not encompass a substantial portion of these works. So each winner is only represented in this volume by up to three photos. All Pulitzer Prize-winning works automatically become parts of the cultural heritage of the United States.

Ruhr University of
Bochum, Germany,
May 2021

H.-D. Fischer

In Memory
of

Karsten Thielker

(1965 - 2020)

The German Photographer was
a Member of the Associated Press Team
that won the 1995 Pulitzer Prize
for Feature Photography

Contents

Feature Photography Awards 1968 - 2020

1968 Award

THE FRUSTRATION OF AMERICAN SOLDIERS IN VIETNAM BATTLE FIELDS IN 1967

by TOSHIO SAKAI, *United Press International*

After they had finished the 1968 voting for the spot news award, the five jury members concentrated on the entries in the feature photography category. Finally, they presented the following six recommendations, listed in order of preference: 1. „Dreams of Better Times" by Toshio Sakai, *United Press International*; 2. „Loosers, Weepers" by Patrick Callahan, *Graphic Newspapers*; 3. A portfolio of „Non-cliche" pictures by Robert G. Lynn, *Cincinnati Enquirer*; 4. and 5. „Flower Power" and „In Praise of Children - Mississippi" by Frank Hay, *Washington Post*, and 6. Illustration for an entire edition of Pictures magazine devoted to „The Soviet Union - After 50 Years" by David Gulick, *St. Louis Post-Dispatch*. The Board accepted the jury's favorite and made Toshio Sakai the Pulitzer Prize winner.

In the previous year the Japanese photographer had crouched with the soldiers of the American B Company, about 40 miles northeast of Saigon. They were behind sandbags and mud banks, surrounded by deep jungle. It was Sakai's first tour of Vietnam, and later he remembered: „There was a commotion in the forest, then all became silent. Birds stopped chirping and insects quieted. My heart was beating fast. A tense atmosphere filled the air." Suddenly, shells exploded overhead, it was a Vietcong attack. The Americans returned the fire, then both sides stopped shooting, and Sakai remembered it as a moment of peace: „I saw a black soldier lying on the bunker and taking a nap. Behind him, I saw another white soldier holding an M-16 rifle, crouching and watching. The sleeping soldier must have dreamt of better times in his homeland. I quietly released the shutter."

Toshio Sakai, born an March 31, 1940, in Tokyo, Japan, graduated from Meiji University in Japan with a B.A. degree. He joined *United Press International* as a darkroom technician in 1964. Only one year later he already became an *UPI* staff photographer. From 1977 to 1985 Sakai was the news agency's chief Far-East photographer. The following year he joined the *Associated Press* in Tokyo. Three years later he left the *AP* and founded his own company, Woodstock Inc. Sakai also free-lanced for *Newsweek*, *Time* magazine and *Reuters*.

DREAMS OF BETTER TIMES

Photo, published June 22, 1967, depicts a scene from a camp of U.S. troops in South-Vietnam. The soldier in the foreground slept on a pile sand bags while his comrade in the background was watching guard. The two troops were of the First Army Division and rested after heavy sniper and mortar fire. They were wearing ponchos to stay dry even though the Monsoon was pouring ceaselessly.

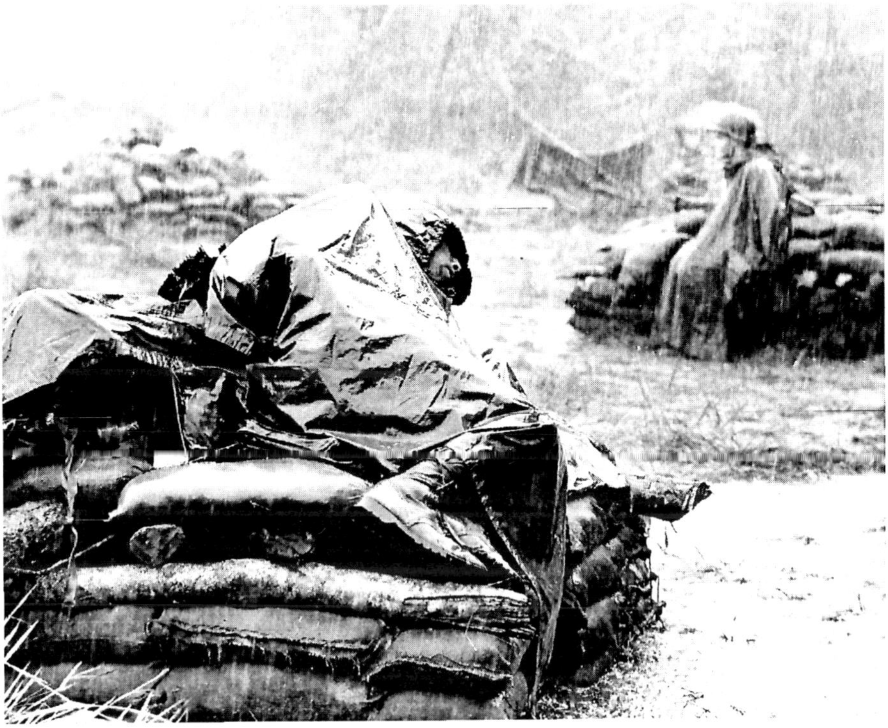

1969 Award

THE ATLANTA FUNERAL SERVICE FOR A MONUMENTAL BLACK LEADER IN 1968

by MONETA J. SLEET JR., *Ebony magazine*

The six jurors of 1969 provided a list of six finalists. They regarded the picture „Locked Out“ by Frank Johnston of *United Press International* as the most impressive submission, thus ranking it first. „This is a feature picture of a news event,“ the members of the jury pointed out, „it tells the story of a significant series of developments in American life ... in a single picture.“ Second place was given to „Mourning“, a series of photos of the funeral of Robert F. Kennedy by Ulrike Welsch of the *Boston Herald-Traveler*. Ranking third was „Biafra“ by Henry H. Gill of the *Chicago Daily News*, followed by „Pfc. Gibson Comes Home“ by John Fetterman of the *Louisville Courier-Journal*. The next ranks came to Roy Miller of *United Press International* and Fred W. McDarrah of *Village Voice*.

But the Board did not accept any of these six propositions and voted instead for a picture that ranked fourth on the jury's shortlist in the spot news photography category, thus awarding the prize to Moneta Sleet Jr. of *Ebony* magazine „for his photograph of Martin Luther King Jr.'s widow and child, taken at Dr. King's funeral.“ In the words of the jury, „this poignant photograph shows the strength of the woman, the comforting of the child and her dignity in the face of deep, personal grief. Although the picture was taken by a magazine photographer,“ the jurors added, Moneta Sleet „was acting as part of a press pool and his picture was widely distributed and printed in many American newspapers.“

Moneta J. Sleet Jr., born on February 14, 1926, in Owensboro, Kentucky, graduated from Kentucky State College with a Bachelor of Science Degree, finished School of Modern Photography in New York and received his M.A. degree in Journalism at New York University, From 1944 to 1946 he served with the U.S. Army as a Staff Sergeant in India-Burma. Sleet worked as an Instructor in photography at Maryland State College in Princess Anne from 1948 to 1949. The following year he joined the *Amsterdam News* of New York as a reporter. One month later Sleet was engaged by *Our World* magazine as a staff photographer, and in 1955 he switched to *Ebony* magazine. Sleet photographed many stations of the civil rights movement.

MARTIN LUTHER KING JR.'S WIDOW

Photo, published April 10, 1968, shows Coretta Scott King and her daughter, Bernice, at the funeral of her husband, Martin Luther King Jr. He was assassinated as he stepped out onto the balcony of his motel in Memphis, Tennessee. It was remarkable that a day prior he had assured people that he was not afraid to die, as he was confident that the oppression of blacks could be overcome one day in the future.

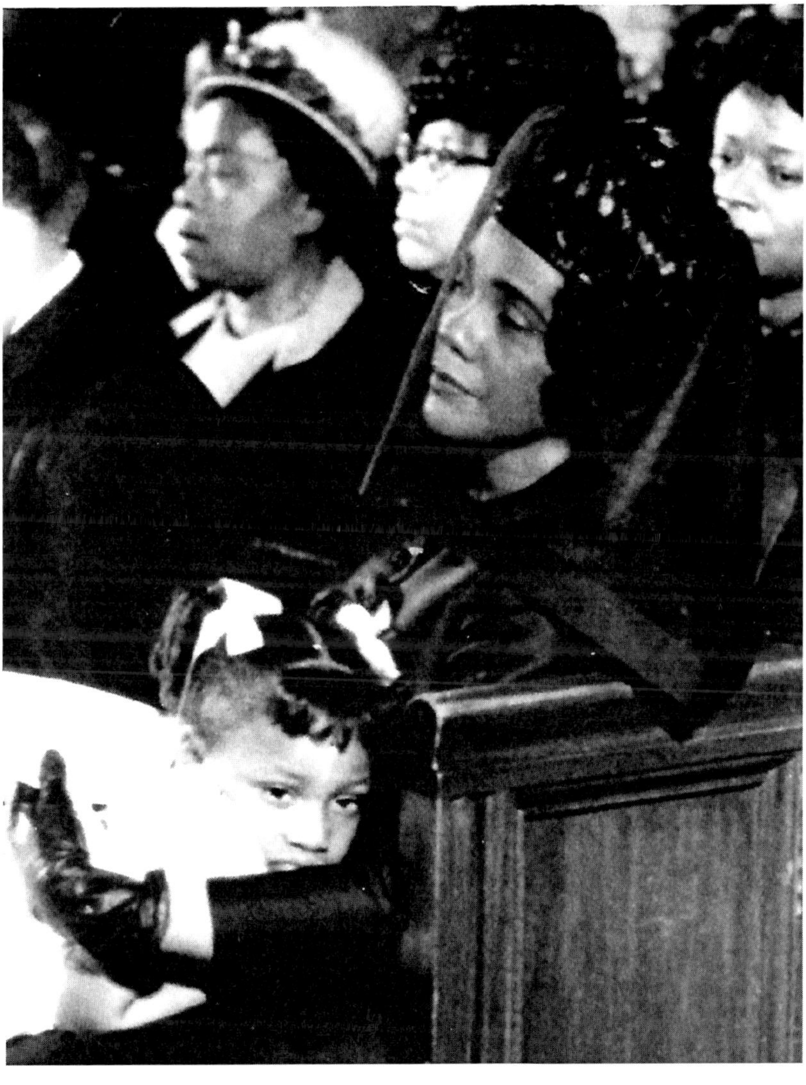

1970 Award

LIVING CIRCUMSTANCES AND POVERTY OF FLORIDA MIGRANT WORKERS IN 1969

by DALLAS KINNEY, *Palm Beach Post*

The 1970 judges chose four finalists, but the two entries chosen as First and Second, the report stated, „were not only quite close to each other in the jury's opinion, but far superior to Third and Fourth choices. First rank was given to a series called „Migration to Misery" by Dallas Kinney of the *Palm Beach Post*. „This photographer captured with extraordinary sensitivity the lives of Florida migrant laborers, as reflected in their faces and in their work", the jury report said. Second rank went to James Atherton of *United Press International* for a „picture of President Nixon and Premier Meir ... as a remarkable example of spontaneity, a happy moment in high places." Third place came to Duane Hall of the *Chicago Sun-Times*, and the fourth rank was given to Lynn Spenoe of the *St. Louis Post-Dispatch*, in both cases the photos dealt with sports actions.

The Board accepted the jury's proposal and declared Dallas Kinney the Pulitzer Prize winner. The photographer of the *Palm Beach Post* had documented in the past many aspects of the region. So he was stunned to discover „The Glades", an agricultural region just half an hour away from the city, where migrant workers labored all day in the fields. „I was an Iowa farm boy and I knew how much work these people were putting into it", Kinney expressed his feelings, „I was unbelievably impressed." He photographed the workers in the fields and at home. „They opened their doors to me", he remembered, „I didn't desire to say 'pity the poor,' but rather to show the strength of people who, through great adversity, were dedicated beyond belief."

Dallas Kinney, born an January 13, 1937, in Buckeye, Iowa, attended the University of Iowa. He started to work as a writer and photographer for the *Washington Evening Journal* of Iowa in 1964. He left the paper two years later and was engaged by the *Dubuque Telegraph-Herald*, Ia., and afterwards by the *Miami Herald*. In 1969 Kinney joined the staff of the *Palm Beach Post* where he got the post of a staff photographer. Later he spent a year with the *Philadelphia Inquirer*, then returned to the *Post*, where he became feature editor. Afterwards Kinney climbed up to president of Concept Associates, a marketing and communications firm.

CROP WORKERS IN FIELDS

Photo, published October 5, 1969, illustrates working conditions of migrant farm workers. They traveled with the harvest seasons from Florida up to Maine, working in the fields and picking any fruit or vegetable that was ripe. The majority of the migrant workers was black. A few years prior to this picture there were counted more than 450,000 workers of that kind in the U.S.

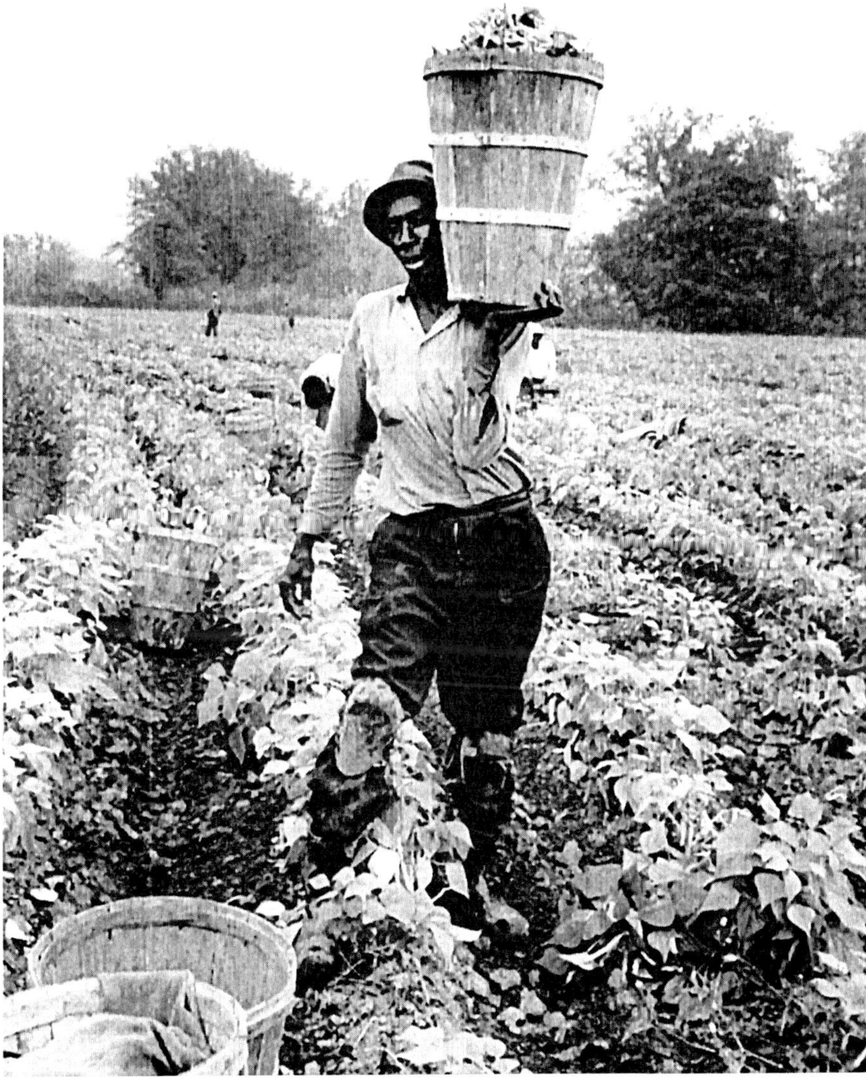

UNHEALTHY HOUSING CONDITIONS

Photo, published October 8, 1969, documents horrible living conditions of migrant workers at a quarter in Pahokee, Palm Beach County, Florida. Many migrant families were staying there from late fall until late January to wait for the next season to begin. The one-room sheds did not have any sanitary facilities. Up to 38,000 migrant workers lived temporarily in the area.

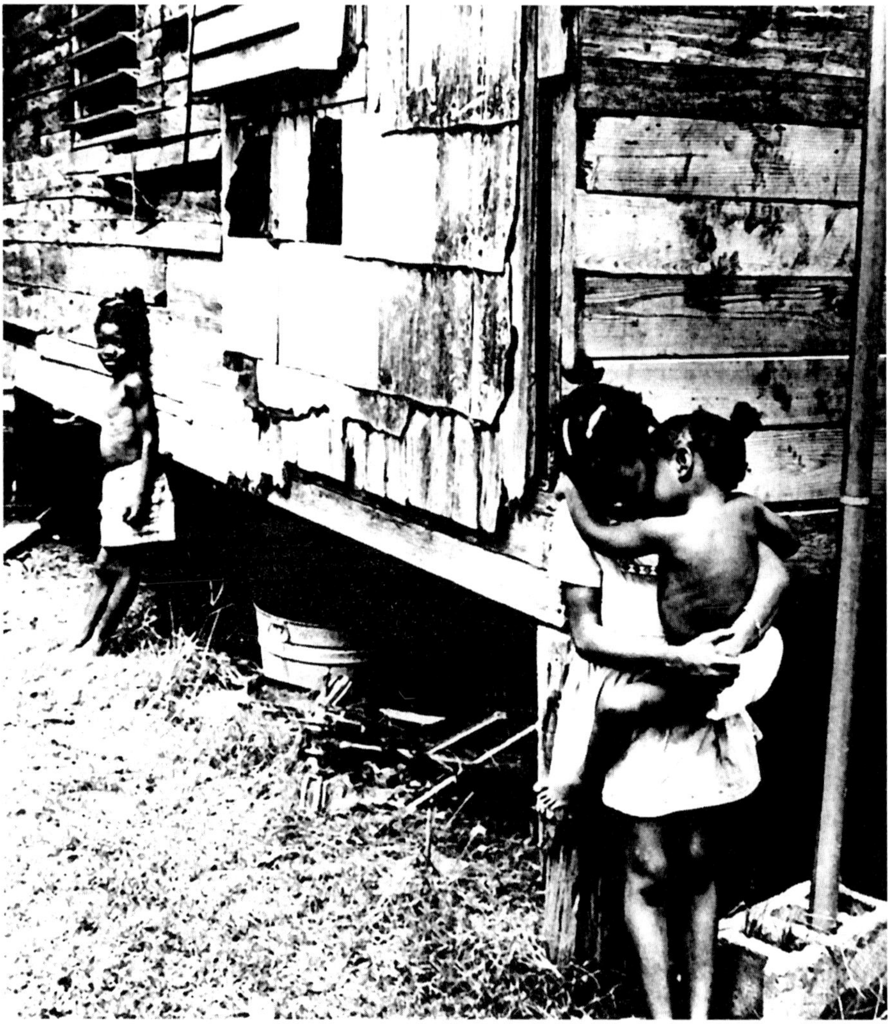

RESTING SENIOR CITIZENS

Photo, published October 8, 1969, shows three retired female migrant workers in Palm Beach County, Florida. They had been traveling with the other farm workers up and down the east coast for all their lives and at an average earned $ 922 per year. Now they were receiving less than $ 80 per month from the government, allowing them only to rent a shack.

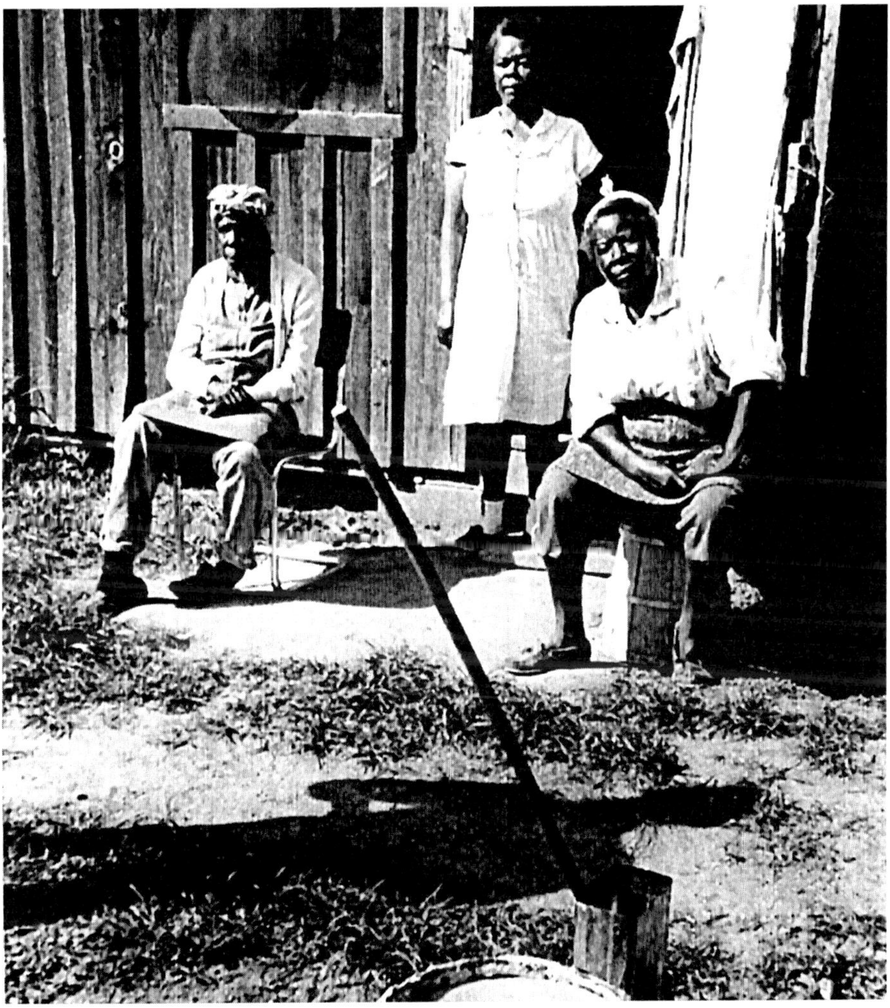

1971 Award

CONDITIONS AT ILLINOIS STATE SCHOOLS FOR THE RETARDED IN 1970

by JACK W. DYKINGA, *Chicago Sun-Times*

The jurors' comments on the three finalists of 1971 were very brief, as the report does not give either the names of the photographers or the medium they worked for. The jury members unaninously recommended, without stating a prefer- ence, two entries of „technical excellence, sensitivity and compassion" and a third choice without any details. One entry, about two Schools for Retarded, was called „an excellent example of a universal, but nevertheless local problem". The other entry had captured „big and little human experiences under the stress of war." The award went to Jack Dykinga of the *Chicago Sun-Times* „for his dramatic and sensitive photographs at the Lincoln and Dixon State Schools for the Retarded in Illinois."

Photographer Dykinga and two reporters had spent four days in two state schools for the retarded to show what life was like in an institution where chronic underfunding had created horrific conditions for the patients. The school officials cooparated, Dykinga remembered, „they were doing what they could, but they didn't have any money. They wanted to put pressure on the governor." Shooting photographs in such a situation, Dykinga said, „is instinctive. You're on cruise control. Afterwards, you have the dreams and nightmares. I can still smell how it smelled."

Jack W Dykinga, born on January 2, 1943, in Chicago, Illinois, started his career with the Metro News Photos Company in 1962. While studying at Procopius College in Lisle, I1., from 1964 to 1965 he was engaged by the *Chicago Tribune*. Then he attended Elmhurst College and switched to the *Chicago Sun-Times* where he took the post of an editorial photographer in 1975. The following year he moved to the *Arizona Daily Star*, but in 1981 he changed his profession and became President of the Southwestern Wilderness Travel and committed himself to the natural world. He still used his ability as a photographer and made pictures on environmental issues in southwestern U.S.A. and Mexico. He brought out quite a number of books on those aspects, like „Frog Mountain Blues", „The Somoran Desert", „The Secret Forest" or „Stone Canyon of the Colorado Plateau."

OVERCROWDED SLEEPING COTTAGE

Photo, published July 26, 1970, depicts a sleeping ward, also called cottage, with many more beds than would be usual. The ward was part of the Lincoln and Dixon state schools for the mentally retarded in Illinois. The schools were the two biggest institutions of that kind in Illinois and in a rather desolate condition, since the state govemment was not providing them with a sufficient budget. Each nurse and child-care assistant had to take care of 25 to 112 children.

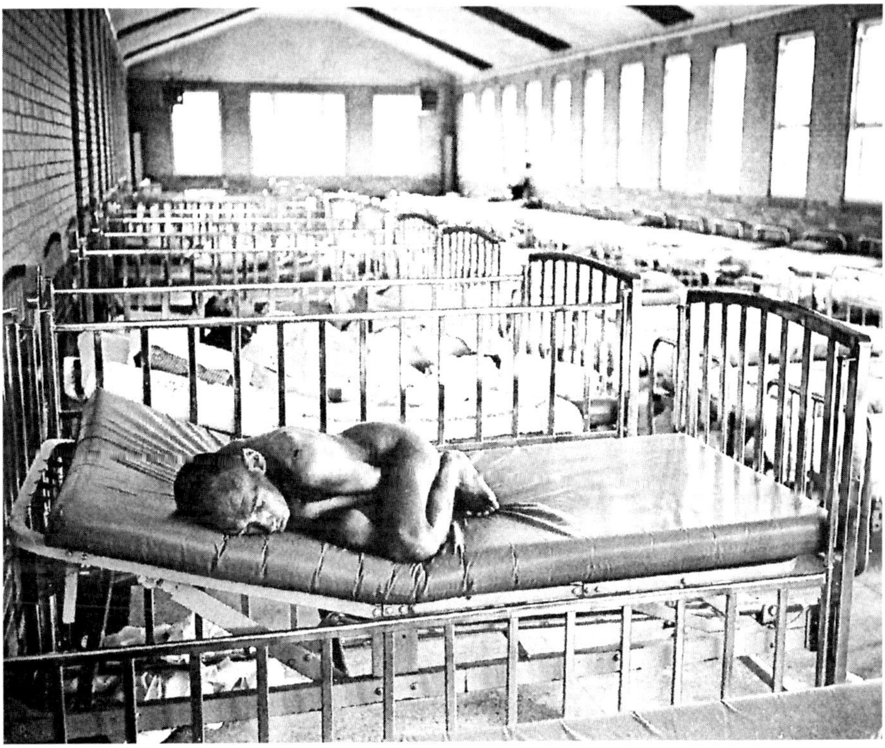

APATHETIC WHEELCHAIR GROUP

Photo, published July 26, 1970, illustrates the conditions under which the students had to live in the school for mentally retarded of Lincoln and Dixon state schools in Illinois. The students were left to themselves for hours as the schools suffered from major shortages in funds and staff. Although the number of students had been reduced in the years before, the situation had not improved.

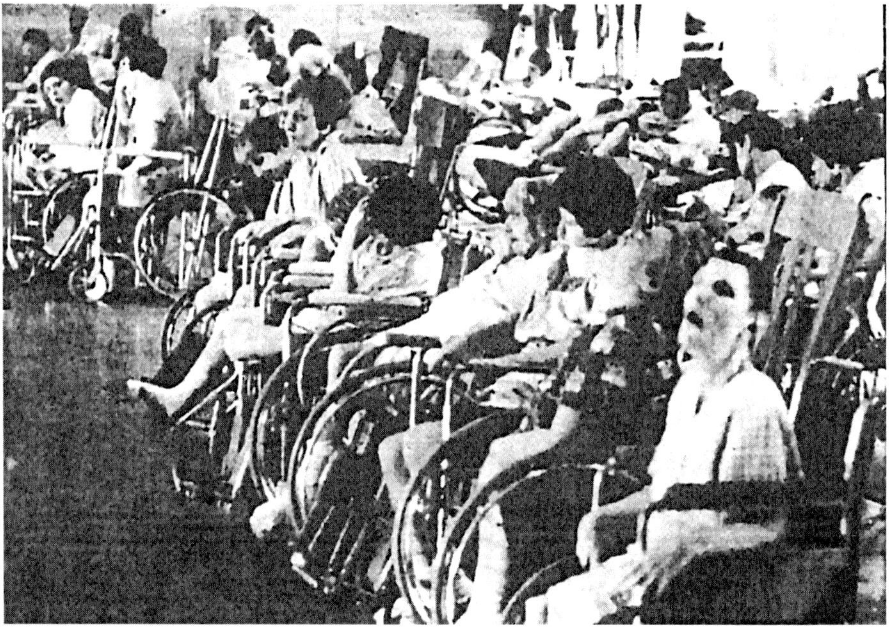

RESIDENTS IN THE DAY ROOM

Photo, published July 27, 1970, shows the students of the Lincoln and Dixon state schools for the mentally retarded spending their day in a hall by themselves. There was not enough funding to hire more staff to care for them, and not enough money for more therapeutic materials either. The residents often sat around for hours. Some of them were only half-clothed or fully naked.

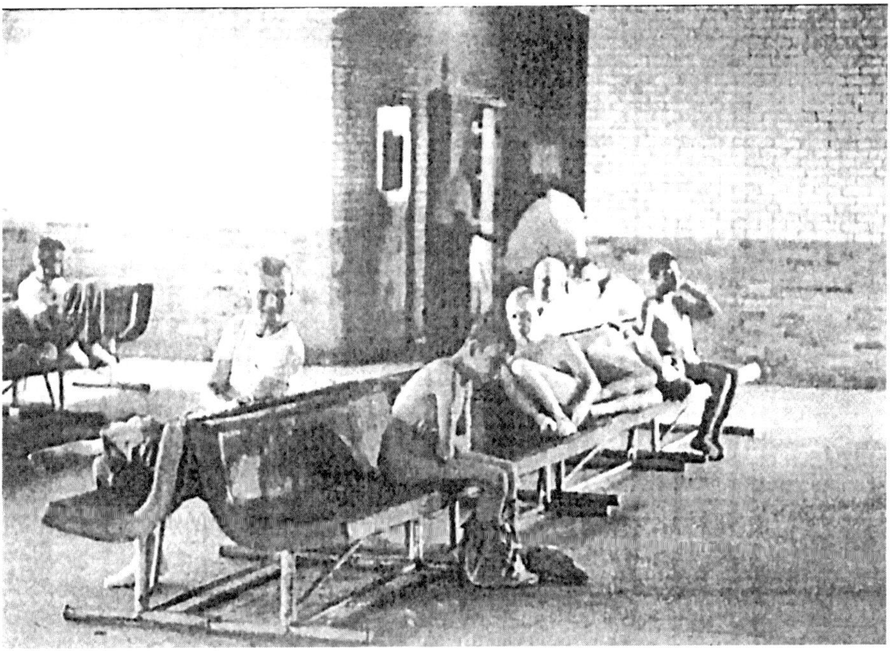

1972 Award

SEVERAL DISCOURAGING FACTS ON THE VIETNAM WAR IN 1971

by DAVE H. KENNERLY, *United Press International*

After sifting through the entries, the jurors of 1972 had quite a few difficulties in agreeing on a clear favorite for that prize. That led to a compromise declaring a first and second place tie, without deciding in favor for or against one of the two photographers in question. Eddie Adams of the *Associated Press* was called by the jury „a photographer who gets movements and meaning into his work, and he frames his photographs with an artist's feel for proportion." Dave Kennerly of *United Press International* had submitted „Vietnam war pictures", acclaimed by the jurors as „a work of art, he captures the story and the drama of the desolation of war; he knows exactly when to snap the trigger." Third rank was given to Erwin Gebhard of the *Milwaukee Journal*, fourth to Ovie Carter of the *Chicago Tribune*, followed by John White of the *Chicago Daily News* as fifth on the shortlist.

The Board was most impressed by the work of Dave Kennerly and therefore made him winner of the Pulitzer Prize „for his dramatic photographs of the Vietnam war." He photographed something beyond battles and bombings. „I took a lot of pictures of bodies and people dying," Kennerly remembered, „but I think the feature side ... , those are some of the best." One photo in particular captured the barren devastation of the war: „I was up in an area where there had been a lot of fighting and the fighting had subsided," Kennerly said, „I was on another hill and saw that soldier walking. To me, that was more the war I saw, in terms of the day-to-day scene. I captured the loneliness and desolation of war."

David H. Kennerly, born on March 9, 1947, in Roseburg, Orgeon, studied at Portland State College from 1965 to 1966 while working for the *Lake Oswego Review*. The photographer then joined the *Portland Oregon-Journal* but switched to *The Oregonian* in 1967. In the same year Kennerly was engaged by *United Press International* where he worked in the Los Angeles bureau from 1967 to 1968, the following year in New York City, and the next station was Washington, D.C. Finally he was assigned to Saigon in 1971. In the following years Kennerly worked for *Life* magazine and *Time* magazine before he joined *Newsweek* as a contributing editor in 1996.

SOLDIER MOVES AMID SHATTERED TREES

Photo, published May 9, 1971, shows an American soldier carefully making his way through a devastated jungle as he approaches a Vietcong dugout. The jungle had been ruined by the Napalm bombs and the ceaseless fighting during the Vietnam War that took place there as long as the vegetation was still intact and soldiers of both sides could hide in it.

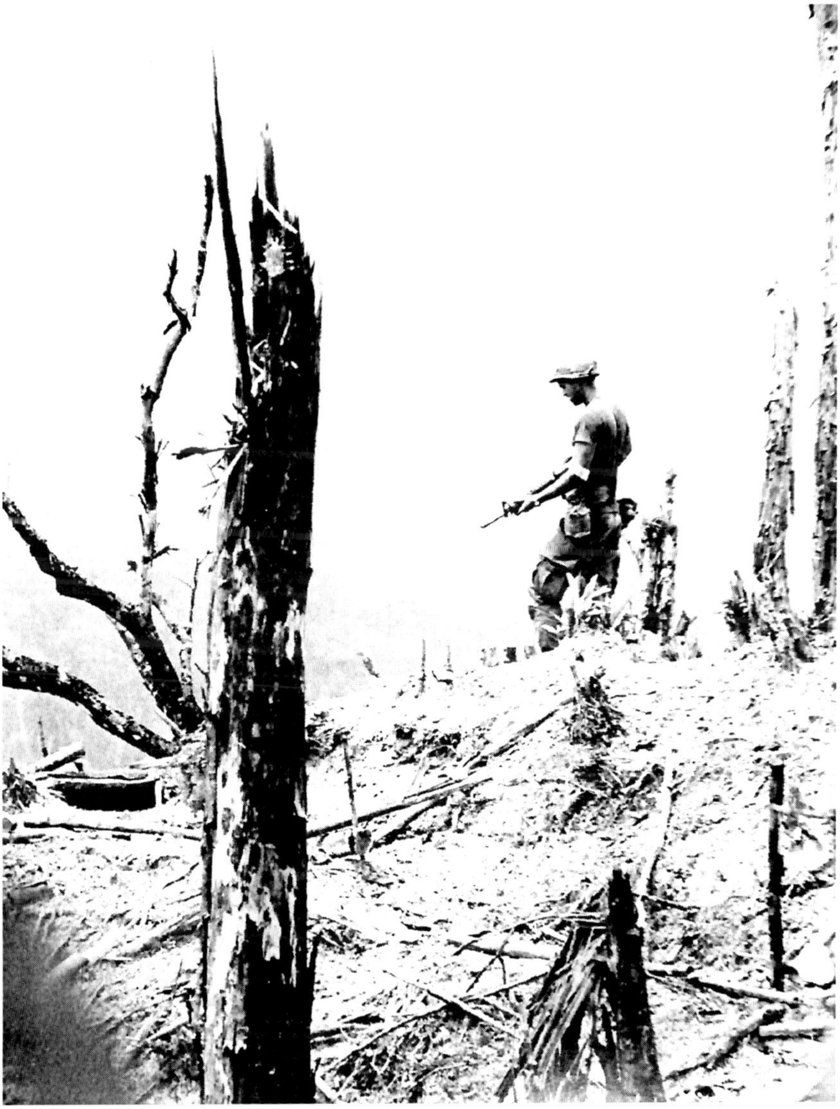

PROTEST OF DISABLED SOUTH VIETNAMESE VETERANS

Photo, published September 8, 1971, depicts a disabled South Vietnamese veteran who discards his artificial limb and sits down in street during a protest days ago. Some thirty disabled veterans waved their artificial limbs at bystanders in front of the Veterans Ministry demanding government aid which had been delayed because of red tape.

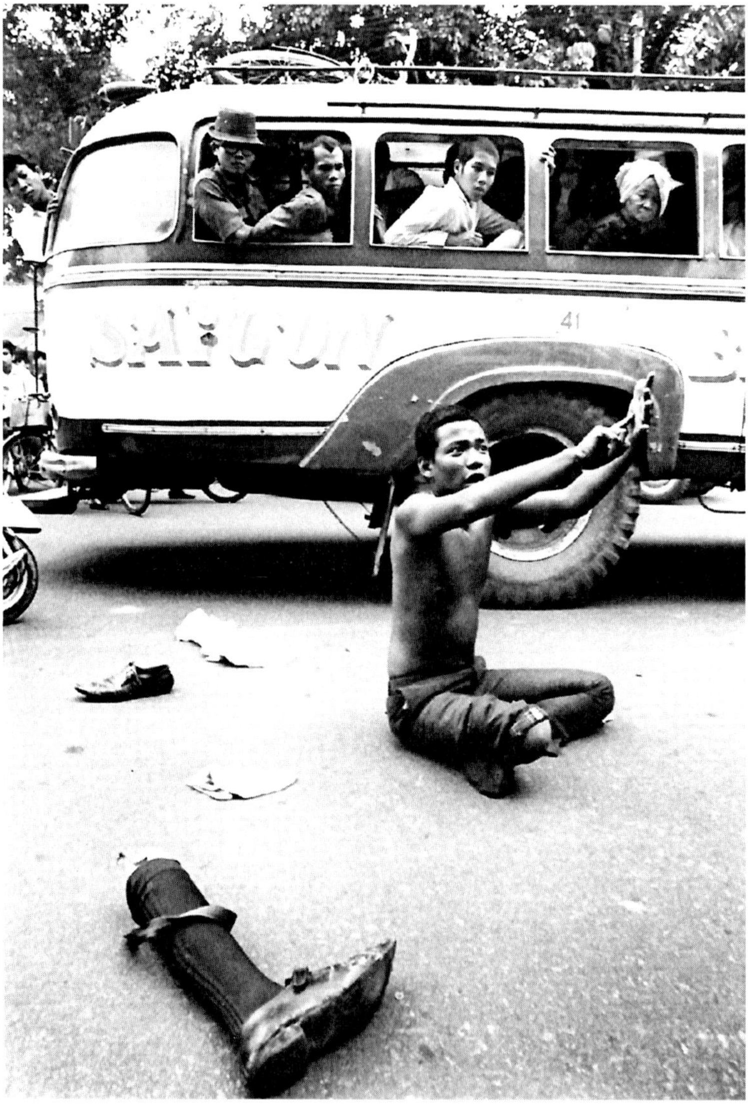

WOUNDED SOUTH VIETNAMESE SOLDIER

Photo, published October 6, 1971, shows how a wounded South Vietnamese soldier is carried to safety by his buddies in Krek, at the edge of the South Vietnamese-Cambodian border. In a combat situation which was termed the biggest single battle in four months, the North Vietnamese and the Vietcong had lost an enormous number of soldiers, estimated at about 350. South Vietnamese troops were later reported to chase the remaining soldiers of North Vietnam and the Vietcong.

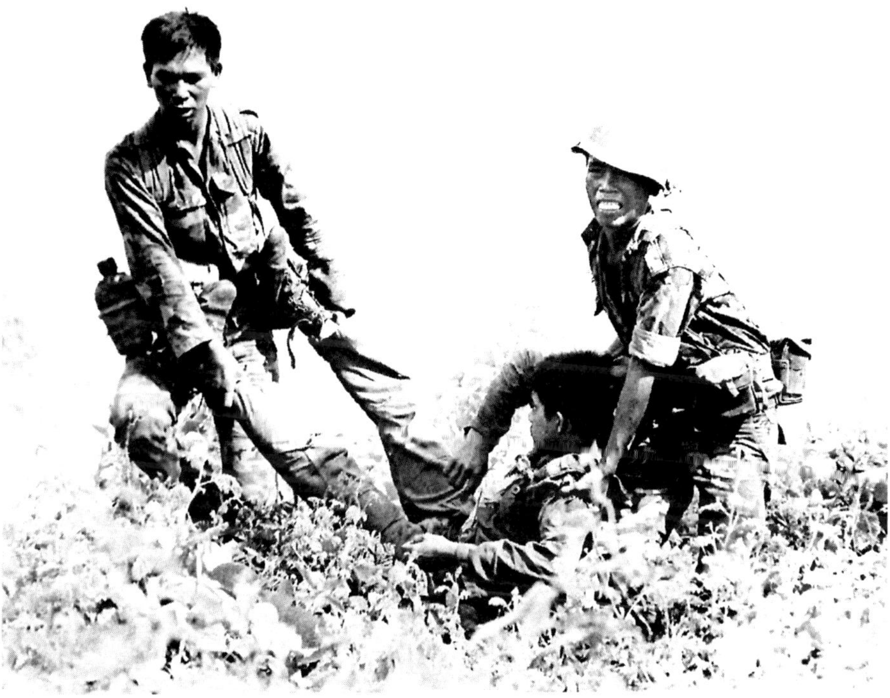

1973 Award

WITNESSING THE BIRTH OF A CHILD IN MIDDLE AMERICA IN 1972

by BRIAN T. LANKER, *Topeka Capital-Joumal*

Like in the spot news category, the jury's remarks about the topics and motifs of the favored 1973 entries in this award group were just as brief. With regard to the works ranking first the jury report did not even state a theme, only pleading for a „joint award“ for Dan Robinson and J. Walter Green. Although both photographers obviously worked for different news media, they had submitted „almost identical shots. Both were in position, both had the idea, and there was only split-second timing between execution.“ A picture with the title „Frog Jumping“ by Walter Zeboski „was our second choice on account of the photographer's ability to capture the spontaneity of the 'coach' urging her entrant on to victory,“ the jurors said, whatever that meant.

The jury had put in third place a photograph by Brian Lanker called „Childbirth“, which was selected by the Board as the Pulitzer Prize winner. Lanker, a photographer at the *Topeka Capital-Journal*, had decided to do a feature about the Lamaze method of childbirth. It took him six months to find a couple willing to be photographed. So Lanker and his camera were in the delivery room with the couple. „During early labor,“ Lanker remembered, „it was obvious to them that I was there. But later on, you have a bunch of doctors and nurses and I was able to blend in ... I was so taken and moved by the whole experience. You're so caught up with the moment and the emotion - fortunately, your professionalism and artistry take over and allow you to do the work while you're experiencing this incredible moment.“ Finally, the baby, a girl, made her appearance, and Lanker's camera captured the moment in several photographs.

Brian T. Lanker, born on August 31, 1947, in Detroit, Michigan, joined the staff of the *Phoenix Gazette* as a photographer in 1966. While working in his job he studied at Phoenix College from whieh he graduated the following year. In 1969 Lanker switched to the *Topeka Capital-Journal*. Beside numerous Regional Photographer of the Year awards he was named National Newspaper Photographer of the Year in 1970. One year after winning the Pulitzer Prize he left the *Topeka Capital-Journal* and moved to the *Eugene Register-Guard* where he served as Director of Graphic Services since 1974.

PREPARATION IN A STERILE HOSPITAL ROOM

Photo, published February 6, 1972, shows Mr. and Mrs. Jerry Joe Coburn prepare for the delivery of their baby in the St. Francis Hospital in Topeka, Kansas. Only recently had the hospital begun to offer a new way of delivery, which was known as the Lamaze method. The most important feature of this method was that the husband was assisting bis wife in the delivery room.

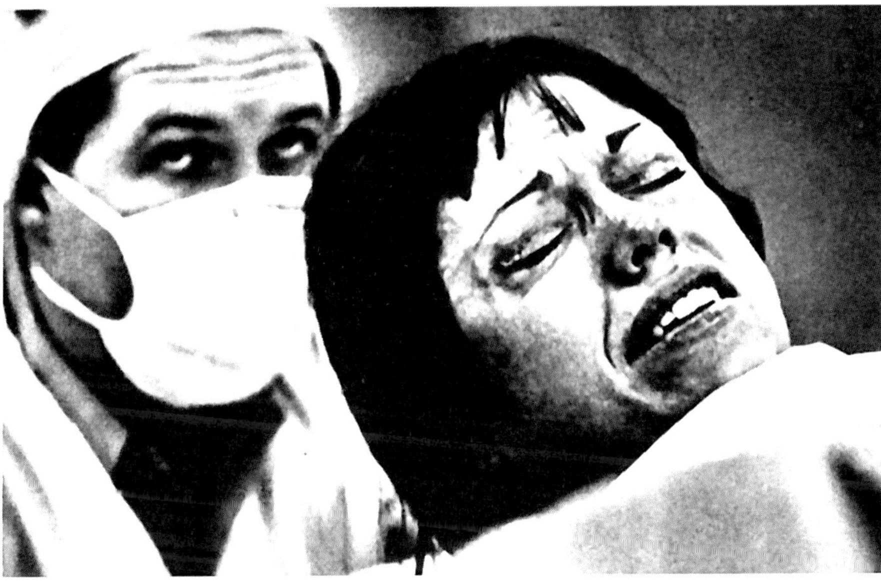

MOMENT OF JOY AFTER THE DELIVERY

Photo, published February 6, 1972, documents the joy and relief of Lynda Coburn who had just delivered her daughter, Jacki Lynn. It was the first child for the Coburns. Her husband, Jerry, who had been assisting her throughout the labor was holding her hands. Just moments before, she had strained every muscle to push the baby out of her body.

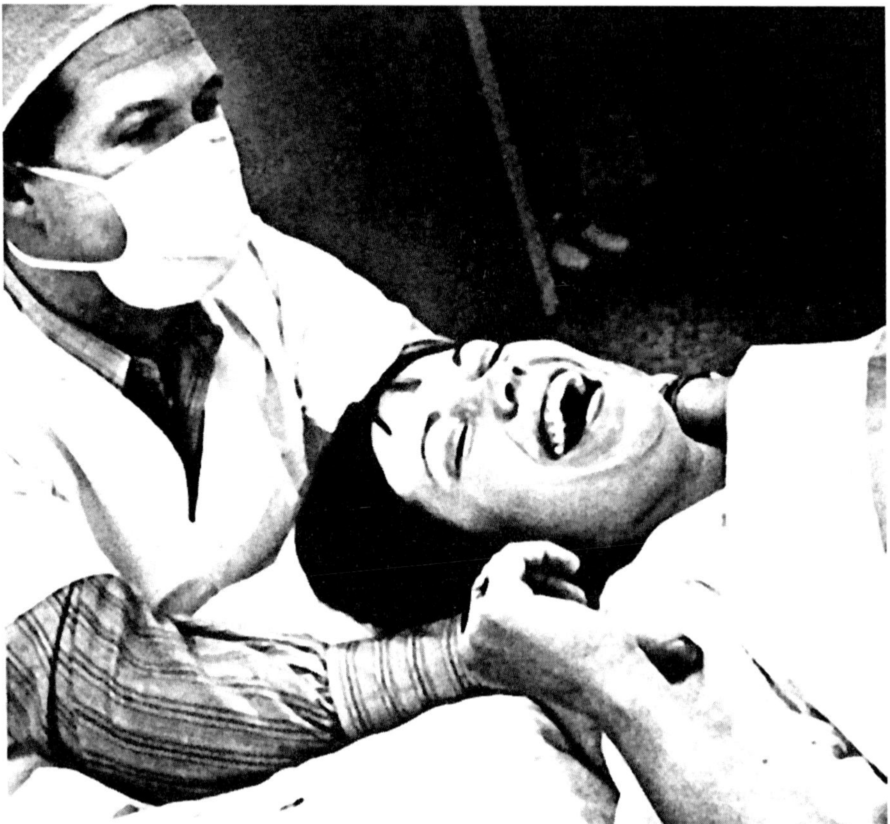

THE BABY GIRL SHORTLY AFTER HER BIRTH

Photo, published February 6, 1972, shows newly born Jacki Lynn Coburn who attended precisely at 11:45 a.m., on Thursday, January 27, 1972, in the St. Francis Hospital in Topeka, Kansas. The birth had been without any complications. Afterwards the father, Jerry, said that he had not thought that it would have moved him so much. Naturally, he had been nervous about going into the delivery room.

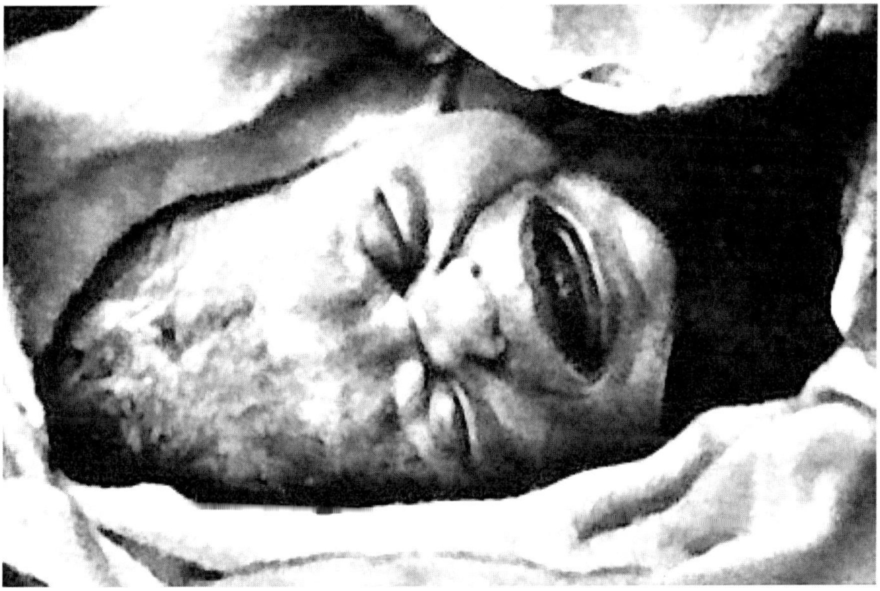

1974 Award

RETURN OF AN U. S. SOLDIER FROM A NORTH VIETNAMESE PRISON CAMP IN 1973

by SLAVA J. VEDER, *Associated Press*

Like in the spot news category, the 1974 jurors of this group also presented to the Board a list of six finalists, but in several cases the report did mention the topic of the respective entry, so that the Board received a few more details than in the other photography award group. The jury's shortlist read as follows: 1. „Cat Woman" by Don Bierman of the *Chicago Daily News*; 2. „Man With Bottle" by John H. White of the *Chicago Daily News*; 3."*Associated Press Package*", including a photo by Slava Veder; 4. „*Milwaukee Journal Package*" by Erwin W. Gebhard; 5. „Wounded Knee Altar" by Max Winter of the *Dubuque Telegraph-Herald*; 6. „Ballerina" by Arthur Ellis of the *Washington Post*.

Once again the Board did not heed the advice of the jury, because it choose the photographer ranking third, Slava Veder of the *Associated Press* package, „for his picture of the return of an American prisoner of war from captivity in North Vietnam." Veder had waited at Travis Air Force Base where families were about to be reunited with long-absent soldiers. „To see them come home brought tears to a lot of people's eyes," Veder remembered, „some of the photographers were pretty well shaken up, as I was, too. There was motion." When a Colonel arrived, „the family had started to run toward him, and that's what caught my eye." Veder raised his camera and clicked the shutter.

Slava J. Veder, born on August 30, 1926, in Berkeley, California, attended Modesto Junior College, the College of the Pacific, Diablo College and Sacramento State College. Since 1945 he did several jobs such as a fireman for the Martinez Fire Department in California, sportswriter for the *Richmond Independent* or working for the Oakland Ice Hockey Club. Veder joined the newsroom staff of the *Alameda Times-Star* in California from 1949 to 1952. He then switched to the *Tulsa World* where he worked as an assistant of the Sunday editor for four years. In 1956 Veder joined the *Concord Transcript*, switched to the *Pittsburg Post-Dispatch* and then worked for the *Oakland Tribune* as a copy editor. The photographer started to work for the *Accociated Press* on free-lance basis and joined the *AP* bureau in Sacramento in 1961 and later was transferred to San Francisco.

BURST OF JOY

Photo, published March 18, 1973, captures the moment of a soldier returning to his family. Lieutenant Col. Robert L. Stirm of the U.S. Air Force had been a prisoner of war in North Vietnam for five years. He was greeted by his wife Loretta and his four children, Lori, Robert, Cynthia and Roger. Together with twenty troops who arrived in the United States on that day, Stirm had been shot down with his bomber and kept in prison.

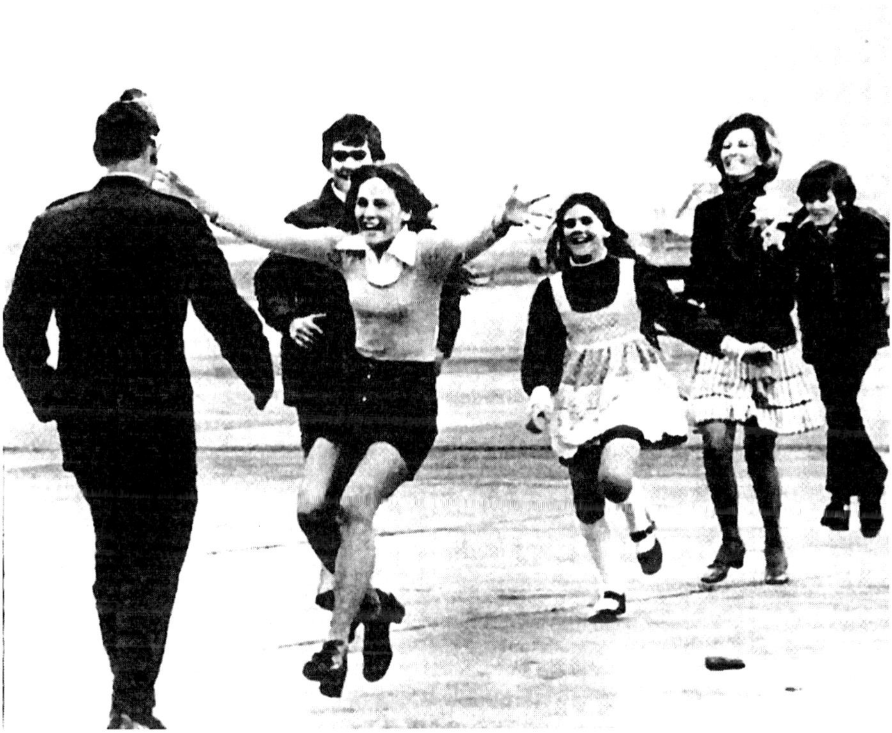

1975 Award

SEVERAL MEMBERS OF THE WASHINGTON ESTABLISHMENT IN 1974

by MATTHEW LEWIS JR., *Washington Post*

The jury of 1975 had a clear favorite, stating in its report that Matthew Lewis of the *Washington Post* should earn the prize. The jurors were „unanimously enthusiastic about the consistently high achievement of this photographer's work, which is characterized by photographic excellence, remarkably versatility, and high intelligence. The work has also been exceptionally well served by its display in the newspaper," the jury report stated. After this commendation, the report continued, „the jury also felt that other submissions of very high quality" included: Earl Seubert of the *Minneapolis Tribune* with a photo of a „woman gleaning rice from the dirt of an unloading area in Cambodia". Larry Spitzer of the *Louisville Courier-Journal* had shot „the aftermath of a tornado graphically shown by the reactions of victims." Ovie Carter of the *Chicago Tribune* was praised „for overall excellence in the presentation of hunger in Africa and India."

Due to the unanimous praise from all members of the jury, the Board did not hesitate to supporrt their reasoning and bestowed the award on Matthew Lewis „for his photographs in color and black and white", all of which depicted various aspects of „the Washington life-style." Lewis had tried to show many facets of the nation's capital, published in the *Washington Post*'s Sunday magazine, *Potomac*. Coaxing some of the city's busy citizens to sit for the camera was difficult. The press secretary of President Richard Nixon, for example, gave Lewis only 20 seconds, and the photographer fired off just five frames. But Lewis not only photographed celebrities but also many other ordinary people in town.

Matthew Lewis Jr., born on March 8, 1930, in McDonald, Pa., was educated at Howard University in Washington, D.C., in 1947. The following year he studied at the University of Pittsburgh. Lewis served with the U.S. Navy as a hospital corpsman from 1949 to 1952. He started to work as an instructor at the audio-visual department of Morgan State College in Baltimore in 1957. He did this job for eight years. Afterwards Lewis joined the *Washington Post* where he worked as news photographer and later on as magazine photographer. After his retirement he worked for the *Thomasville Times* in Georgia.

TV ANCHORMAN

Photo, published on February 17, 1974, shows David Brinkley who was one of the most prominent Washington-based TV anchormen und commentators on election night coverage. Because of his critical commentaries, he was on Richard Nixon's enemy list during the Nixon Presidency.

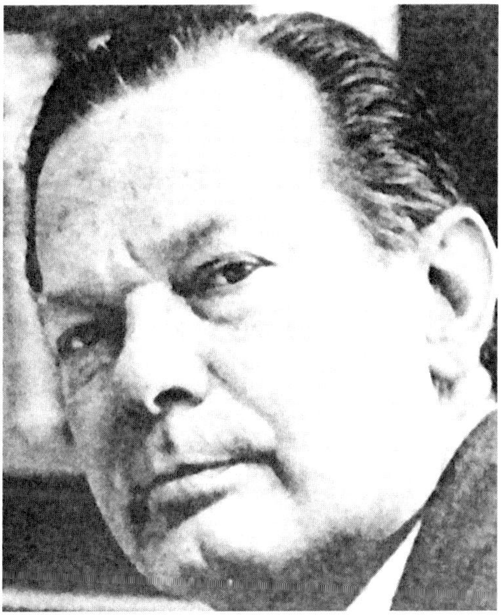

ATTORNEY GENERAL

Photo, published July 7, 1974, shows William B. Saxbe who took over as U.S. Attorney General in early January 1974, when the administration of President Richard B. Nixon was consumed by crisis in connection with the Watergate Affair.

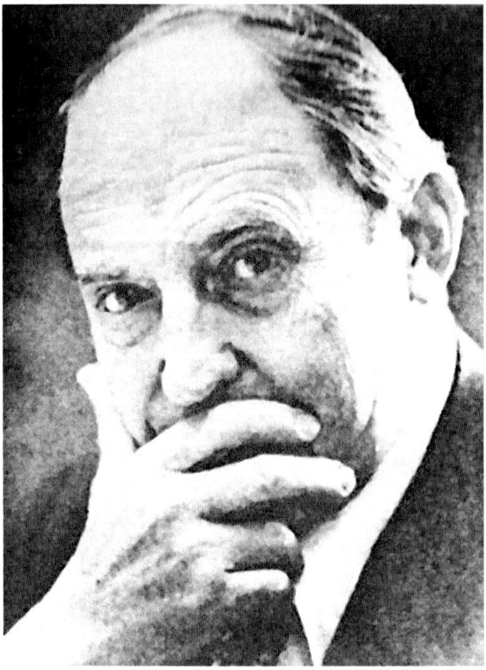

TRIAL LAWYER

Photo, published September 15, 1974, shows John J. Wilson who was the combative and outspoken trial lawyer who represented two top Nixon Administration aides in the Senate Watergate hearings in 1973, presided over by Senator Sam J. Ervin.

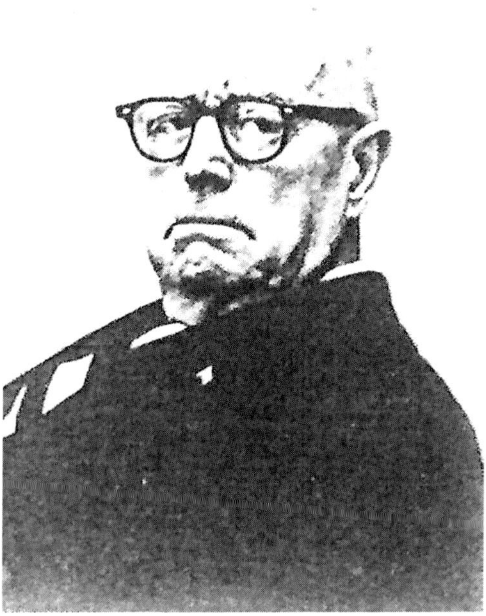

1976 Award

STRONG CONTROVERSIES ON BUSING IN LOUISVILLE'S SCHOOLS IN 1975

by CORT BEST ET AL., *Louisville Courier-Journal* and *Times*

The 1976 jury report contained three propoitions for the Pulitzer Prize in this award group: 1. Brian Lanker of the *Eugene Register-Guard*: his album was „a clear choice of the jury for first place". 2. Gerald Gay of the *Seattle Times*: no details were given. 3. Michael O'Brien of the *Miami News*: „his album included several feature sequences". In addition, „the jury voted to award an honorable mention because of the unusual photographic quality" of Robert Modersohn's work in the *Des Moines Register and Tribune*. The Board did not follow any of these proposals, but rather put the entry ranking second in the spot news category into the feature group and made it a Pulitzer Prize-winner. This is how the award went to the *Louisville Courier-Journal and Times* photographic staff „for a comprehensive pictorial report on busing in Louisville's schools."

After a federal court had ruled that students in Louisville, Ky., must be bused to achieve racial integration and equal education for all, protests and riots came up. Keith Williams, one of the photographers who covered the story for the *Courier-Journal*, remembered: „There was apprehension on both sides - the students who were predominantly black being bused out to predominatly white counties, and people in predominatly white who didn't want to be bused into the city. For the kids, here you are going to a neighborhood you've never gone to before. You've seen protesting and throwing rocks and you're going into that neighborhood where those protesters came from." The newspaper's photographers caught many of the facets of the school integration crisis and were decorated for their work with the Pulitzer Prize.

Altogether seventeen photographers of the *Louisville Courier-Journal and Times* took part in the realization of the pictures for this group award. The coverage was credited to the following staff members: Cort Best, Michael Coers, Stan Denny, Melissa Farlow, C. Thomas Hardin, Tom R. Hays, Bud Kamenish, Frank Kimmel, Charles W. Luster, Bryan L. Moss, Richard Nugent, Paul Schuhmann, Pam Spaulding, Larry R. Spitzer, Robert Steinau, William Strode and Keith Williams. On the following pages, only a few examples of the exhibit are reprocduced to give an idea about the controversial situation in Louisville by the time of the busing problem.

WISH TO RETURN TO HIS FORMER SCHOOL

Photo, published August 28, 1975, shows Joseph Bell in a bus that was about to take him to his previous school, the Martin Luther King Elementary School in Louisville, Kentucky. The eight-year-old boy had visited his new school, Jacob Elementary, which he was going to attend with the beginning of the new school year in September, 1975. Adecision of the U.S. Supreme Court had made this transfer necessary.

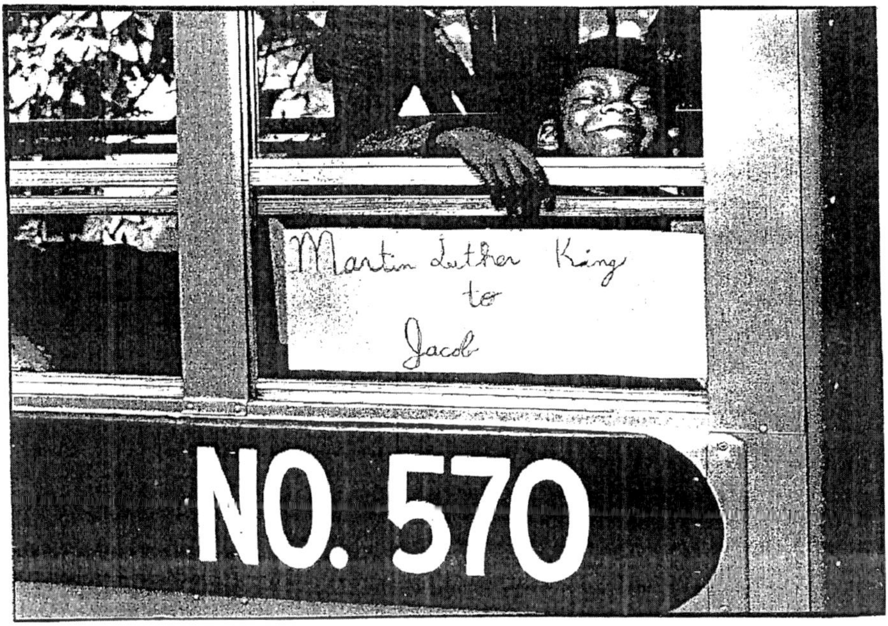

TWO BOYS IN EMPTY CLASSROOM

Photo, published September 4, 1975, shows how Mark Stewart, seated, shook hands with a new boy in his class, Darrel Hughes, both eight years old. Apparently, they were the only two in their classroom in the Greenwood Elementary on the first day of the new school year. This was due to two reasons: the busing did not run as smoothly as planned so that many students came in late. Many families boycotted the U.S. Supreme Court's decision by not sending their children to school.

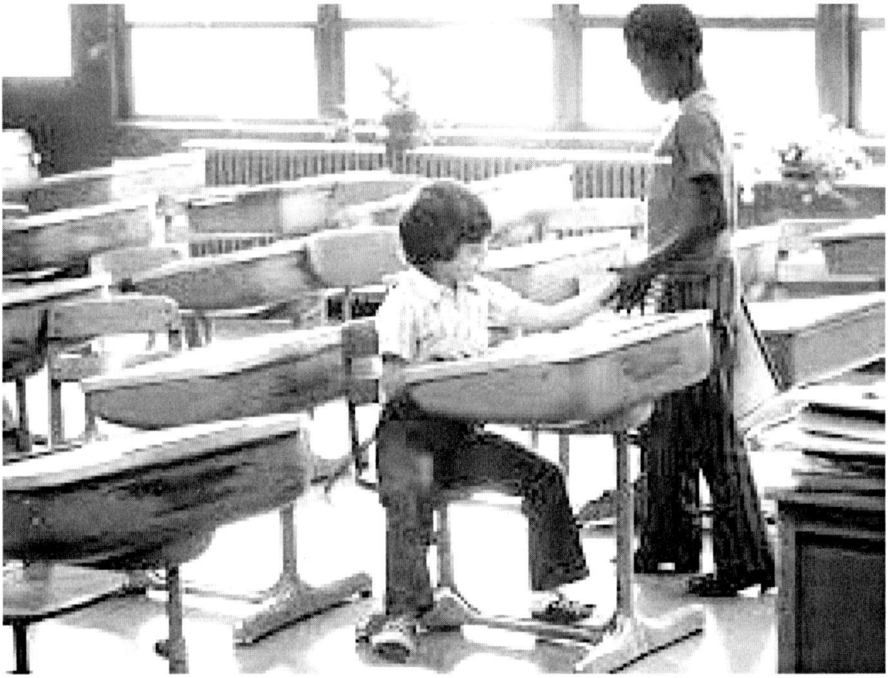

POLICEMAN ESCORTES SCHOOL BUS

Photo, published September 8, 1975, shows State Trooper Lonnie Hughes safeguarding a bus which transported students to the Fairdale High School. This was part of the precautions taken by the State Board of Education to ensure safe busing in Jefferson County, Kentucky. They were posting guards next to the buses on the third day of the new school year because it had come to several incidents in the days before.

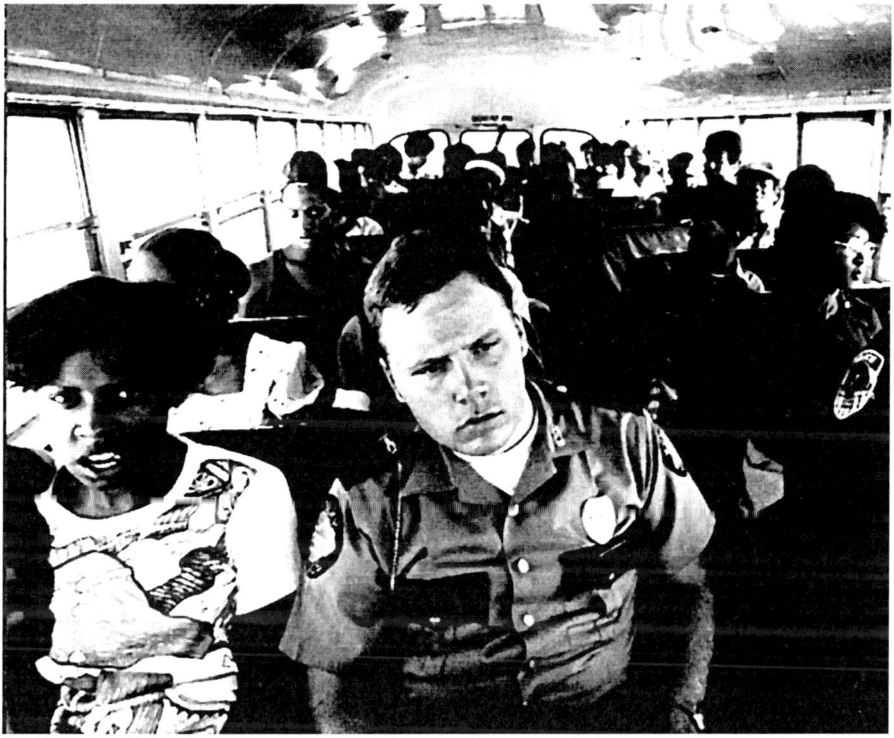

1977 Award

THE CHATTANOOGA ARMED FORCES DAY PARADE AT A RAINY DAY IN 1976

by ROBIN L. HOOD, *Chattanooga News-FreePress*

The jurors of 1977 selected three photographers' work in the following order: Robin Hood of the *Chattanooga News-Free Press*, it can be read in the report, „easily captured the jury's first place votes with his pieture of a legless Vietnam veteran hugging an infant at an Armed Forces Day parade. The pomp and ceremony was on the street marching by but the emotion and feeling of a man who had given more than most captured the essence of the day." Second place went to Ricardo J. Ferro of the *St. Petersburg Times* „for his portfolio of faces of the elderly ... Sometimes there is desolation, sometimes an all-encompassing aloneness." Third rank was given to Albert Goya of the *Miami Herald* for his picture „Blind Kids See Lincoln". The photo showed „blind youngsters on a trip to Washington reaching up to touch, to stroke, to feel the face of Abraham Lincoln" at the Lincoln Memorial.

The Board voted for the contender ranking first, Robin Hood of the *Chattanooga News-Free Press*, „for his photograph of a disabled veteran and his child at an Armed Forces Day parade." The photographer, himself a Vietnam veteran, had walked the sidelines of the parade, taking pictures for his newspaper. „I had just finished photographing a group of small Vietnamese children who had been relocated to Chattanooga as war refugees and were now watching the parade and waving small American flags," Hood remembered, „I felt the real story was not in the pomp and ceremony of the parade, but in the emotions of the spectators viewing it. .. Here was a man who had made a great sacrifice, lost in the crowd, biting his lips, who paid a high prize" in the war, loosing both of his legs. Hood had released the shutter immediatedly.

Robin L. Hood, born on September 22, 1944, in Chattanooga, Tn., attended local public schools and studied art at the University of Tennessee in his home town from 1962 to 1966. The following year he enlisted in the U.S. Army where he served as second lieutenant since 1969. He advanced to first lieutenant the following year. From 1970 to 1971 Hood served as an information officer with the First Air Cavalry Division in Vietnam where he had to photograph military activities and escort news media through operating areas. After his return the photographer joined the *Chattanooga News-Free Press* in 1971.

DISABLED VIETNAM VETERAN

Photo, published May 15, 1976, depicts a Vietnam veteran and his child watching the annual Armed Forces Day Parade in Chattanooga, Tennessee. Eddie Robinson, who had lost both legs in the Vietnam War, observed the glamor of the hour-long parade.

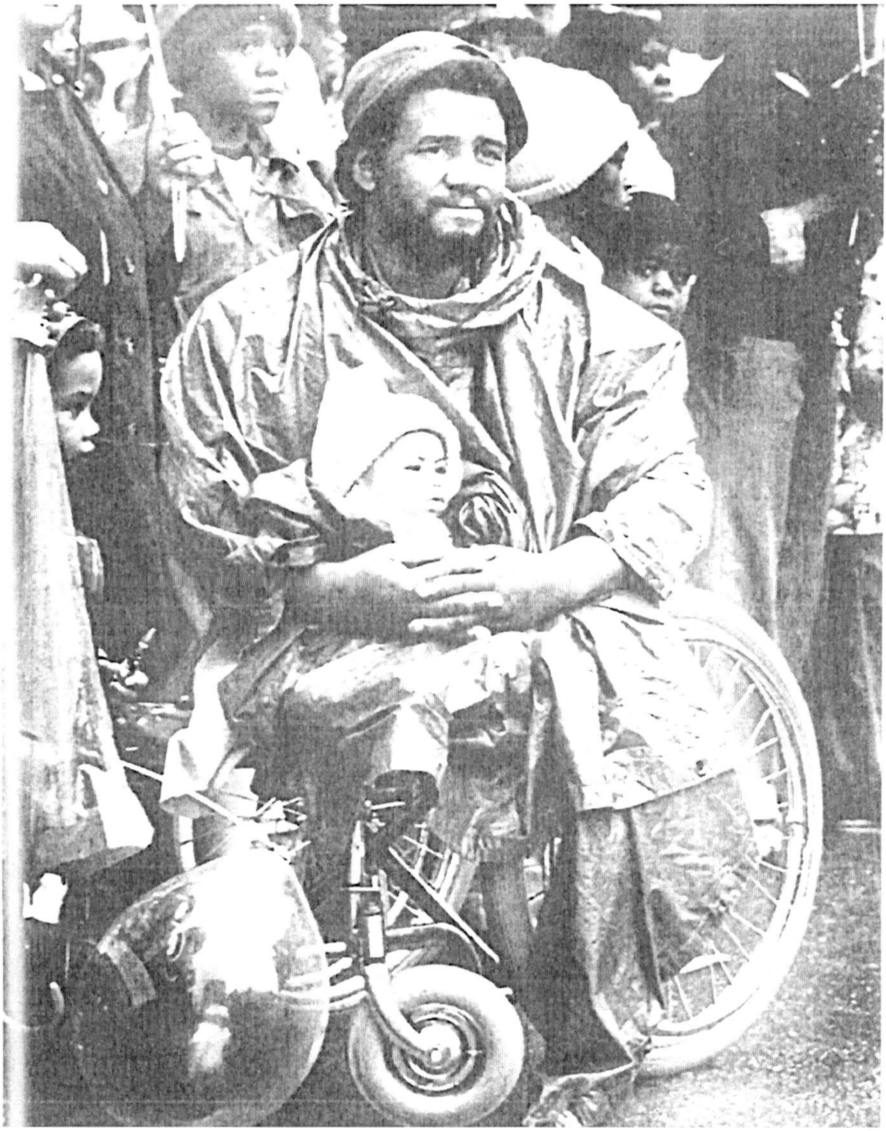

1978 Award

WHITE-RULED RHODESIA AND OPPOSING GUERILLA ACTIVITIES IN 1977

J. ROSS BAUGHMAN, *Associated Press*

The 1978 committee's choice for first place came to Ross Baughman of *AP* „for his vivid pictorial description of one of the year's major news stories, the ... guerilla war in Rhodesia... Baughman was not capturing an instant flash event; rather, he was carefully depicting one part of a nasty war - the plight of black prisoners captured by the Rhodesian army. Two of these pictures ... warrant attention... But the most moving picture showed a prisoner with a rope around his neck being marched along by two Rhodesian cavalry men on horseback." Second choice in the eyes of the jurors was a sequence entitled „Taking Jesus to Jail" by lohn H. White of the *Chicago Daily News*, „especially the photograph of the person holding a tattered Bible." Third place came to Michael O'Brien of the *Miami News* „for his sensitive and extensive series on the Culmer Ghetto in Miami."

The Board decided in favor of Ross Baughman of the *Associated Press* „for three photographs from guerilla areas in Rhodesia." The *AP* photographer had traveled with a cavalry unit which had the mission to seek out anti-government guerillas and destroy them. „1 was just coming along as the newcomer," Baughman remembered, „just trying my best to get into the field and take real pictures and get a firsthand story. I couldn't stand just accepting the government's press releases ... On my troop's mission, they forced all the men in one village to live up in push-up stance on the ground. It was very hot that day ..., they're holding that positions for forty-five minutes in the sun ..." Most of Baughman's film documenting increadible tortures were confiscated by censors, but he could hide three rolls of film before he was forced to leave Africa.

J. Ross Baughman, born on May 7, 1953, in Dearborn, Mi., graduated from Kent State University with a B.A. degree cum laude in 1975. He started his career as a staff photographer and writer at the *Lorain Journal* in Ohio. He got the post of a contract photographer and writer for the *Associated Press* in 1975 to cover Africa and the Middle East. In 1978 he was co-founder of the *Visions International* news agency. He became director of photography at the Day Publishing Company before he was named photo editor of the *Washington Times*.

ROPE AROUND PRISONER'S NECK

Photo, published December 3, 1977, shows a black captive in Rhodesia. The rope around his neck served as a securitive means, so that the caught man could not escape. According to the photographer, the Rhodesian troops would used this way of apprehending a suspect. The rope was tied to a horse and the cavalry then forced the man to run behind the horse; sometimes he would be dragged behind the galopping animal.

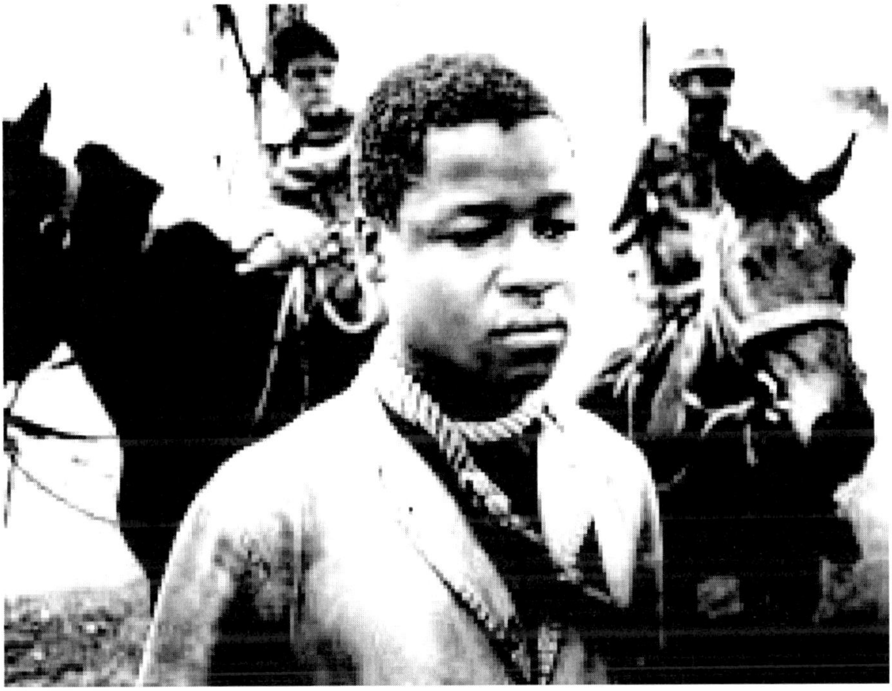

SOLDIER HOLDS ENEMY NEWSMAN

Photo, published December 3, 1977, illustrates the brutal methods of soldiers of the white regime in Rhodesia fighting against black guerillas. The lieutenant, 19-year-old Graham Baillie, had been beating the black man with a bat, in order to find out where the guerillas were. The lieutenant paused only when the black man, Moffat Ncube, was unconscious. He later died of the injuries.

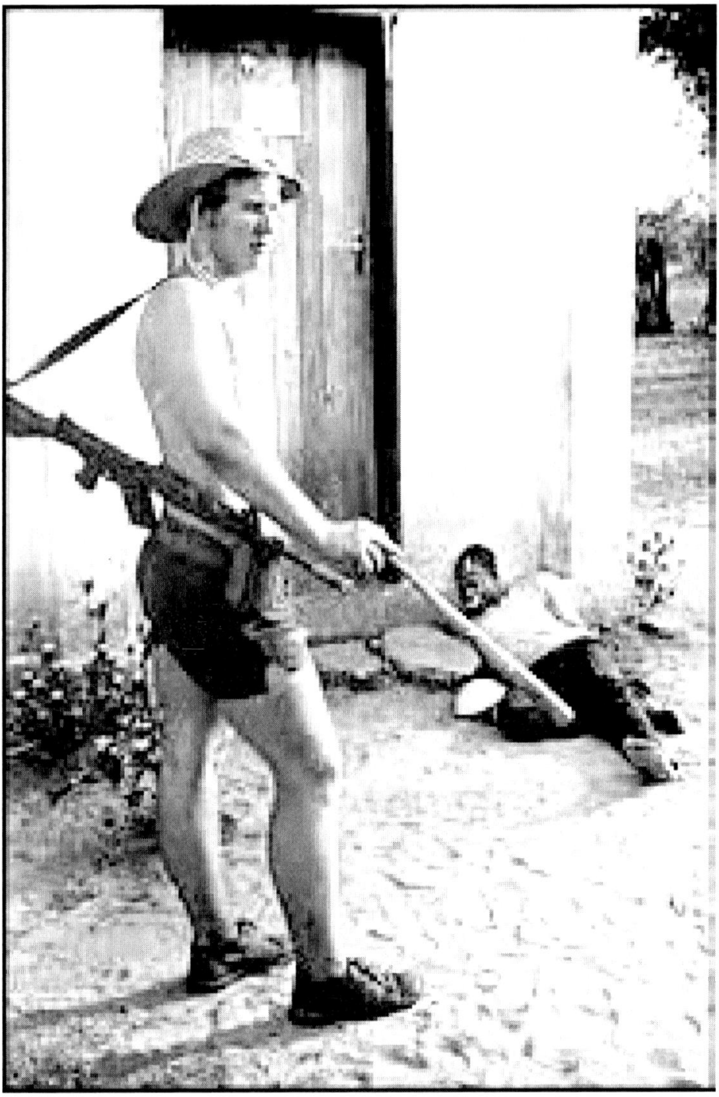

PRISONERS IN MIDDAY SUN

Photo, published December 3, 1977, shows a Rhodesian soldier interrogating a group of prisoners near Kikidoo. He forced them to remain in push-up stance for forty-five minutes. The soldier wanted answers as to the whereabouts of guerillas who had been raiding nearby. The prisoners who broke down during the push-ups were taken behind a house and knocked out. Then a trooper would fire a shot into the air.

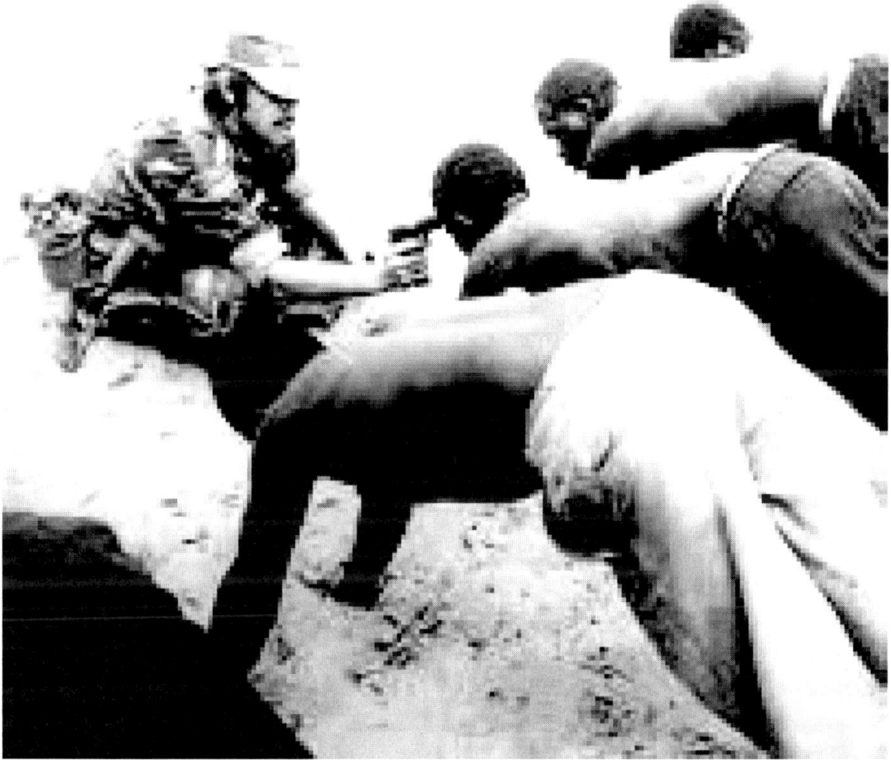

1979 Award

THE DESTROYING POWER OF A NEW ENGLAND BLIZZARD IN 1978

by MIKE ANDERSON ET AL., *Boston Herald American*

The 1979 jury's list of three suggestions had in first place the photo staff of a New England newspaper, the *Boston Herald-American*. The group of photographers, it can be read in the report, „displayed resourceful use of photography and team effort in producing detailed and imaginative coverage of a disastrous storm. The photographers were faced with telling the story of the worst blizzard in the history of New England. They did so with wide ranging, dramatic photographs that accentuated the human element." Ranking second was Gordon N. Converse of the *Christian Science Monitor* who „went to China to see if he could photograph the 'real China' as reflected by its people. His pictures are sensitive and perceptive selections of subjects that depict a warm, friendly and busy people." Third on the jury's shortlist were Bill Marr and Nick Kelsh of the *Columbia Daily Tribune* from Missouri for a picture series called „Youth imprisoned."

The Pulitzer Prize went to the photo staff of the *Boston Herald-American* „for photographic coverage of the blizzard of 1978." After heavy snowfall and frightening hurricane-force winds thousands of people were stranded all along the New England coast. As the water and ice floes took over coastal towns, terrified residents climbed onto roofs and second floor porches to escape their flooded homes. Beside of the newspaper's chief photographer, Kevin Cole, staff photographer Paul Benoit was determined to cover the besieged coastal town of Revere. He endured a grueling ten-hour trek, alone and on foot, through a blinding storm and a rising flood of water. After drying his camera in an oven, he went straight to that part of town hardest hit, working three days and nights without sleep. Other *Herald-American* photographers covered the region, photographing the blizzard's destruction.

This group award was bestowed to the entire photography staff of the newspaper for its coverage of the blizzard that hit eastern Massachusetts early in February 1978. The sixteen staff photographers were: Mike Anderson, Paul Benoit, Dennis Brearley, Kevin Cole, Gene Dixon, Stanley J. Forman, Ted Gartland, Frank Hill, Bob Howard, Angela Kaloventzos, Ray Lussier, Roland Oxton, Leo Renahan, John Thompson, Dick Thomson and M. Leo Tierney.

RESCUE WORKER IN ACTION

Photo, published February 12, 1978, depicts a scene after a blizzard had destroyed countless towns in New England by putting them under water, ice and snow: A rescue worker was trying to pull an evacuation boat to the front door of a house in Revere, Massachusetts. Thousands of people had to be evacuated from their homes.

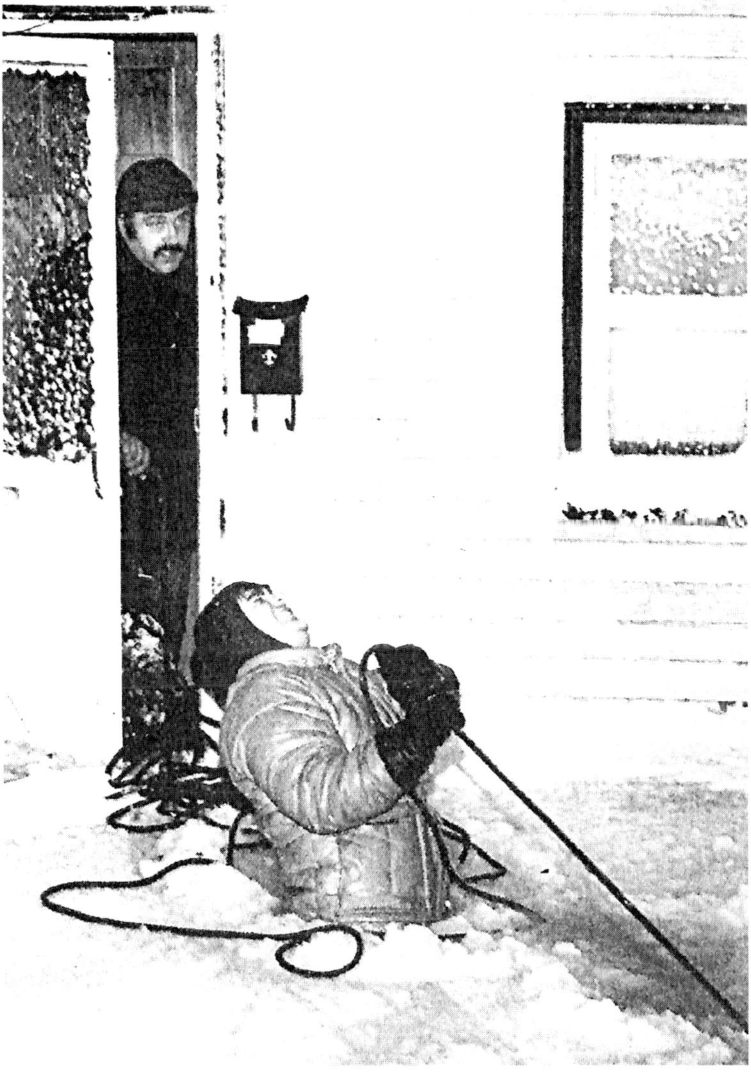

STRANDED CARS ON HIGHWAY

Photo, published February 12, 1978, illustrates the situation in New England after the blizzard had wiped out normality. Hope ran out for about 3,000 drivers left stranded on Route 128, the major beltway around Boston. They were trapped in their cars while more snow was falling and the wind reached up to 120 miles per hour.

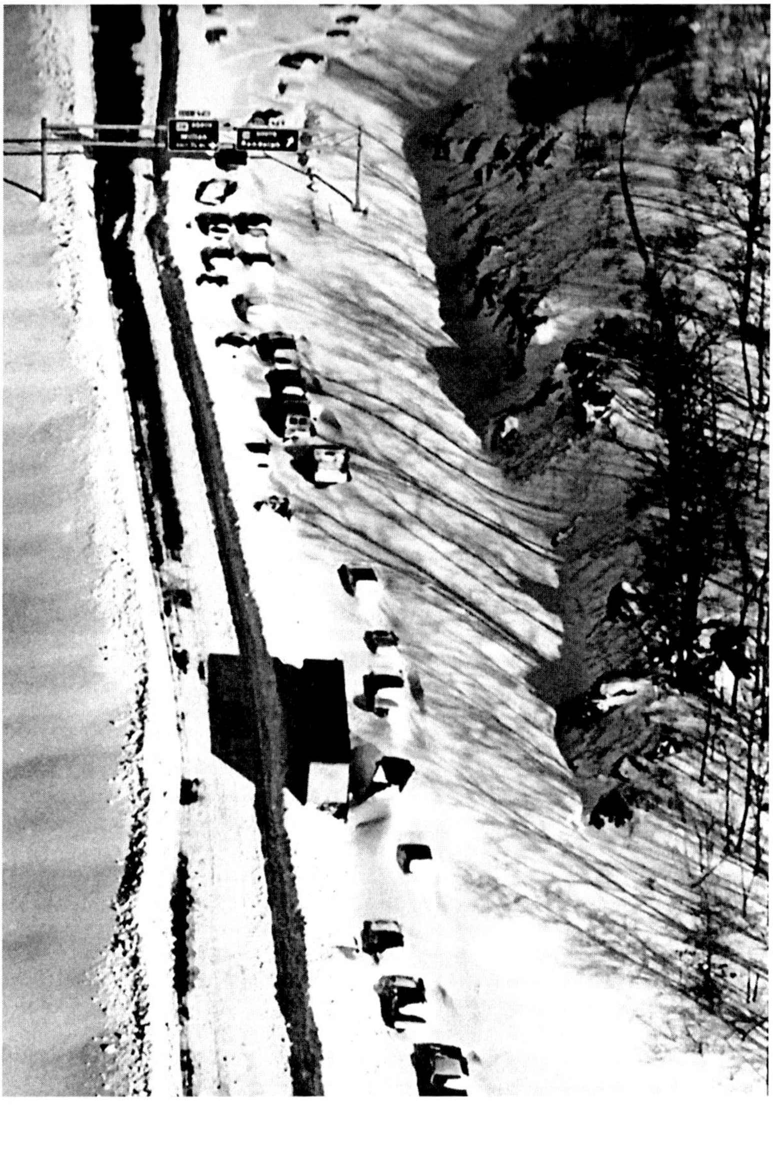

LIGHTHOUSE IN ANGRY SEA

Photo, published February 12, 1978, shows the Minot Lighthouse near North Scituate, Massachusetts, with giant waves roaring against it. The blizzard had transmuted the sea in a turmoil, flooding numerous towns by the seaside and leaving 10,000 people homeless. The lighthouse, however, seemed to resist the heavy waves.

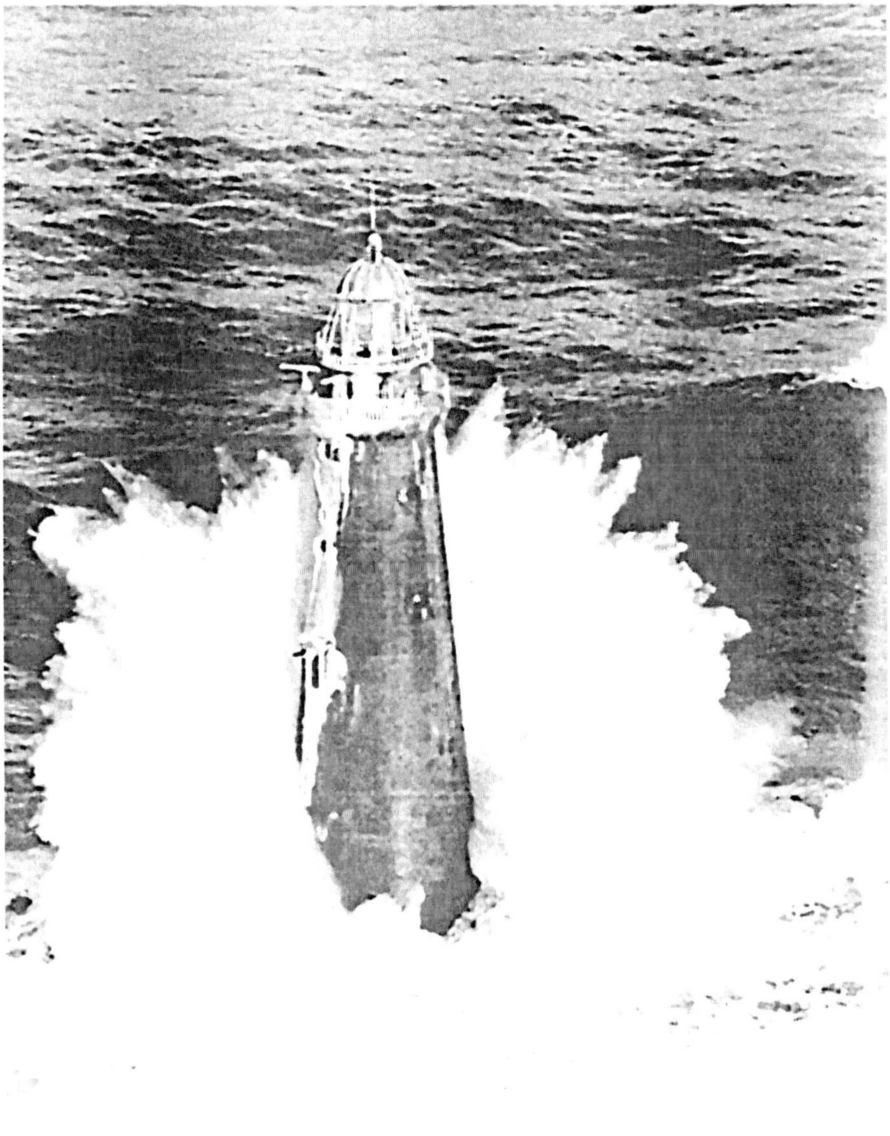

1980 Award

THE LONELY AND ASCETIC LIFE OF THE TEXAS WESTERN COWBOY IN 1979

by ERWIN H. HAGLER, *Dallas Times Herald*

When in 1980 the jury members were discussing the ranking of the chosen candidates, they even went so far as to make explicit exactly how they had voted in each of the three cases of finalists. The five members of the jury, as can be read in their report, „were unanimous in their selection of Erwin H. Hagler's series on the Western Cowboy. The jurors felt that Hagler revealed in pictures the passing of an American institution, and revealed the story with great industry and sensitivity. Further, the jurors agreed that the photographs are representative of the highest technical and compositional skills of American photojournalism."
Three of the five jurors, the report goes on, „recommended John J. Sunderland's 'Dying in a Hospice' entry'" from the *Denver Post* as the second choice. ,Only two of the five jury members voted for the third place exhibit, David A. Kryszak's photos „Children in Cambodia", published in the *Detroit News*.

As a result of the unanimous praise heaped on the person at the top of the jury's list the Board accepted the proposal and honored Erwin H. Hagler with the Pulitzer Prize. The photographer had wanted to get pictures of the long cattle drives and the life of the cowboys in the Texas cattle country, where he slept in a bunkhouse and got up at dawning each morning. Since he was not much good on a horse, Hagler followed the cowboys on foot or by pickup car, photographing everything they did - eating, resting, driving cattle, roping steers. The cowboys, always reserved, were not sure how they felt about having him around. Hagler eventually found himself up in a helicopter with a pilot-cowboy. „We got up there", Hagler remembered, „and he started doing all this crazy stuff to get the cows moving, loops and dives ... The guy flew using only one hand on the controls. It was really a sight."

Erwin H. Hagler, born on August 7, 1947, in Fort Worth, Tx., attended Eastern Hills High School in his home town and graduated from the University of Texas in Austin with a Bachelor of Architecture degree in 1971. In the same year he joined the *Waco News-Tribune* as a staff photographer but switched to the *Fort Worth Star-Telegram* the following year. Since 1974 Hagler then was engaged by the *Dallas Times-Herald*. In 1988 he left the newspaper job to become a freelance photographer.

TEXAS COWBOY

Photo, published December 9, 1979, depicts a symbolic, typical scene of the life of a cowboy in the South-West of the United States. The cowboy in the photo worked about ten hours a day. On the day pictured he and his colleagues were preparing the herd of cattle for branding. At this stage of the branding operation, the cowboys were rounding the cattle up, riding down cows that ran loose and directing the herd towards the fenced area of the ranch.

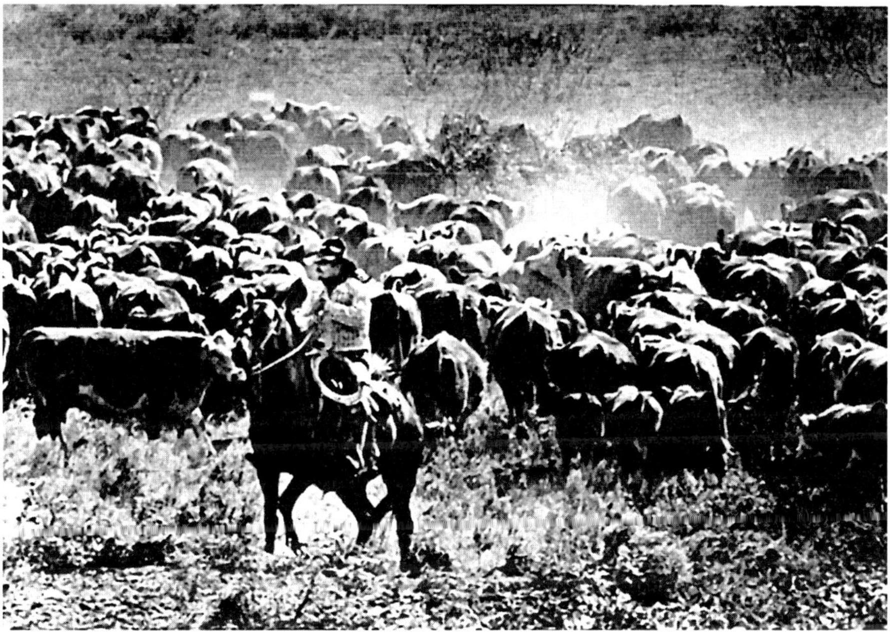

WORKING CONDITIONS

Photo, published December 9, 1979, shows the cowboy Butch Morris working the cattle to round up. His day, as everybody else's, had begun at 5:30 in the morning when the chow bell had woken all cowboys on the Pitchfork Ranch, founded in 1883. The cowboys had hurried to the cookhouse where they were served a hearty breakfast. That had helped them do a good job when they had been galopping a herd of cows counting 300 to a holding pen.

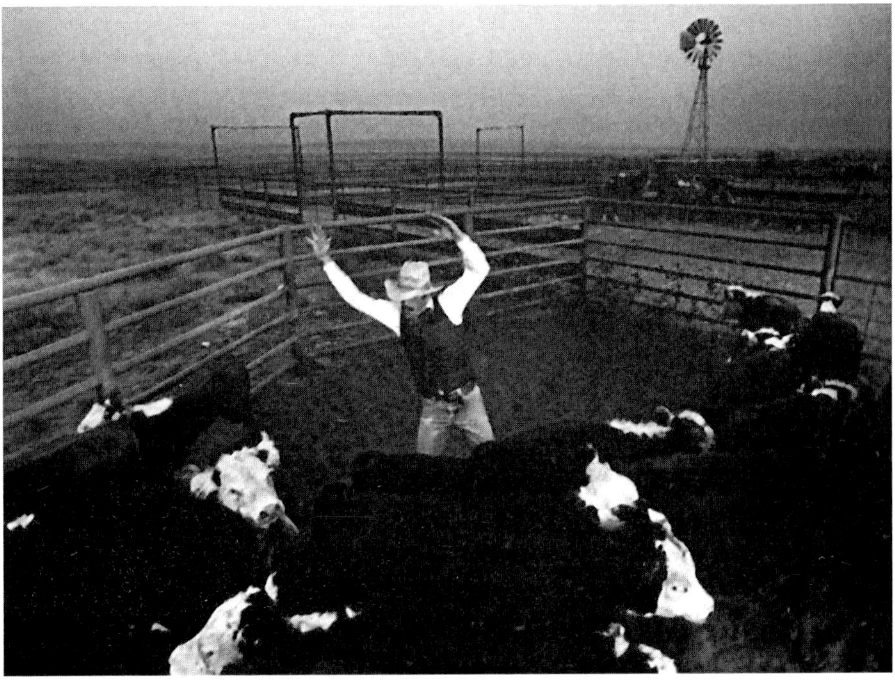

HELICOPTER COWBOY

Photo, published December 9, 1979, shows a pilot-cowpoy in full action above the ranch area. He coordinated with the ground crew by directing strays back to the herd.

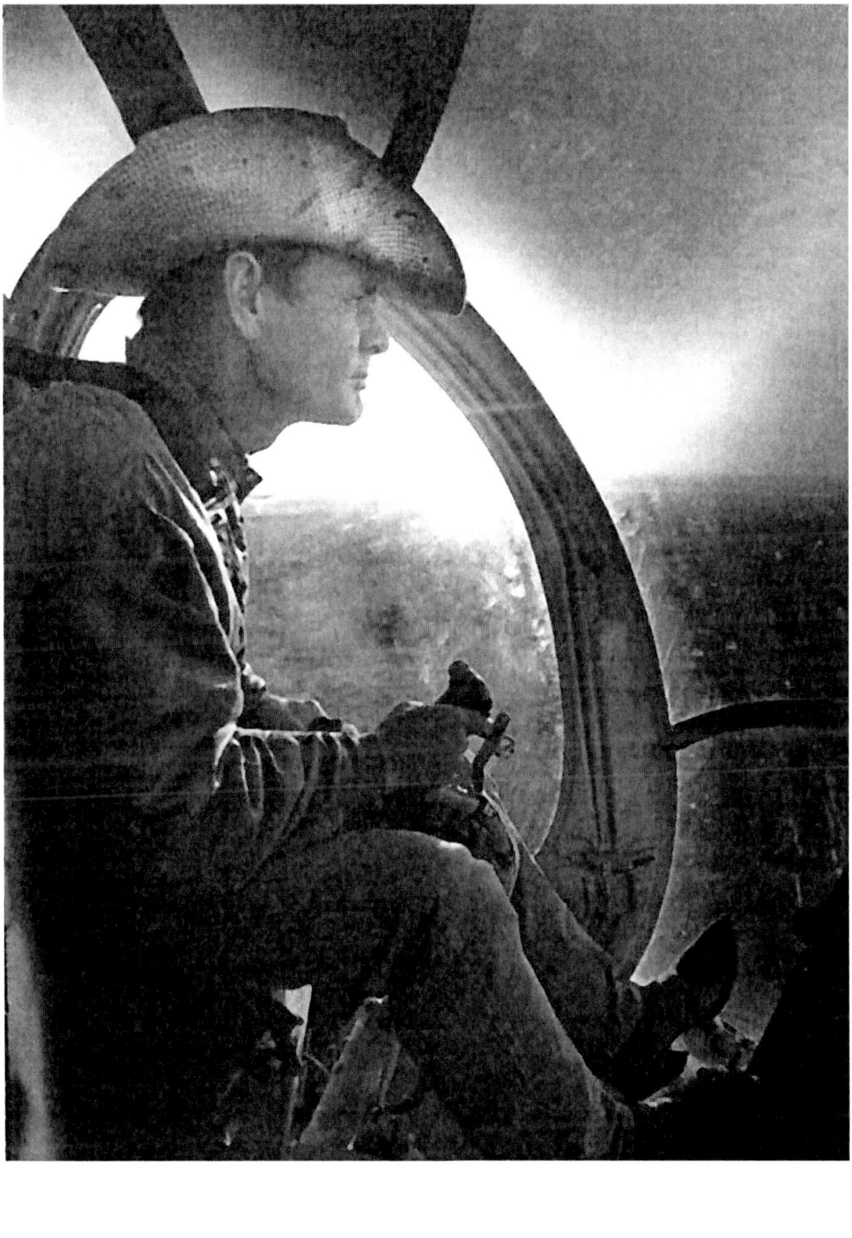

1981 Award

THE LIVING CONDITIONS IN THE MICHIGAN STATE PRISON AT JACKSON IN 1980

by TARO M. YAMASAKI, *Detroit Free Press*

First on the 1981 shortlist of the jury's finalists was Taro Yamasaki of the *Detroiut Free Press* for „displaying great courage, coupled with a rare sensitivity". He had thoroughy documented „the terror and emptiness of a huge correction institution. He detailed interviews and stark, candid photographs portray life behind bars in an engrossing, human way. With an eye for detail and timing he demonstrates the qualities of an outstanding photographer," the jury report stated. Next on the list was Paul Beaver of the *Jackson Clarion-Ledger*. He had provided „ an excellent documentary and pictoral essay on the cotton culture of the Delta region in Mississippi." Third rank came to Micheal C. Hayman of the *Flint Journal* from Michigan. He had photographed portraits of the auto workers in his region, he showed them „on the job, at leisure and leaving for warmer climates," the jury report said.

The Board was convinced by the merits of the entry at the top of the jury's list, so the prize was given to Taro M. Yamasaki of the *Detroit Free-Press* „for his photographs of Jackson, Mich., State Prison." The photographer had stayed ten days inside the prison and enjoyed unprecedented freedom because weeks later Michigan voters were going to be asked to approve a ballot proposal to increase prison funding. The prison officials were receptive to Yamasaki's undertaking, wanting to demonstrate the dangerous overcrowding that existed in the Southern Michigan State Prison. „There were very few guards," the photographer remembered, sometimes one guard with hundreds of inmates. „The inmates trusted me", he said, „but they also figuered they could kill me."

Taro M. Yamasaki, born on December 19, 1945, in Detroit, Mi., attended Cranbrook School in Bloomfield Hills and studied Journalism at the University of Michigan. In 1968 he moved to New York City to learn photography in the streets. He had to work in various jobs to finance it, e.g. as a fashion photographer's assistant. In 1973 he moved back to Michigan and got the job as a staff photographer at the *Detroit Free-Press* four years later. Since 1983 he worked as a freelance photographer for magazines like *Time, Life, People, Sports Illustrated, Fortune and Forbes*, and he also taught classes at Michigan University School of Art and Design.

MANY PRISON CELLS

Photo, published December 14, 1980, decipts a part of the largest walled prison in the United States, the State Prison of Southern Michigan at Jackson, one hour off Detroit. The prison was designed and constructed to hold 4,000 convicts. At the time the photos were taken, 5,700 prisoners were living there. The reason that there were still empty cells was that only half of the convinced felons needed to be in the high-security section of the prison.

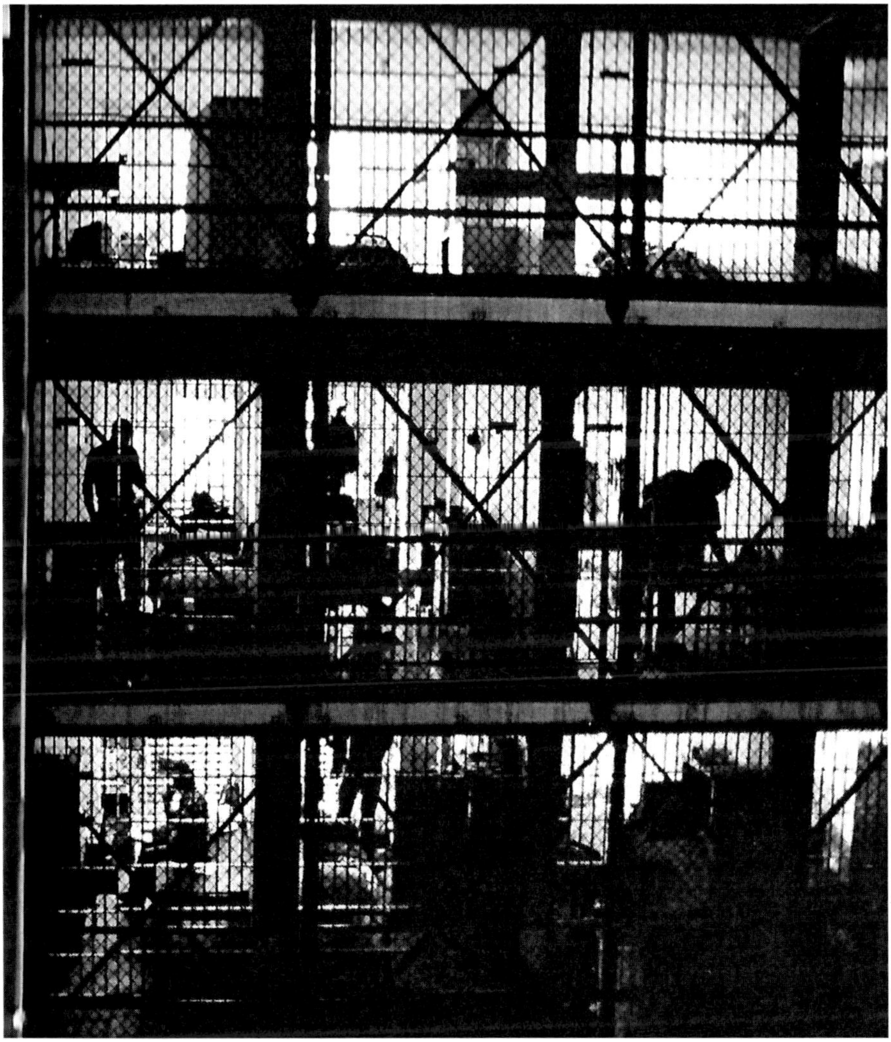

SUPERVISING GUARD

Photo, published December 17, 1980, shows a floor in block eleven in the maximum-security section of the State Prison of Southen Michigang at Jackson. The block was one of two honor blocks in Jackson Prison. There was a waiting list of inmates who sought to be tansferred to these blocks because the blocks were equipped with color TV and lounge area etc. To get onto the waiting list, the inmates had to have a clean record for at least six months.

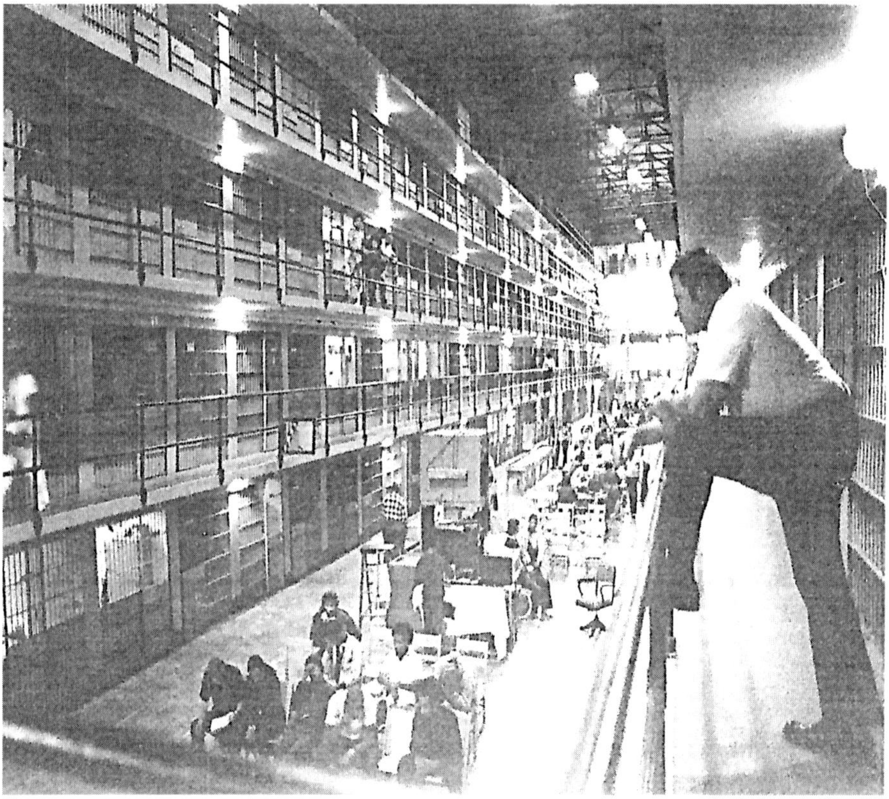

OBSERVATION OFFICER

Photo, published December 20, 1980, documents a typical day in Jackson Prison in Michigan. An observation officer surveyed the outer part of the prison. As a result, few inmates had ever really physically escaped from the maximum security area.

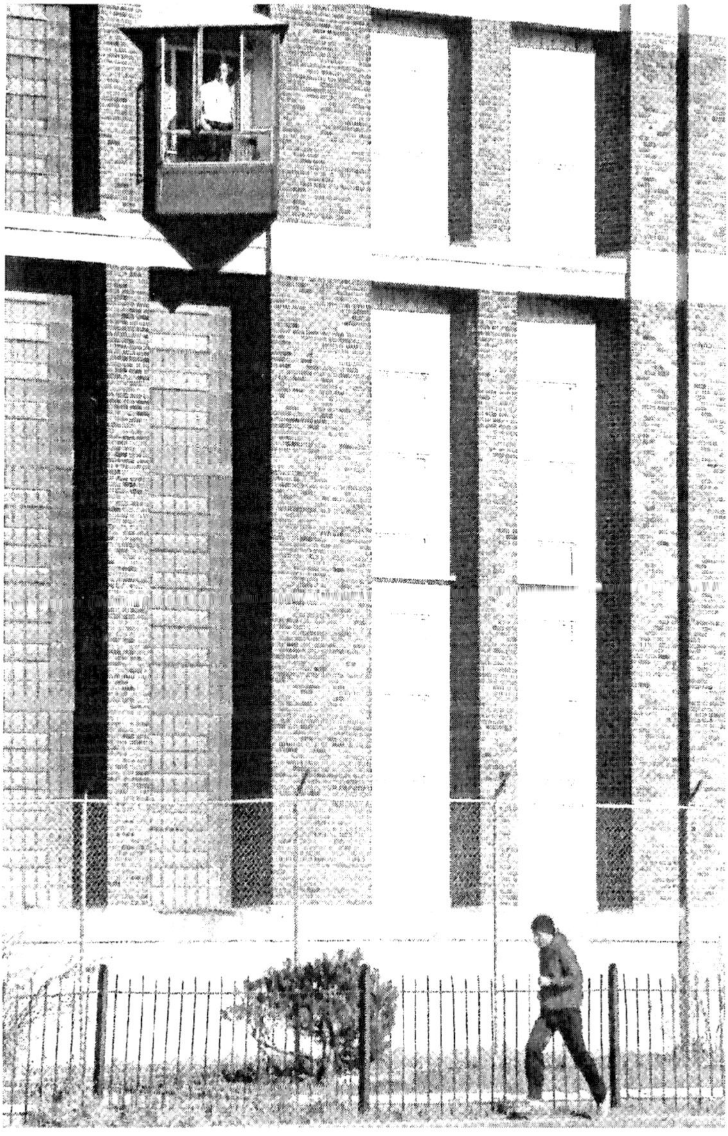

1982 Award

ARMY MEMBERS, POLICE DUTIES AND MUSIC EDUCATION IN ILLINOIS IN 1981

by JOHN H. WHITE, *Chicago Sun-Times*

According to the 1982 report, the jury was „struck by Mr. White's ability to produce excellent photographs with great consistency. While the subject matter is commonplace, his execution is extraordinary. The body of his work reflects a blend of humor, warmth and compassion recorded with a creative eye and technical excellence. The jury concludes this is the first place entry." After this praise for the exhibit by John H. White of the *Chicago Sun-Times*, it was Walter C. Stricklin of the *Florida Times-Union* who reached second place. The jurors „found a body of photographs which recount with drama, emotion and understanding the problem faced by a family confronting the death of one of its members." Third rank went to Ellis Reed of the *San Francisco Examiner*. The jurors stated that his „photographs captured the harsh realities of daily life in the San Francisco public housing project known as 'Pink Palace'".

The winner was John H. White „for consistently excellent work on a variety of subjects" from the Greater Chicago area. When he earned the prize, he had been photographing Chicago for more than thirty years. „I live in the city," he once confessed, „I breathe the city is everything. There's the lakefront, there are the parks, I can see as good a sunrise in the City as anywhere in the world." White's award-winning portfolio reflected a year in the life of the city and his work. The purpose was to share slices of life from all walks of life; to be the psalm of the life of people. The photographs were from news situations, but not hard news.

John H. White, born on March 18, 1945, in Lexington, N.C., graduated from Central Piedmont Community College in Charlotte with an associate of applied science degree. From 1966 to 1968 he served as a photographer in the U.S. Marine Corps in Quantico, Va. In 1969 he started to work as a photojournalist at the *Chicago Daily News*. The following year he was a volunteer photography teacher at Southside Art Center in Chicago. In 1978 the photographer switched to the *Chicago Sun-Times*. In the same year, White became instructor in photojournalism at Columbia College in Chicago. He was a finalist for the Pulitzer Prize in 1981 before he earned the award the following year.

SEARCHING POLICE OFFICER

Photo, published March 30, 1981, documents the law enforcement's attempts to fight gangs in a public housing project. In the photo, the police officer was searching for weapons in the Cabrini-Green building. It was part of the Near North Side public housing project in Chicago, Illinois. The living conditions in the Cabrini-Green house were determinated by violent clashes between two gangs.

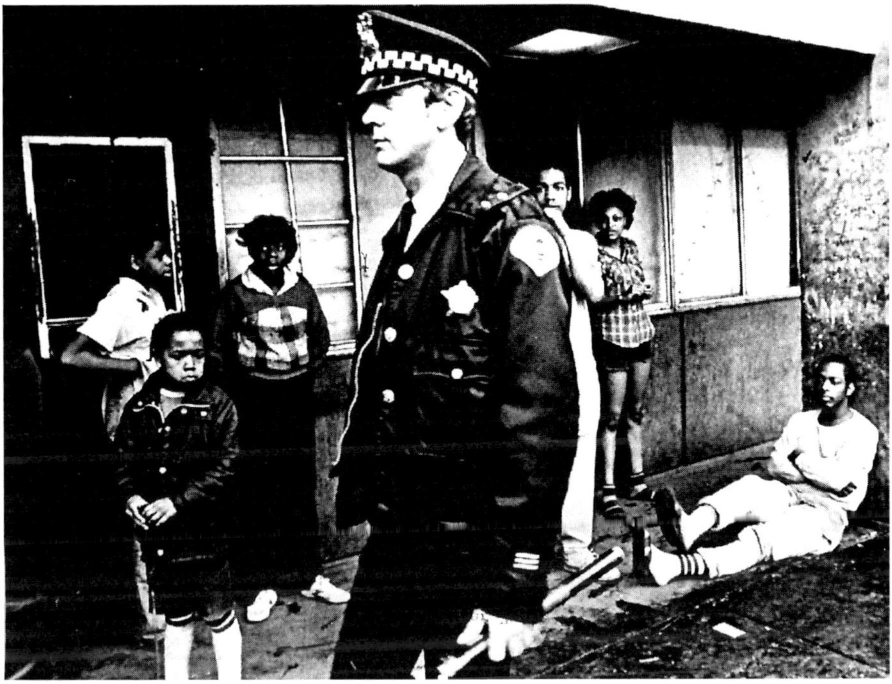

SPECIAL VIOLINIST TECHNIQUE

Photo, published April 22, 1981, shows two girls practicing one violin together. They were students at the Haag-Levinton Suzuki Academy of Performing Arts in Des Plaines, Illinois. The academy taught according to the Suzuki technique which stressed the hearing memonry of students rather than reading the music.

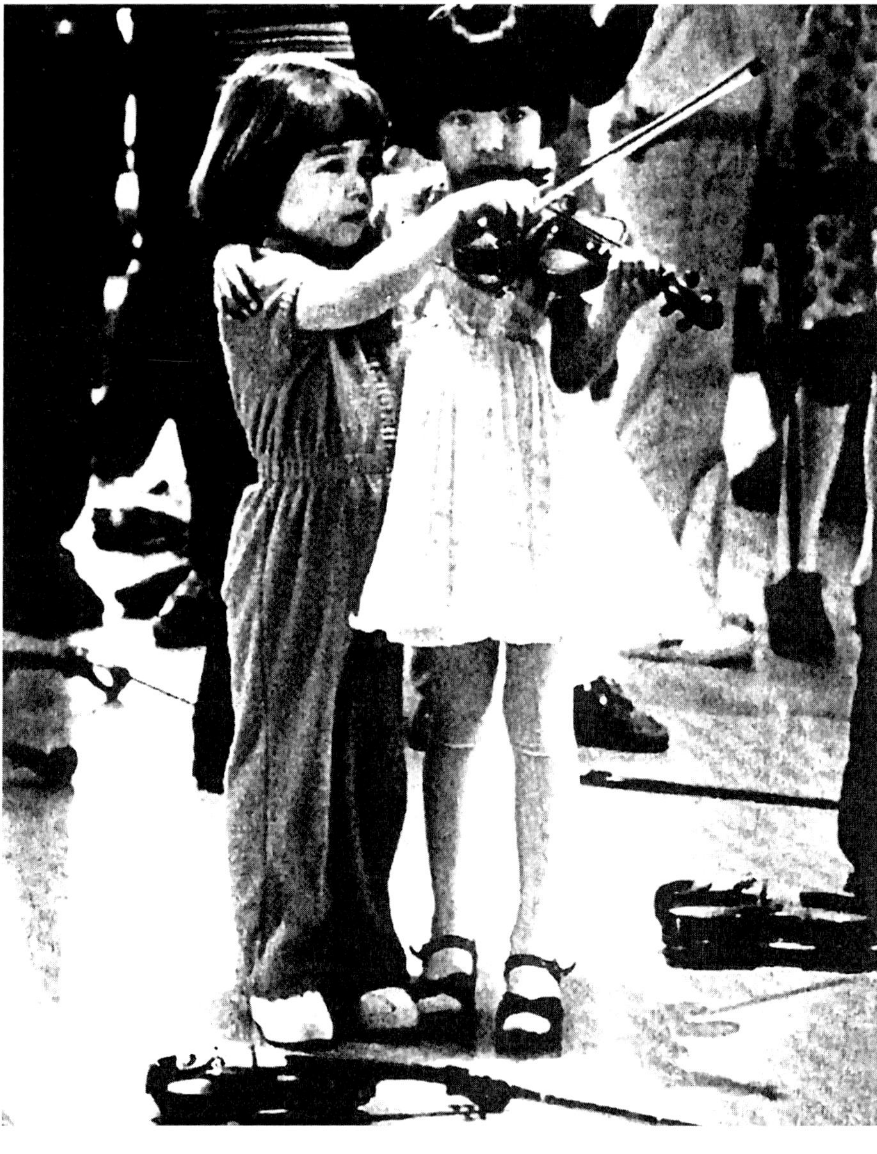

NATIONAL GUARD GROUP

Photo, published June 21, 1981, demonstrates the high moral despite adverse conditions. The Illinois Army National Guard medical group was singing while marching in the rain during summer camp training at Fort McCoy, Wisconsin. Their motivation was mainly accounted for by the fact that they are volunteers. Ten years prior, the Guards had made negative experiences with a draft.

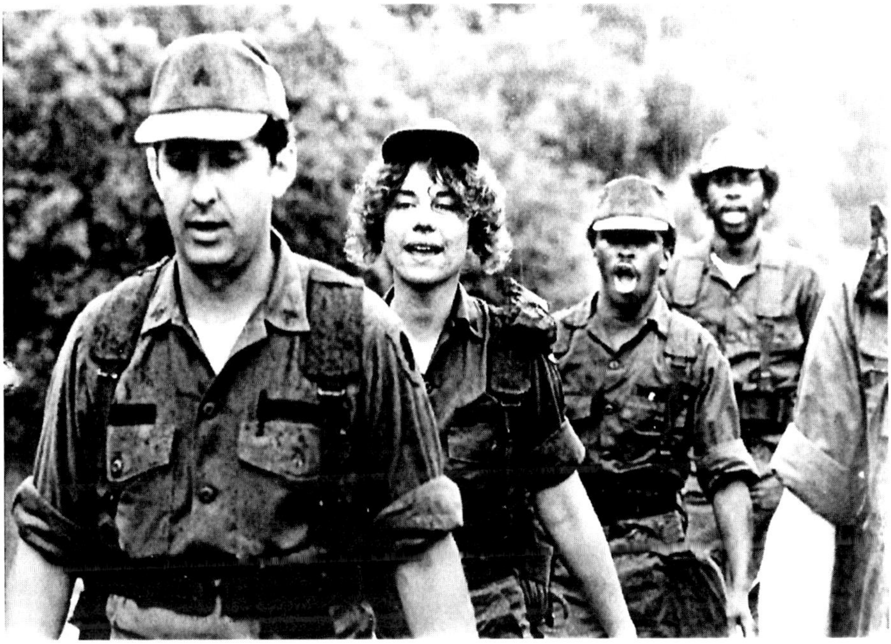

1983 Award

LIFE AND DEATH DURING THE EL SALVADOR CIVIL WAR IN 1982

by JAMES B. DICKMAN, *Dallas Times-Herald*

The jury's recommendations of 1983, which included two entrants removed from the spot news pictures classification and placed in this award category, were: James B. Dickman of the *Dallas Times-Herald* „for his picture story 'El Salvador - The Killing Ground', the aftermath of a series of bloody battles." Barron Ludlum, also of the *Dallas Times-Herald*, was praised by the jurors „for his picture story of the courageous battle of an eight-year-old to survive a congenital liver malfunction, this struggle was shared by her mother." The third name on the list was that of John H. White of the *Chicago Sun-Times*, who had won the preceding year, „for his portfolio of pictures which cover the tapestry of life in Chicago, from the grief of a child of Tylenos victim to a tooth operation on an elephant and almost all elements of our society in between."

The jury „was unanimous in its decision selecting Dickman's work as the finest of these three and of what we found to be an extremely strong field of contenders." So the Board accepted this proposal and gave James B. Dickman the Pulitzer Prize „for his telling photographs of life and death in El Salvador." The photographer and some of his colleagues from other newspapers had been in the capital San Salvador, we „the military started shooting guerillas right in front of us," he remembered, „we were around the side of a building, staying low, trying to get pictures. I photographed soldiers dragging away bodies. Nobody tried to stop us... One of the difficult parts is to keep your focus literally and figuratively on what you are there for. Hopefully you are documenting it so people back home can see it and it will have an impact."

James B. Dickman, born on March 25, 1949, in St. Louis, Missouri, studied at the University of Texas at Arlington from 1967 to 1969. Afterwards he joined the McKinney Job Corporations of Texas as a photographer. His first newspaper job was at the *Denver Post* before he moved to the *Dallas Times-Herald* in 1970. Since 1987 Dickman freelanced for *Life, Times, National Geographic, Fortune, Sports Illustrated* and other magazines. Once, he spent three months living in a stone-age village in Papua-New Guinea for *National Geographic*, and he also was a potographer on several book series.

WOMAN TAKEN FROM HER HOME BY DEATH SQUAD

Photo, published July 18, 1982, decipts a scene of the civil war in El Salvador, showing a woman who had been forced out of her home by the troops. On election day, the guerillas had tried to keep voters away from the ballots while soldiers had stepped in. In the following battle a dozen guerillas had died. The woman and her husband's tiny cabin had been in the line of fire that had been exchanged between the death squad and the guerillas in San Antonio Abad, a suburb of San Salvador.

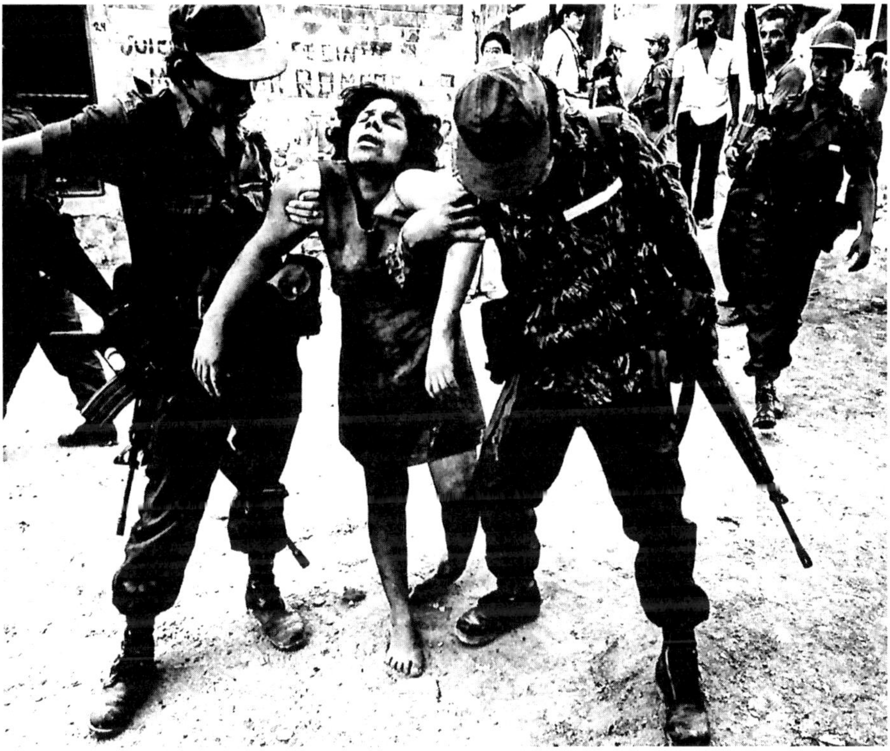

INNOCENT CHILDREN IN RAMSHACKLE REFUGEE CAMPS

Photo, published July 18, 1982, shows a refugee girl in the La Virtud camp in Honduras. The girl had fled the chaotic situation in her home-country of El Salvador where the civil war still raged. Many of the children in camps like La Virtud were orphans. The camp accomodated up to 5,000 refugees. Among them were so-called campesinos who were not used to living so close to other people. This fact added to the already difficult living conditions.

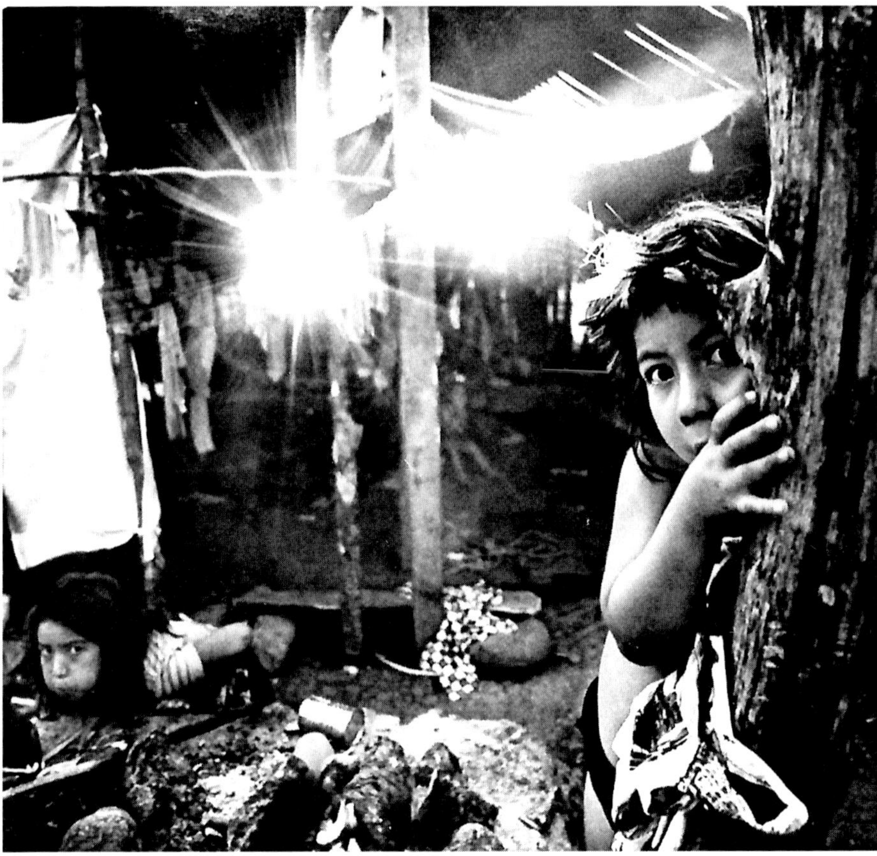

BODY OF A FAMILY MEMBER PLACED ON A TABLE

Photo, published July 18, 1982, shows a mourning ritual of a family in El Salvador. They exhibited the body of a family member on the table in the middle of the room. The man had died in the course of the civil war during which the leftist guerillas were fighting against the so-called death squad. The civil war in El Salvador had begun when a small leftist group in the border area to Honduras had claimed that a portion of the Honduran land belonged to El Salvador,

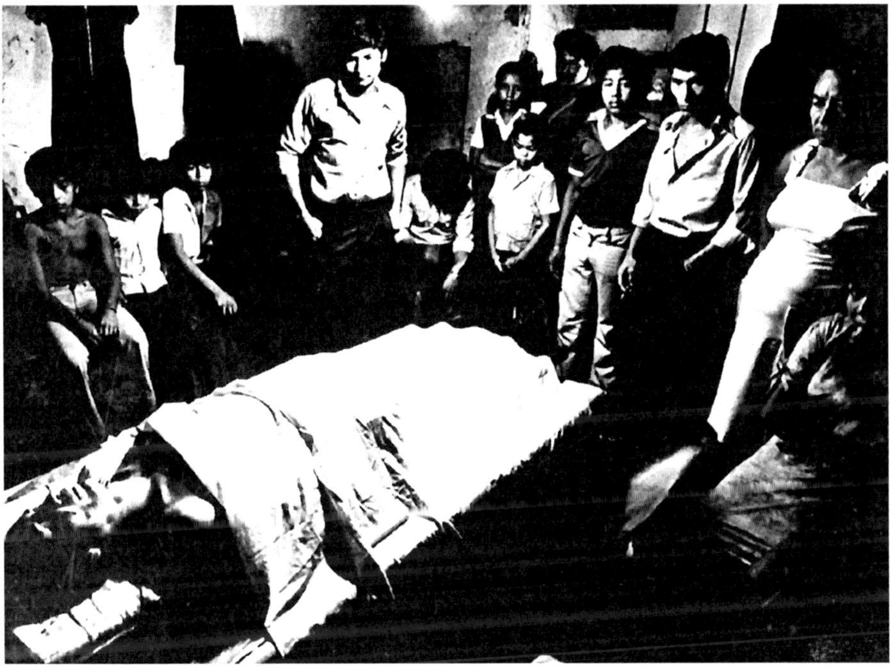

1984 Award

THE MANY EFFECTS OF STARVATION IN ETHIOPIA DURING 1983

by ANTHONY SUAU, *Denver Post*

In 1984 turned out that the entry ranked third in this category had been moved by the Board to the spot news group, where it won, so that there were only two finalists left for the feature award. One of them was David Woo of the *Dallas Morning-News* who had presented „a moving series of fifteen color photographs... depicting children as the victims of war“, the jury report stated; it was the commitee's first choice by a 4-to-1 vote. „The pictures show the loneliness of children displaced by war in Central America,“ the jurors said, „the photographer captured mood, emotion and the despair in some of the children's eyes... We were particulary impressed with his ability to focus on one subject in each picture, avoiding the busyness found in much color photography.“ The jury's second choice was an entry of work by Anthony Suau of the *Denver Post* for pictures telling „a tragic story of starvation in Ethiopia in vivid terms“ and other motifs.

The Board gave the prize to Anthony Suau „for a series of photogaphs which decipt the tragic effects of starvation in Ethiopia and for a single photograph of a woman at her husband's gravesite on Memorial Day.“ Anthony Suau had been at a cementery when he saw a woman holding the tombstone. „I positioned myself with a longer lens,“ he remembered, and „within a few minutes she embraced the tombstone again. I made about six frames. And I realized immediately that it was a very intimate moment.“ Suau waited outside the cementery, and when the woman appeared, he approached her and told her that he made photos when she embraced the tombstone. He wanted to make sure that she gave her permission to publish the picture, and she was delighted. That motif is shown on this book's front cover.

Anthony Suau, born on October 16, 1956, in Peoria, Il., graduated from the Rochester Institute of Technology. After a three-month internship he was engaged by the *Chicago Sun-Times* as a staff photographer in 1979. He switched to the *Denver Post* two years later. In the same year, Suau was named Illinois Press Photographer of the Year. His pictures were also published by the photo agency Picture Group in national magazines like *Time, Business Week, U.S. News and World Report*, etc.

ETHIOPIAN FAMINE CRISIS

Photo, published September 16, 1983, shows that World Vision, a christian relief organization delivers food by small planes to a resote region of Ethiopian's Gondor province. A famine began in Northern Ethiopia that eventually killed as many as one million people within the next twelve months due to drought and civil war.

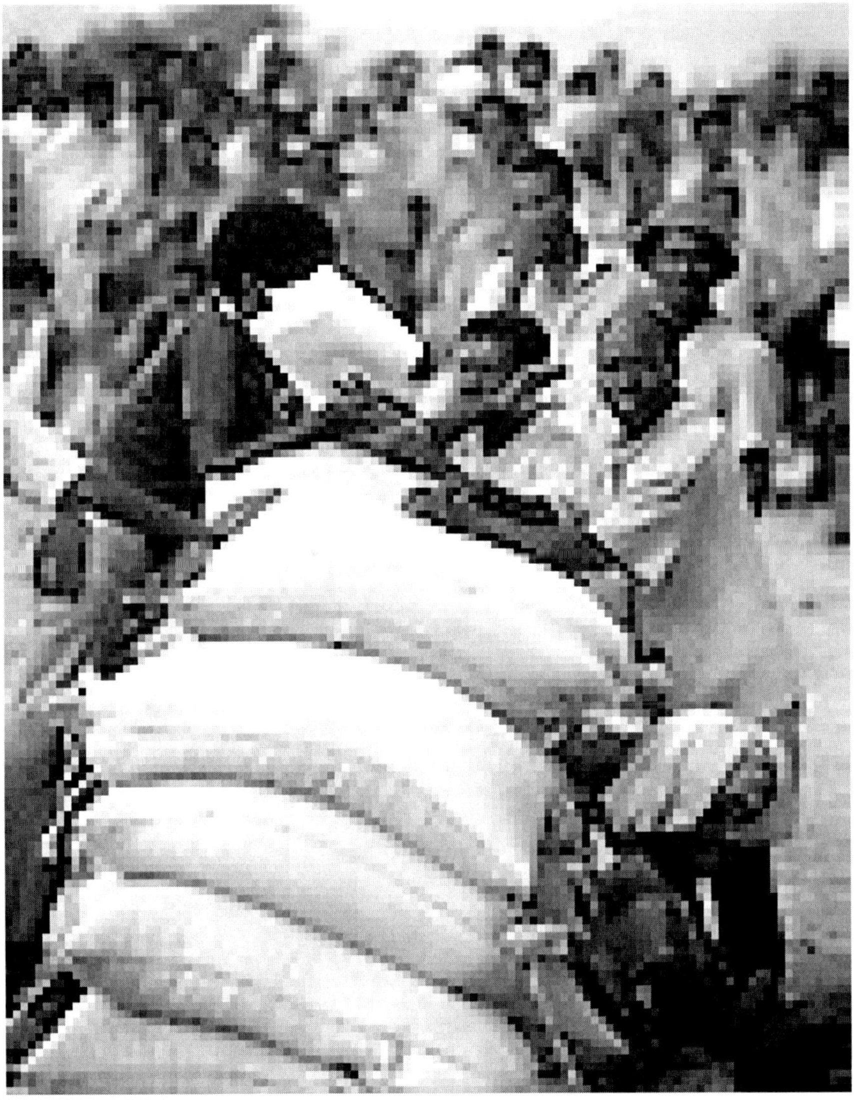

HUNGRY ETHIOPIAN BABY

Photo, published November 27, 1983, decipts a starving three-year-old boy in Ethiopia. The severe hunger castastrophy caused the deaths of 200,000 people. Although closer to the Soviet Union, the United States and Europe sent most food imports to the country.

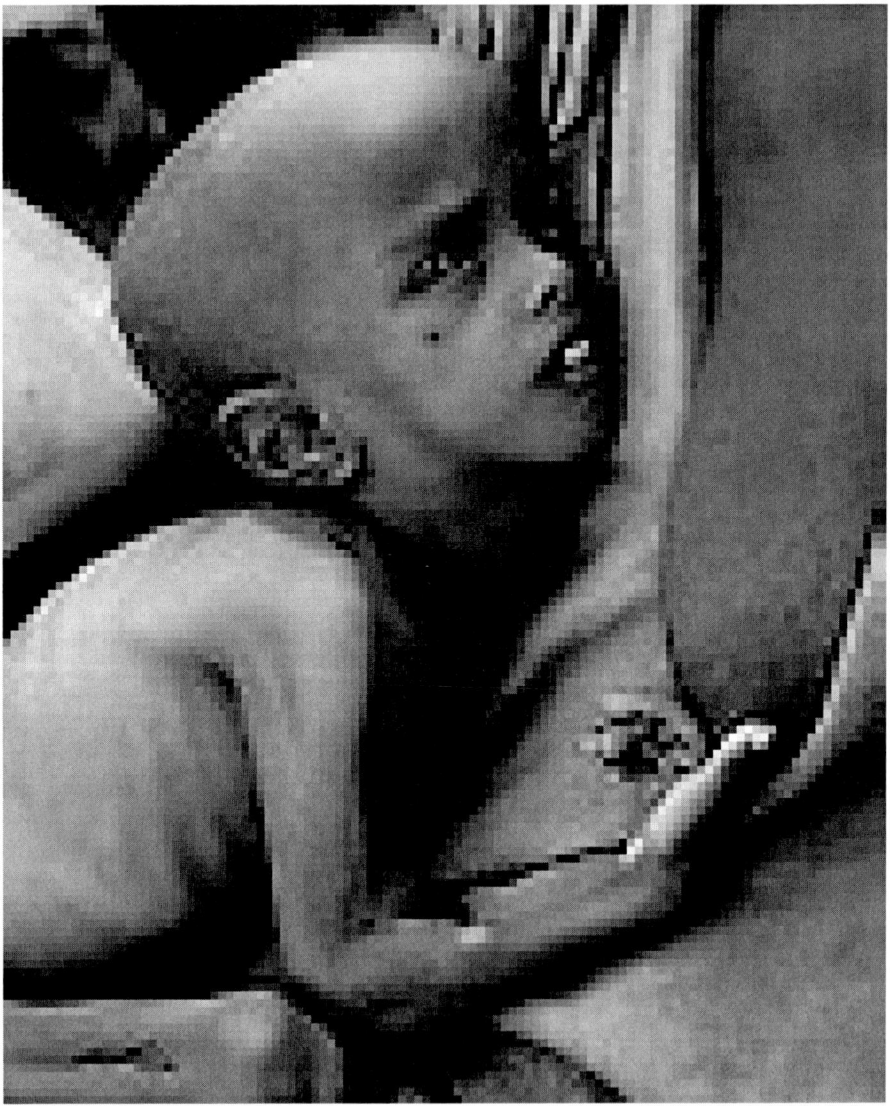

WOMAN AT A WATER HOLE

Photo, published November 27, 1983, illustrates the search of an Ethiopian woman for water. Due to the drought, she had not had water in three days. She had been walking a day to reach this waterhole which had dried out to a mud hole.

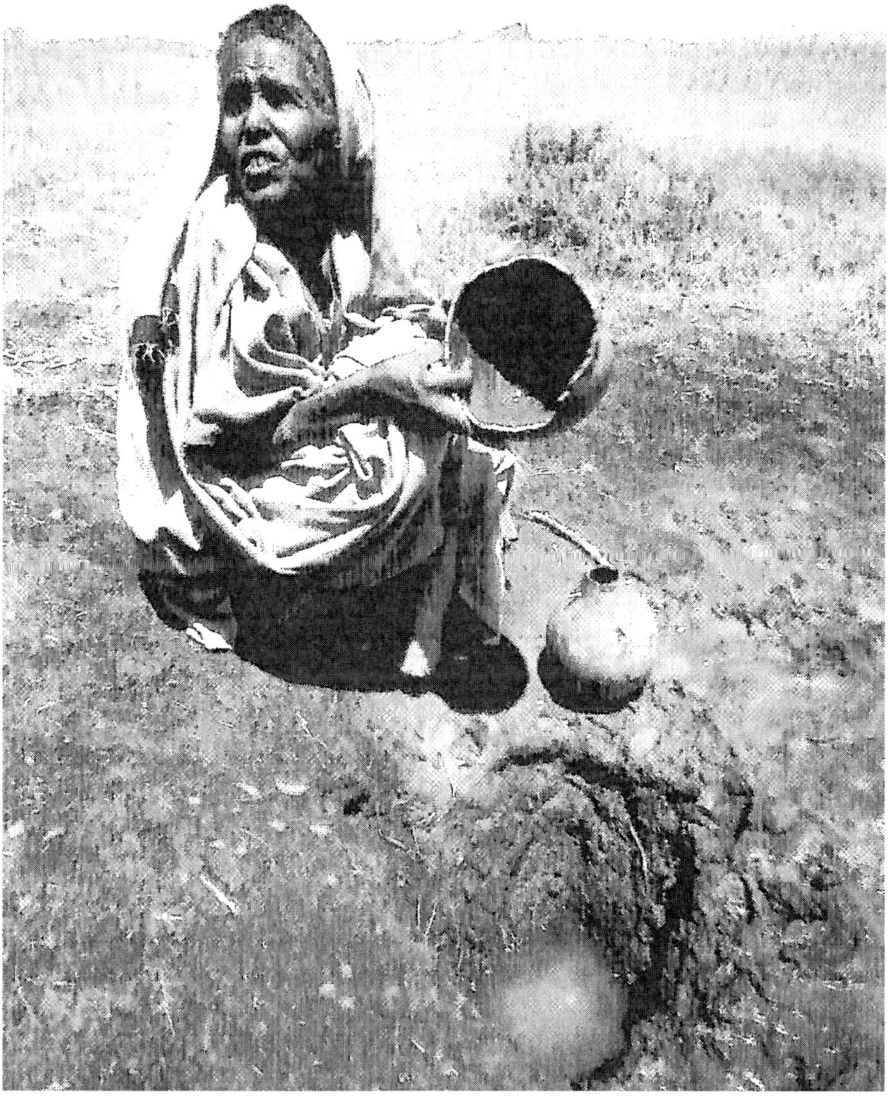

1985 Award

ILLEGAL MEXICAN IMMIGRANTS AT THE UNITED STATES BORDER IN 1984

by STAN GROSSFELD, *Boston Globe*

The 1985 jurors listed the three nominations in this category as follows: Stan Grossfeld of the *Boston Globe* who had presented two stories, one on Ethiopia, the other one on illegal aliens on the U.S. border with Mexico. In the eyes of the jury, both stories showed an „impressive close-up, human element as well as stunning overall shots, a great variety and strong impact." Another finalist was Stormi Greener of the *Minneapolis Star-Tribune* who had shown „pictures of a dying girl that celebrated her life rather than emphasized her dying," the jury report said, „the best photo is of her and friends smiling." Sebastian Salgado Jr. from *Magnum Photos* of Paris was the third contestant on the shortlist for presenting pictures of „strong, beating reality of Ethiopia, with simplicity and high drama in the seriens and good combination of the general and the specific."

The Board gave the Pulitzer Prize in this category to Stan Grossfeld of the *Boston Globe* „for his series of photographs of the famine in Ethiopia and for his pictures of illegal aliens on the Mexican Border." It was quite a surprise that Grossfeld was not the only winner in the Feature Photography category because the Board also declared Larry C. Price of the *Philadelphia Inquirer* winner in this award group. Both earned the Pulitzer Prize in equal parts, and for both it was already their second honor of this kind.

Stan Grossfeld, born on December 20, 1951, in New York City, graduated from the Rochester Institute of Technology with a Bachelor of Science in Professional Photography degree in 1973. He then started to work as a staff photographer at the *Newark Star-Ledger*. Two years later he switched to the *Boston Globe*. While working as a photographer Grossfeld graduated from Boston University with a Master in Journalism degree in 1980. He published the book *Nantucket: The Other Season* in 1982. The following year he was promoted to be chief photographer of the *Boston Globe*. Stan Grossfeld was made the recipient of the 1984 Pulitzer Prize in the spot news category for his series of unusual pictures which reveal the effects of war on the people of Lebanon. Two years after earning his second Pulitzer Prize, Grossfeld moved up to Associate Editor of the *Boston Globe*.

MEXICANS TRY TO MOVE INTO THE UNITED STATES

Photo, published September 9, 1984, shows a group of Mexicans trying to enter the United States illegally by crossing the Rio Grande river, wading neck-high in the murky water. They wanted to work on the okra fields at El Ranchito, Texas. However, they had no move back towards the Mexican side of the river when a United States Border Patrol Agent came by. The number of illegal immigrants from Mexico to the U.S. was estimated to have skyrocketed in recent years.

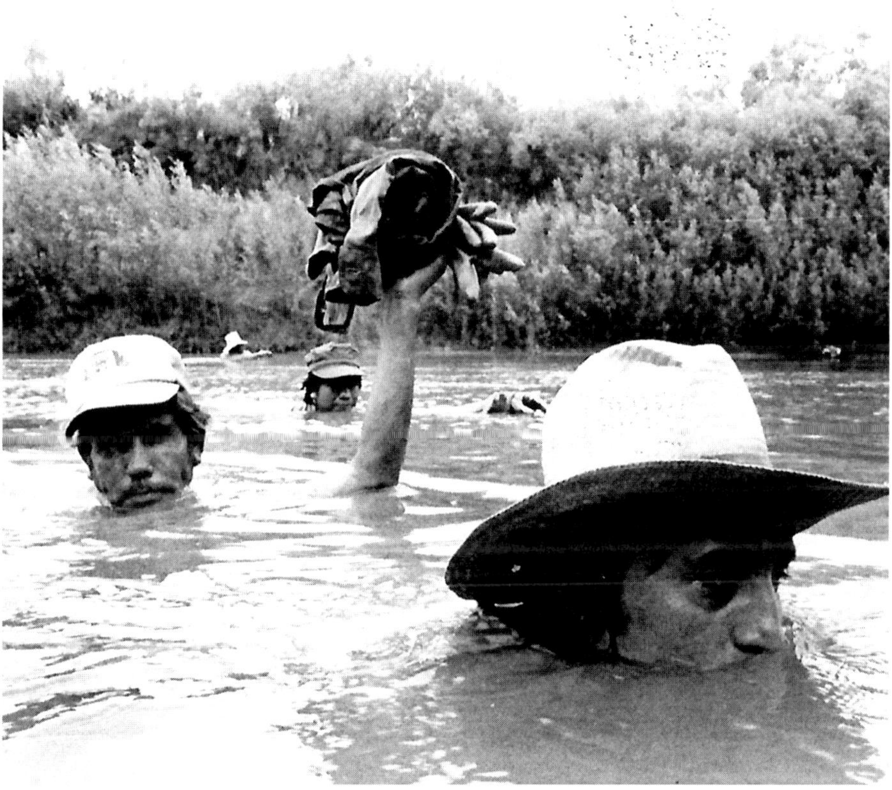

1985 Award

WAR VICTIMS OF THE CIVIL WAR IN EL SALVADOR DURING 1984

by LARRY C. PRICE, *Philadelphia Inquirer*

Price, the second winner in the 1985 feature category, could not be found on the jury's list in this award group. Instead, his merits were told on the shortlist in the spot news category, from where the Board had switched the entry to the feature group. Without saying anything about the content of Price's exhibit, the jury report only told in general wording that he had shown „initiative in getting where the action was; he came up with exceptional photos out of dangerous situations, showed the desperation of the situations.“ When Price earned the award, he was praised by the Board „for his series of photographs from Angola and San Salvador depicting their war-torn inhabitants.“

The photographer remembered El Salvador as a dangerous story because „you never knew where the enemy was, you never knew what was waiting for you around the corner“. Particularly menacing were the right-wing death squads, which murdered more than 50,000 civilians in thirteen years. „These death squads,“ Price said, „would target neighborhoods in El Salvador, summarily execute people, throw them into the back of a truck, driven them out and throw out their bodies.“ The dead were often taken to a field of volcanic lava outside San Salvador. „ I drove over late one afternoon“, Price remarked, „there had been a whole fresh round of killings. The remain of that persons had been dumped a couple of days before. There were a lot of fairly fresh bones and skulls.“

Larry C. Price, born on February 23, 1954, in Corpus Christi, Tx., began his career with taking photos for the Corpus Christi Ray High School newspaper. He attended Sam Houston State University in Huntsville before he tranferred to the University of Texas in Austin in 1976 where he worked for the student newspaper *Daily Texan*. The following year he received a Bachelor of Journalism degree. He then joined the *El Paso Times* where he stayed for two years. Afterwards he was engaged as a staff photographer by the *Fort Worth Star-Telegram* in 1979. Larry C. Prince was awarded the 1981 Pulitzer Prize in the spot news photography category for pictures from Liberia. In 1983 he switched to the *Philadelphia Inquirer* where he got the post of a photojournalist. After winning his second Pulitzer Prize he moved to the *Baltimore Sun*.

FAMILY FLEES FROM EL SALVADOR

Photo, published March 25, 1984, shows a Salvadorian family leaving the region of Jucuaran, in order to evade the fighting which had not ceased since guerillas came to the area six months earlier. The family crossed the Rio Grande de San Miguel climbing the remains of the bridge that used to be there. The Marxist guerillas had destroyed the bridge as they wanted to keep the government soldiers away. However, the troops found another way to enter the region and the fighting commenced.

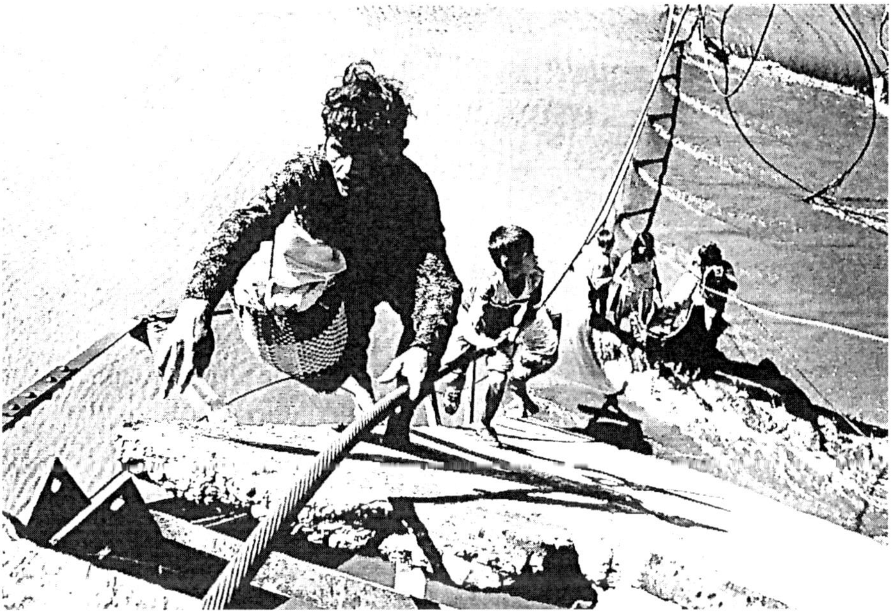

FOOD FOR SALVADORIAN CHILDREN

Photo, published March 25, 1984, portrays one of the many refugees that the civil war in El Salvador created. The boy was in the Mesa Grande refugee camp in southern Honduras. Run by the United Nations, the camp provided shelter and food under extremely difficult conditions. Although the Salvadorians had fled the dangerous situation in their home state, they were not completely safe in the neighboring country. The Honduran government strongly advised the refugees to stay inside the camp as they might be subject to attacks outside the camp walls.

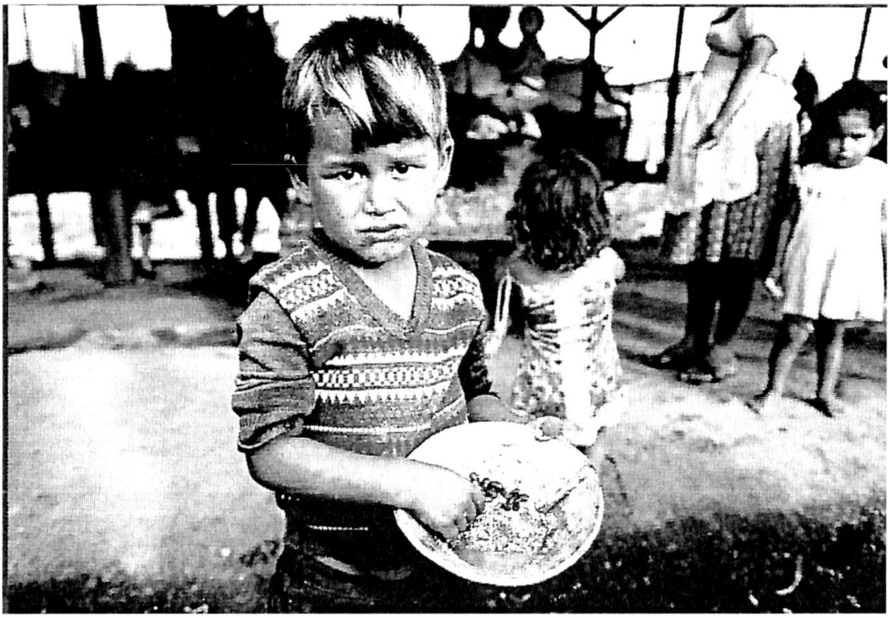

VICTIMS OF NUMEROUS KILLINGS

Photo, published July 8, 1984, explains that the dead of the civil war often taken to El Playon, a field of volcanic lava outside of San Salvador. The picture shows the remains of a person that had been dumped a couple of days before, a lot of fairly fresh bones and skulls.

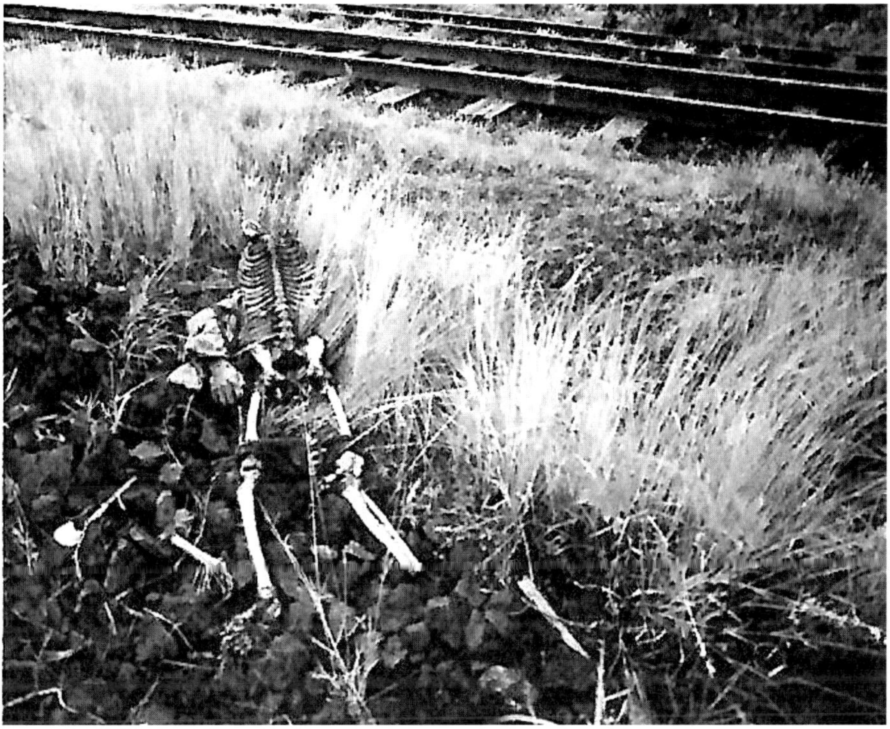

1986 Award

HOMELESS PEOPLE AT THE STREETS OF PHILADELPHIA IN 1985

by TOM GRALISH, *Philadelphia Inquirer*

The three finalists of 1986 had covered different social problems. Tom Garlish's photos of the Philadelphia homeless, published in the *Philadelphia Inquirer*, in the eyes of the jury „brought these people out of the wary city's statistics of the 1980s. His portraits not only showed the plight of these people but society's response to the readers could easily recognize their own reaction for this urban phenomenon, which gave the pictures a certain quality.“ The civil strife in South Africa was the theme by David J. Leeson of the *Dallas Morning-News*. „This strife lives today,“ the jury report stated, „in the voices, faces and actions of the people of South Africa. David Leeson's portraits of these people... represent both superb feature photography and distinguished journalism.“ Michael S. Wirtz of the *Dallas Times-Herald* had „documented the decline and despair of American farmers“ and reached third nomination.

The Board did not hesitate in announcing Tom Gralish of the *Philadelphia Inquirer* winner of the Pulitzer Prize „for his series of photographs of Philadelphia's homeless.“ The photographer had stepped out his life and into the lives of the city's street people. „I didn't know much about these guys,“ Gralish remembered, „so I decided to show what their day is like. I wanted it to be straight-forward 'doc photography' - go out and see what you can find.“ He had walked the streets with his camera, and he „hooked up with one little group. It was like a community - enough vendors to be nice to them, enough steam grates, a liquor store nearby, a hospital, lots of commuters to panhandle - everything they needed... People like it when you pay attention to them. These guys had disdain for society and the rules; that's why objected to the shelters. They saw themselves as the last free men.“

Tom Gralish, born on July 12, 1956, in Mount Clemmens, Mi., lived in England, Japan and the Philippines and in many regions of the United States during his childhood. He was engaged by the *Las Vergas Valley Times*. His pictures were distributed by the *United Press International* bureaus of Dallas, Tx.; Detroit, Mi.; Minneapolis, Mn., and Kansas City, Mo. In 1983 he joined the staff of the *Philadelphia Inquirer*. He became director of photography for the *Inquirer*'s Sunday Magazine.

LIFE IN WINTER ON SIDEWALK

Photo, published February 2, 1985, shows a homeless man called Walter living on a sidewalk heating gate. Walter talkes to himself and rants to people on the street. Everyone knows him; people who live and work in the neighborhood give him change so that he can buy some food.

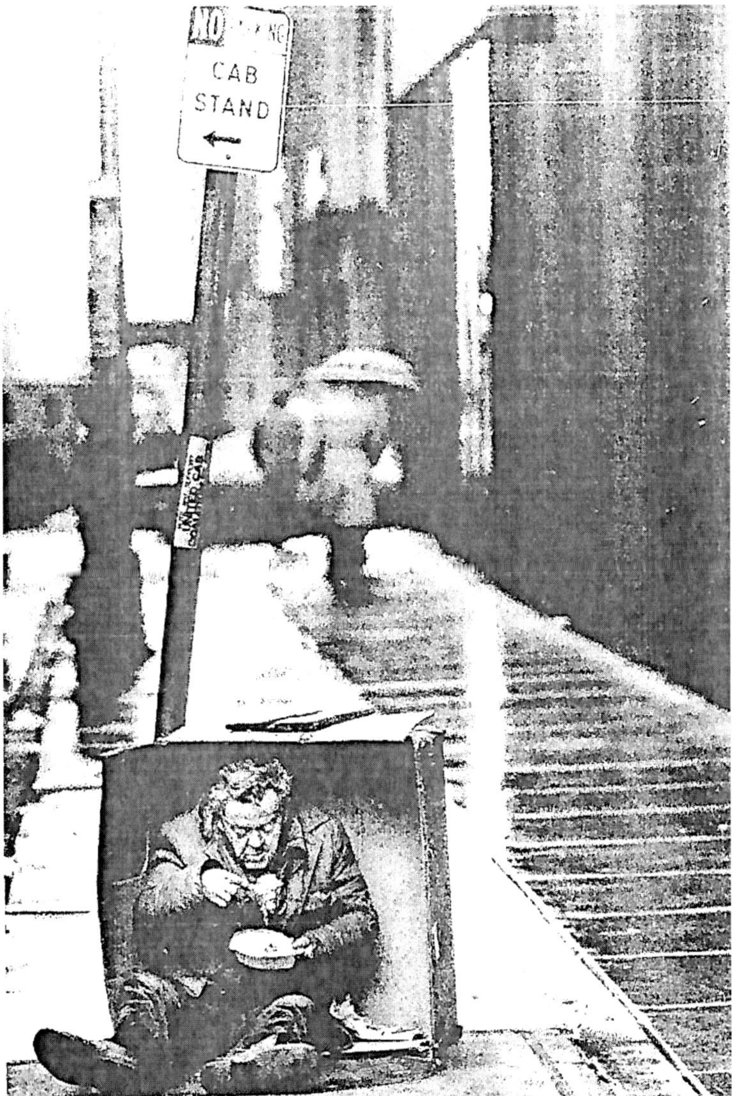

BEGGING AT HOT-DOG VENDOR

Photo, published April 7, 1985, shows a homeless named Carlos talking with the sausage vendor, Tony Thomas. After he had immigrated to the United States from Greece, Thomas admitted he was surprised to see that in a rich country such as the U.S. there were homeless people whereas in Greece he claimed nobody was living on the streets. Thomas got to know the homeless young man when he set up his vendor stand near the grate where Carlos lived.

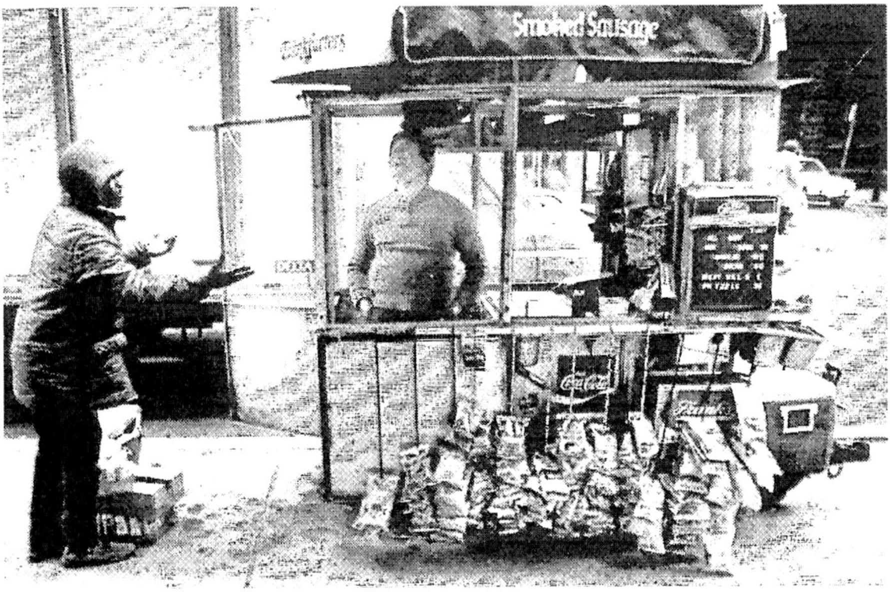

WATCHING RESTAURANT COSTUMERS

Photo, published April 7, 1985, decipts a typical scene for homeless people in the streets of American cities; watching other people eat in restaurants while they are starving. While they could always find a place to sleep by themselves, the homless had to beg for food every day. Most of them did not get a welfare check because they did not have a permanent address. Therefore the means to get food on a regular basis were limited: they had to either beg for money to buy food.

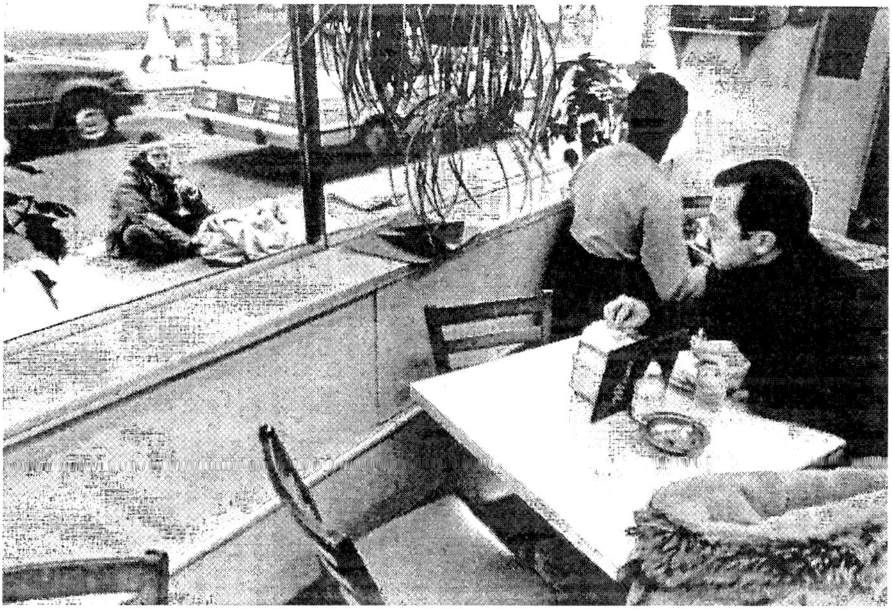

1987 Award

THE SHATTERED ECONOMIC DREAMS OF AMERICAN FARMERS IN 1986

by DAVID C. PETERSON, *Des Moines Register*

An unusual theme was mentioned right at the beginning of the 1987 jury report. The entry by Cheryl Nuss of the *San Jose Mercury-News* „chronicled the diversity of AIDS victims and the emotional toll exacted by the diseas on the victims themselves and those around them... A strong example of powerful photojournalism." David Peterson's photos, published in the *Des Moines-Register*, were called by the jurors „an excellent portrayal of the human drama of the farm tragedy. The photographer took issues crucial to the newspaper's circulation area and communicated well the complex story. The reader feels personally present as events progress toward the quietly dramatic conclusion." April Saul-Zerby of the *Philadelphia Inquirer* had presented to the jury „the finest example of sensitive photography with no feelings of intrusion, despite strong cultural barriers to the presence of an outsider", but no details about the theme were mentioned.

In the end the Board picked David Peterson of the *Des Moines Register* and made him winner of the Pulitzer Prize „for his photographs depicting the shattered dreams of Americam farmers." The photographer had taken a leave of absence from his job at the newspaper to tell the farmers' stories which was not easy. „Farmers put their guard up," Peterson remembered, „it can take them a long time to warm up to the camera." Peterson spent much time with the Steffes couple who lost their farm. „The symbol for the death of a farm... was the wooden white cross," the photographer explained, „once I started shooting they seemed to forget about me and became lost in their thoughts... They were together in their grief but seemed lost and apart in their hopelesness."

David C. Peterson, born on October 22, 1949, in Kansas City, Mo., graduated from Kansas State University with a Bachelor of Science degree in Art Education in 1971. Two years later he received another Bachelor of Science degree in Journalism of the University of Kansas. From 1975 on he worked for the *Topeka Capital-Journal* as a staff photographer. He then switched to the *Des Moines Register* in 1977. In the mid-1980s, he applied for a Nikon/ National Press Photographers Association grant to cover the farm crisis in depth and took a sabbatical from the newspaper.

COUPLE FORCED TO SELL THEIR FARM

Photo, published December 7, 1986, illustrates the consequences of the crisis of farming that had been going on for six years. The crisis was especially severe in Iowa where many couples and families were forced to sell their farms. Pat and Elmer Steffes from Audubon, Iowa, lost their land through foreclosure after they could not pay their debts anymore and had to make a whole new start.

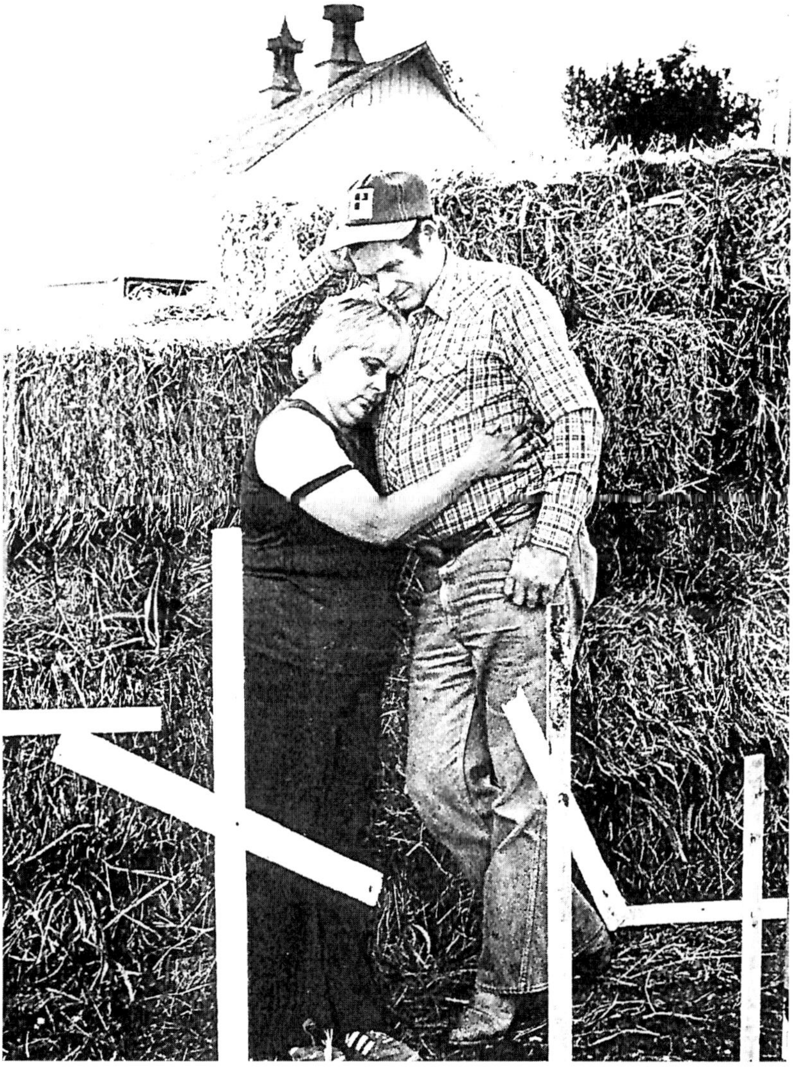

SELLING THE FARM AND MOVING TO TOWN

Photo, published December 7, 1986, decipts Ellen Fleener, 88, who has prepared to move into town and give up her farm life. However, she could not find a buyer for her property.

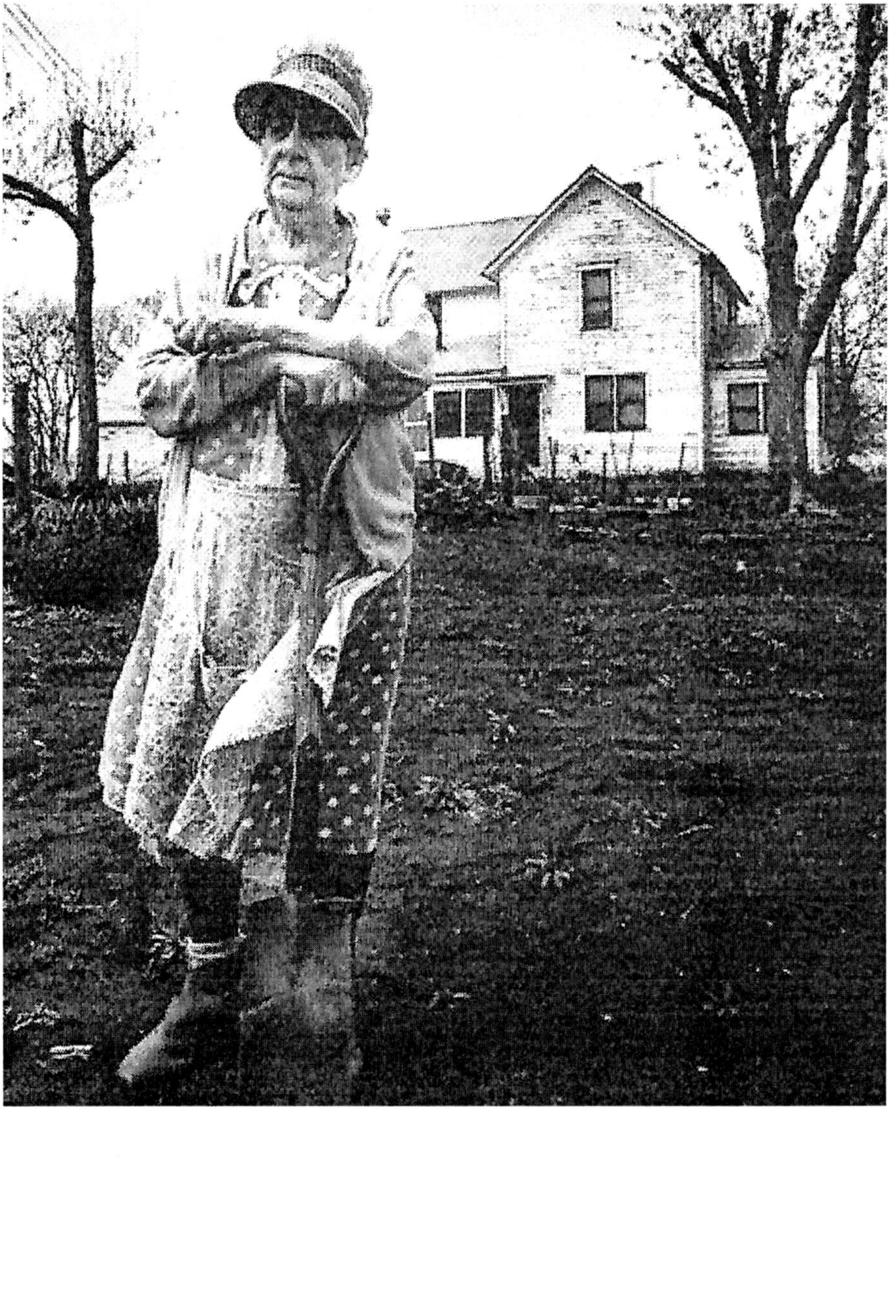

ONE HUNDRED-YEAR OLD FARM SOLD

Photo, published December 7, 1986, shows Roger and Kathy Taylor with their twelve-year-old son, Jarrod. They had to sell their farm which had been owned by their family more than a hundred years. They were facing a $ 300,000 debt that they were unable to work off and had to sell their property of more than 400 acres.

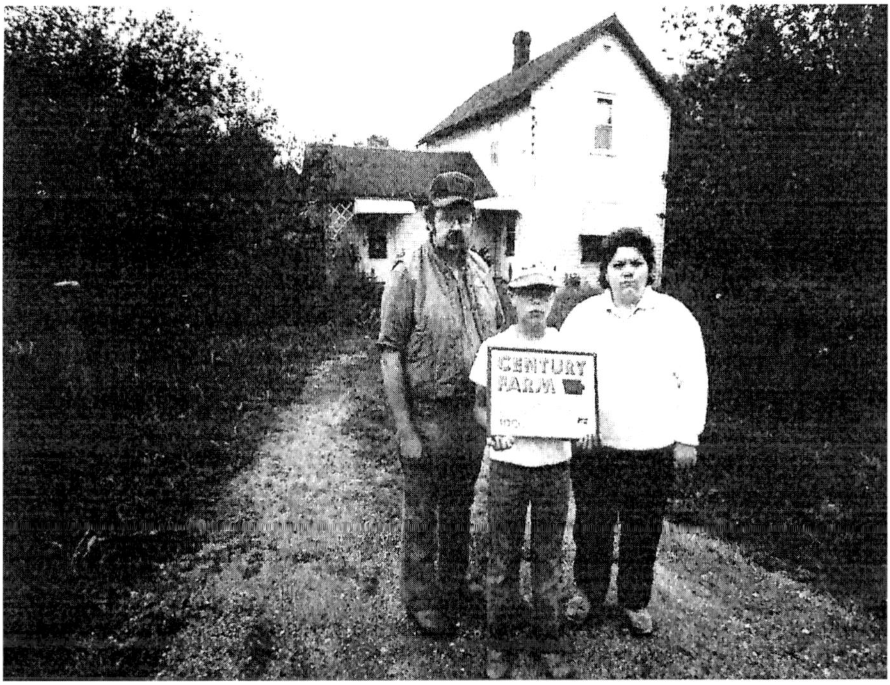

1988 Award

PORTRAITS OF THE GRADUAL DECAY OF DRUG CONSUMERS DURING 1987

by MICHEL DU CILLE, *Miami Herald*

According to the 1988 jury report, George Widman of the *Associated Press* had „captured the hopelessness, and despair of the homeless in one photograph with a subject who appears almost as an apparition." Although the Vietnam War was long over, photos of that kind were still news, the jury members stated re an entry by Barbara J. Reis of *USA Today*. Her „photograph, taken on Veteran's Day at the Wall in Washington", the report said, „bridges the gap between generations as a disabled Veteran and an elderly woman clutch hands in remembrance." Third photographer on the jury's list was Michel C. du Cille of the *Miami Herald* who had presented moving pictures about cocain and cracks users. He „had to go close, perilously close to his subjects to show the tragedy, pain and despair of crack. The jury believes," the report continued, „Mr. du Cille could only have taken photographs at great personal risk."

This explosive topic was also deemed to be most outstanding by the Board, and thus Michel du Cille was honored with his second Pulitzer Prize for his pictures of Miami's Graveyard area. „Everyone had been painting it as a black inner-city problem," du Cille explained, „ set out to show that people in all walks of life were involved." For weeks the photographer hanged out in the 'Graveyard', photographing lives fading to ruin. „You have to be there and they have to get to know you, they need to feel comfortable with you... There is a certain line of humanity that you have to draw and you say 'I have to step over this line and be human'", du Cille stated. His pictures moved people and stimulated change, the complex was cleaned up and crackheads disappeared.

Michelangelo E. du Cille, born on January 24, 1956, in Kingston, Jamaica, graduated from Indiana University with a Bachelor's degree in journalism in 1981. He then joined the *Miami Herald*. In 1986 Michelangelo E. du Cille won the spot news photography Pulitzer Prize, shared with Carol Guzy. By the time he earned his second Pulitzer award in 1988, Michel du Cille moved to the *Washington Post* to become the newspaper's picture editor.

MAN SMOKING CRACK FROM A PIPE

Photo, published April 5, 1987, decipts a man who had converted a beer can into a pipe so that he could smoke crack through it. Michael had bought three pieces of crack and had planned to take them home, but in the end he could not wait any longer and smoked them in broad daylight. Michael had left his family in Detroit and talked about getting off the drug while he was constantly searching for more. He had started smoking crack when he had moved to Miami.

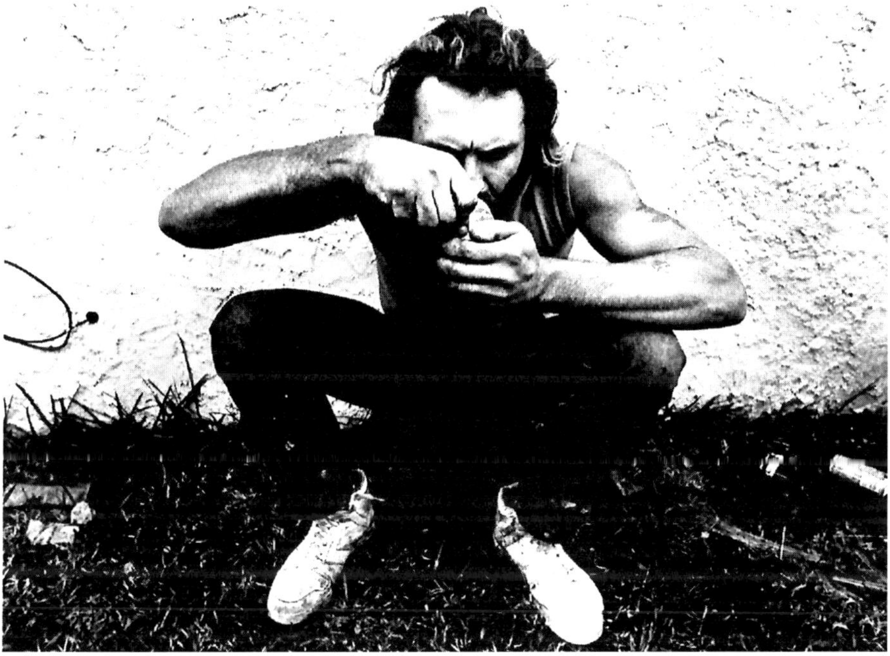

WOMAN TEMPTED INTO CRACK SCENE

Photo, published April 5, 1987, illustrates the demise of the apartments in „the Graveyard", a housing project in Miami, Florida. Pat, the woman in the photo, sat in a apartment that had been converted into a crack den. In her opinion, the name of the project derived from the fact that most drug-addicts look and act like zombies that only have drugs on their minds and nothing else. Probably being addicted to drugs herself, she only had a milk crate left to sit on.

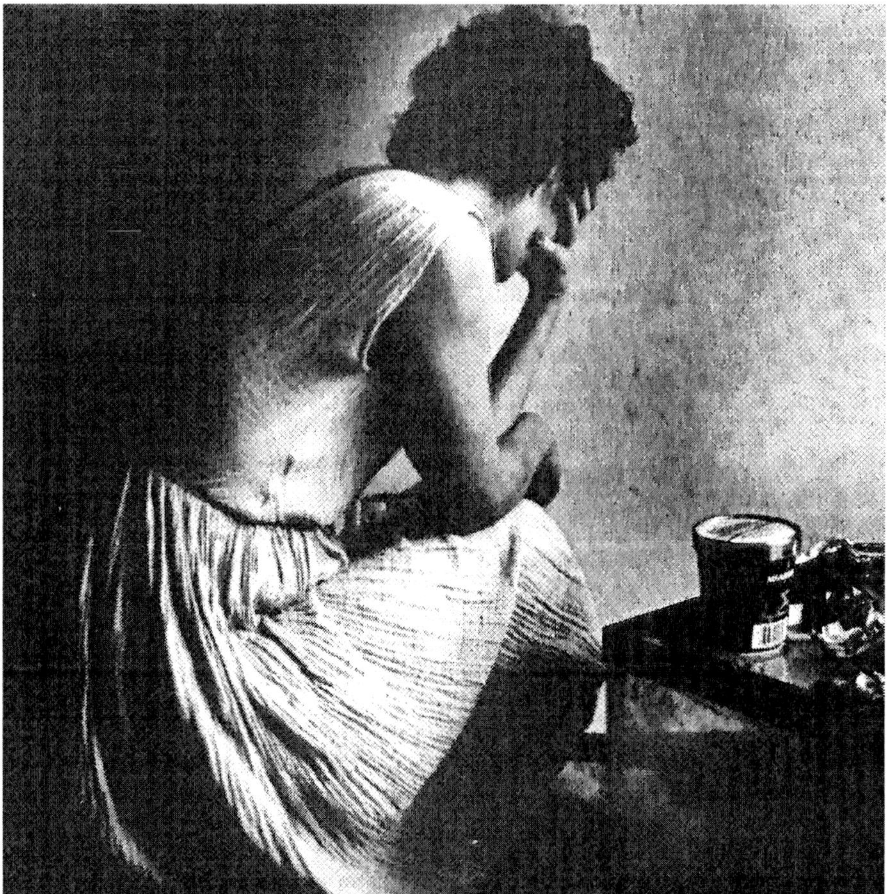

WEEPING MAN AFTER HIS ARREST

Photo, published April 5, 1987, reveals the desperation of a man who had been apprehended during a police raid in a housing project in Miami, Florida. He begged the police to let him go because he did not want his kids to know why he had been arrested. He was but one of many who had come to the „Graveyard" to buy drugs. Crack only cost ten dollars a piece which made it easy for many people to purchase.

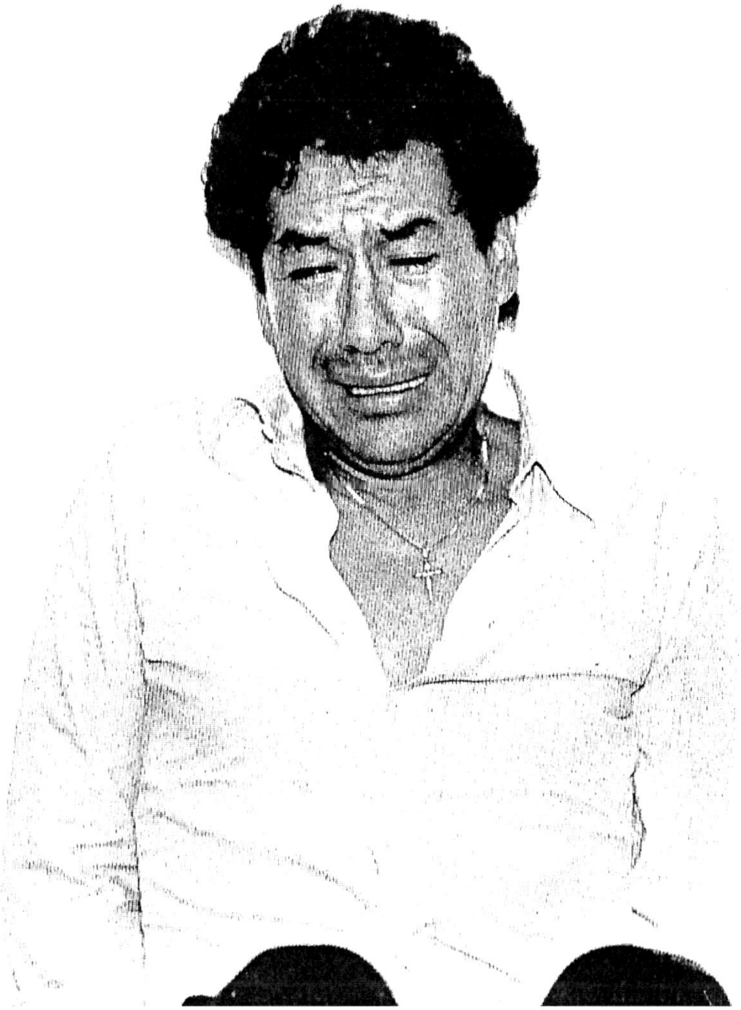

1989 Award

SOME FACTS OF STUDENT LIFE AT A DETROIT HIGH SCHOOL IN 1988

by MANNY CRISOSTOMO, *Detroit Free-Press*

Donna Bagby of the *Dallas Times-Herald* was mentioned first on the 1989 jury's shortlist, but no theme of her exhibit was given. Her entry, in the words of the jurors, „reflected the timeless quality and the strong composition expected in a feature entry.“ Manny Crisostomo of the *Detroit Free-Press*, it was said, „had built, frame by frame, a moving and permanent record of a special place and time. The photos speak eloquently of both the unchanging flavor of life in an urban American high school and the 1980s reality of drugs, youthful pregnancies and weapons in the classroom. Few newspapers,“ the jury added, „would grant a photographer the time to visit and revisit a local high school for a whole school year“ as Crisostomo did. Frederic Larson of the *San Francisco Chronicle*, third contestant on the list, had visited Hiroshima and Nagasaki forty-three years after atomic bombs had devastated both cities. His portfolio „eloquently recaptured the human toll of suffering and shattered lives.“

The Board chose Many Crisostomo of the *Detroit Free-Press* and gave him the prize „for his series of photographs depicting student life at Southwestern High School in Detroit.“ The photographer had spent 40 weeks at the school after the superintendent had given permission to take pictures. Crisostomo's intention was „to photograph the things that make high school tick, - classes, students, teachers, athletics, as well as the socioeconomic factors away from the classroom that have an impact on the students.“ He found Southwestern „just like any other high school in America..., problems with dating, with proms, with homecoming. We talked, laughed and argued about the city and the world. I saw a lot of them mature and come to grips with impending adulthood.“

Manny Crisostomo, born on November 28, 1958, in Sinajana, Guam, attended the University of Guam and the University of Missouri. He entered newspaper work as a staff member of the *Columbia Missourian*, joined the *Jackson Citizen-Patriot* and the *Detroit Free-Press* where he was promoted to be staff photographer. His publication credits included *Life, Time, Newsweek, Pacifica*, the *Los Angeles Times* and the *Honolulu Star-Bulletin*.

THREE OUT OF FOUR DROPPED OUT

Photo, published June 26, 1988, shows four friends who originally met in Southwestern High School in Detroit. Only one of them, John Jerome, at the far left of the picture, was still attending that school. The others, Dawn Glabosky, Weaver and Darren Carnes all had left school without a diploma. The four friends were heading downtown Detroit to go to the Motown Hoedown. For the next school-term, Jerome had promised himself not to skip classes anymore.

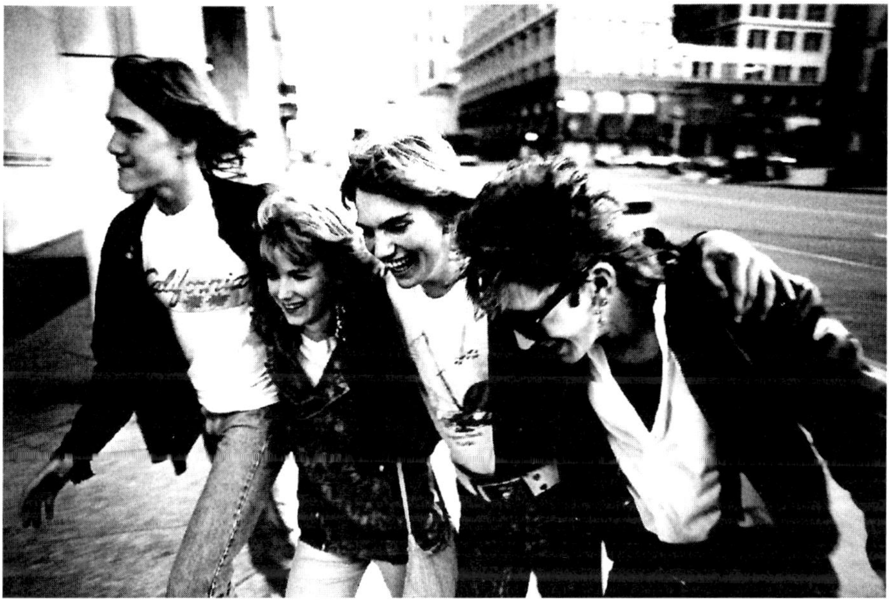

LINING UP FOR GRADUATION CEREMONIES

Photo, published June 26, 1988, shows the senior students of Southwestern High School in Detroit waiting to go on stage and receive their high school diploma. The garduates were only a small part of students who had entered the high school after finishing junior high. This was due to the increasing rate of drop-out students. The situation in high schools had deteriorated in many regions of the U.S., however, the change was particulary severe in Detroit.

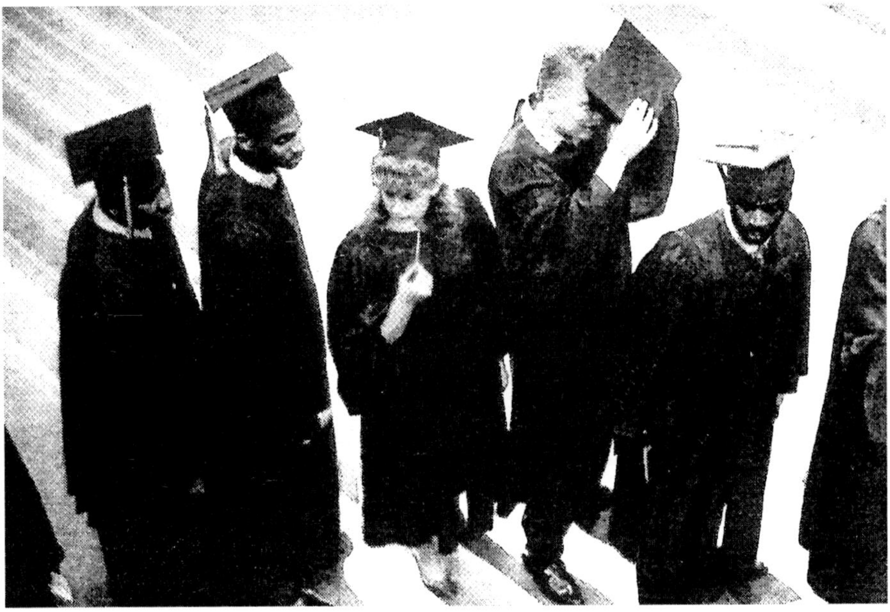

EMJOYING A STUDENTS' GARDEN PARTY

Photo, published June 26, 1988, decipts the first part of an evening during which high school graduates celebrated their diploma. Before going to the prom at their high school, the students met for a garden party. The young women and men all attended Southwestern High in Detroit. The young man in the foreground of the photo was Senior Ray Ponder who was proud of his achievements because he had reached his self-set goals: Ponder had managed to maintain his 3.5 grade point average.

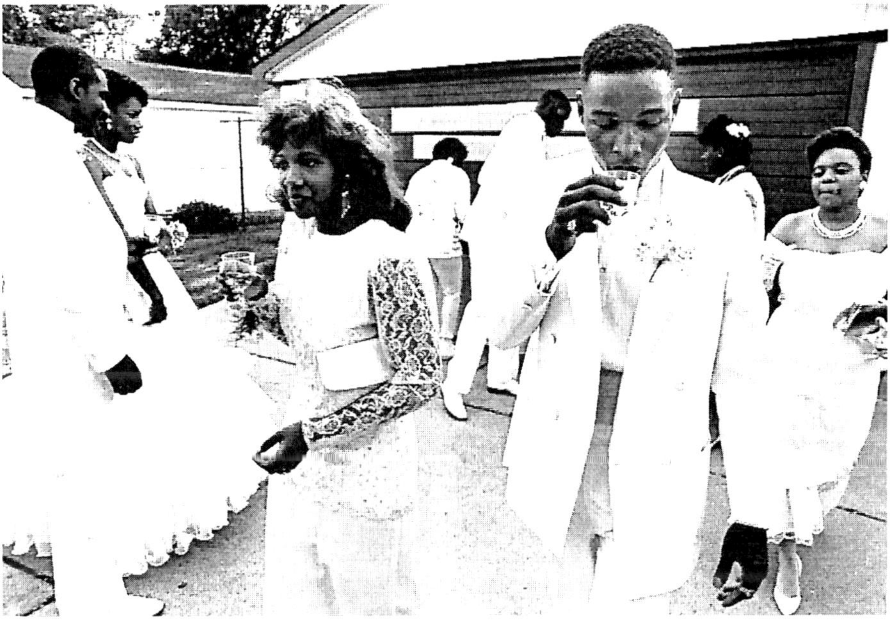

1990 Award

THE POLITICAL UPRISINGS IN CHINA'S CAPITAL BEIJING IN 1989

by DAVID C. TURNLEY, *Detroit Free-Press*

Photographers of the *Anchorage Daily News*, who had covered the tanker accident of the „Exxon Valdez", were mentioned first on the jury's list of 1990 and praised for the „human elements" in their pictures about „this environmental tragedy." John Tlumacki of the *Boston Globe* was among the three finalists for his „memorable images.... readers will never forget" from Berlin in the days of the German reunification process. Sara Greener-Brown of the *Minneapolis Star-Tribune* was mentioned next for moving photos about „Child Abuse". „This photo story", the jury report started, „breaks new ground journalistically: we've written about the tragedy of tried abuse but few have succeeded of illustrating it. The public service aspect of this project: very, very strong... The photographer's ability to work into the story was remarkable." Although all three finalists were cited for their amazing competence, the Board chose non of them. Instead it declared David C. Turnley of the *Detroit Free-Press*, featured in the spot news category, as winner „for photographs of the political uprising in China and Eastern Europe."

The photographer had been in Beijing when thousands demonstrated for democratic reform. „I found students in Tiananmen Square playing guitars and singing Beatles songs", Turnley remembered, „I felt like I was going to experience what it was like to change the status quo." What he photographed instead was a massacre. „To see the youth of that society having their dreams crushed was very disillusioning", he said. From China he moved to Germany by the time the Berlin Wall came down. „People were almost silly with euphoria", he remembered, „it was just such an unexpected, complete shift in the status quo.Turnley followed the democratic wave to Czechoslovakia and then to Romania, before he later confessed: „I'm still reeling from the roller coaster of emotions of that year."

David C. Turnley, born on June 22, 1955, in Fort Wayne, In., attended the University of Michigan from which he graduated with a B.A. degree and then studiend at Sorbonne University in Paris, France. He started his newspaper career in 1978 as a staff photographer at *Northville Sliger Home Newspapers*, Mi. Two years later David Turnley switched to the *Detroit Free-Press*.

MAN KILLED AT TIANANMEN SQUARE

Photo, published June 4, 1989, decipts one of the many victims of the violent clashes between the Chinese military forces and the Chinese people in Beijing. In mid-April, 1989, students in the Chinese capital had started to demand freedom and democracy in their country in mass demonstrations. Soon over 50,000 students demonstrated peacefully. More and more people joined them and supported the students' movement. On June 4, tanks were rolling onto Tiananmen Square. They did not stop for people standing in their way.

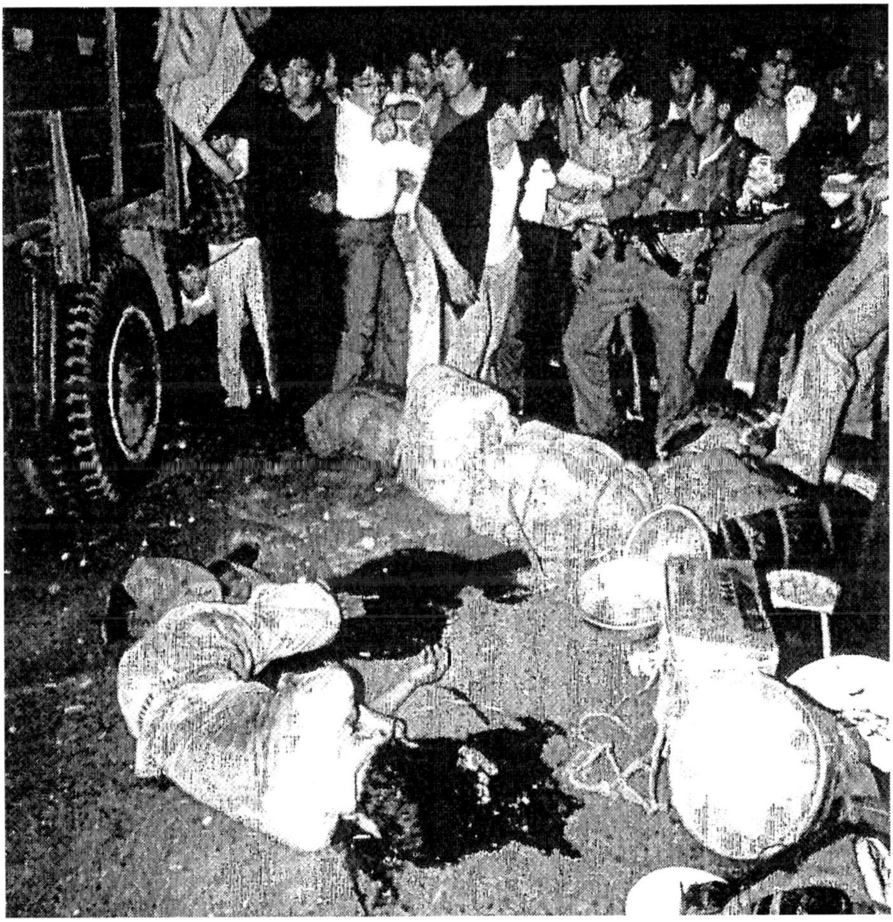

A MOTHER MOURNS THE DEATH OF HER SON

Photo, published June 5, 1989, decipts family members trying to comfort a grief-stricken mother who has just learned of the death of her son, a student protester killed by soldiers on Tiananmen Square on June 4. Many other families also had no idea what happened to their children.

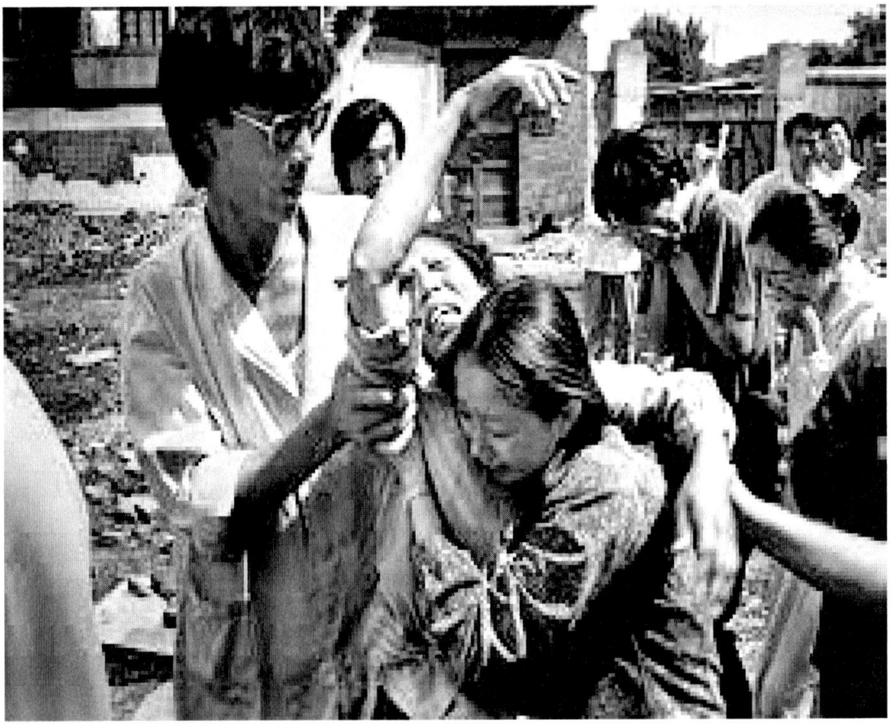

DAYS AFTER THE BEIJING MASSACRE

Photo, published June 7, 1989, decipts the city of Beijing after the movement for democratization of China had been violently crushed. Since the demonstrations had begun in mid-April after the death of reformist politician Hu, the government had condemned the movement and claimed that its initiators were only attempting to disturb the peace in China's society. However, when the students started to convince the public of their goals, the government decided to put an end to their protests in early June.

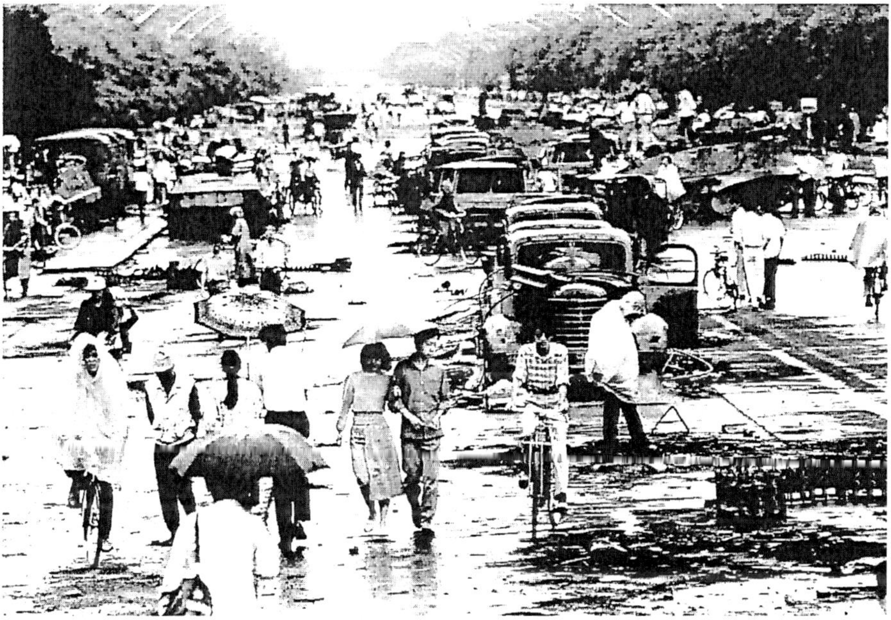

1991 Award

ORPHANED CHILDREN LIVING IN POST-COMMUNIST ROMANIA IN 1990

by WILLIAM D. SNYDER *Dallas Morning-News*

The 1991 jurors stated in their report that photographer William D. Snyder of the *Dallas Morning-News* had covered „the fall of the communist dictator in Romania" which „opened the door for Western journalists to reveal the horrorof an oppressive regime" that did not care for orphaned children. Ronald Costes of the *Philadelphia Inquirer* had depicted „A 60-Year-Old Returning to High School, a human story" of unusual feelings. Jay Mather of the *Sacramento Bee* had submitted „beautiful pictures of Yosemite National Park."William Snyder received the Pulitzer Prize „for his photographs of ill and orphaned children living in subhuman conditions in Romania."

„It was horrible, absolutely horrible", Snyder remembered, „I was a human being, someone you could touch and see. The kids were all over me. I had a son about two years old. I just kept projecting him in that situation, it was very difficult. A lot of the workers didn't care about the children, they did the bare minimum. They swaddled the infants so that they wouldn't roll around and create problems, - therefore restricting motor growth and coordination. I had always been a run-and-gun photographer. Going to Romania changed everything for me. This wasn't about pictures, this was about people, defenseless, helpless people. It was no longer just pictures to be taken, it was stories to be told."

William D. Snyder, born on July 1, 1959, in Henderson, Ky., entered the newspaper work already at the age of fourteen by photographing local school football games for the *Henderson Gleaner*. Two years later when he received the driver's license he was promoted to be „weekend" staff photographer. Snyder attended Boston University for one year. He then studied at Rochester Institute of Technology, where he was named College Photographer of the Year. He received a B.S. degree with highest honors in 1981 and directly started to work as a staff photographer for the *Miami News*. Two years later Snyder was elected Region 6 Photographer of the Year by the National Press Photographers Association. In the same year he switched to the *Dallas Morning-News* where he got the post of a general assignment photographer. William Snyder won his first Pulitzer Prize in the explanatory journalism category in 1989 before he earned the feature photography award two years later.

ON THE WAY TO GATHER FOOD

Photo, published August 5, 1990, depicts an examplatory scene in an orphanage in Romania: At the Gradinari orphanage in Vulturesti, the nurse Mimi Rizescu was taking care of twenty children. She had to leave them alone when she went to a neighboring building where she gathered food for the afternoon meal for the children. The photo illustrated the depressing state in which the buildings of the orphanage and foremost the orphans themselves were in. In Romania, therewere more than 500 orphanages which ran under equally bad conditions.

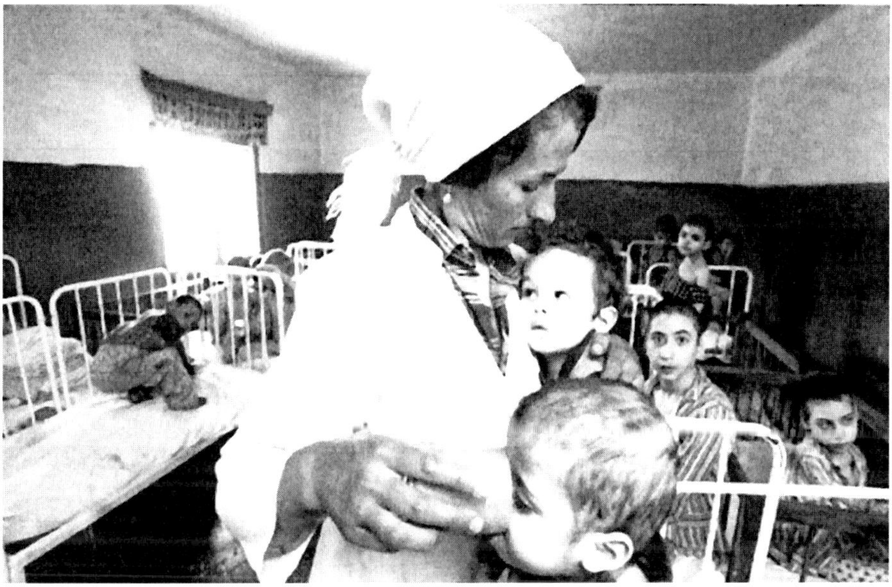

RESPONSIBLE FOR TWENTY CHILDREN

Photo, published August 21, 1990, shows Mimi Rizescu taking care of two children simultaneously at the orphanage for mentally and physically handicapped children in Vulturesti, Romania. While she only had to look after twenty children, her two colleagues each had fifty children under their supervision. Many children had to share a bed with others as the facilities were very poorly equipped. In addition, the state-run orphanages' budgets were drastically cut in the depression that followed the downfall of the communist regime in Romania.

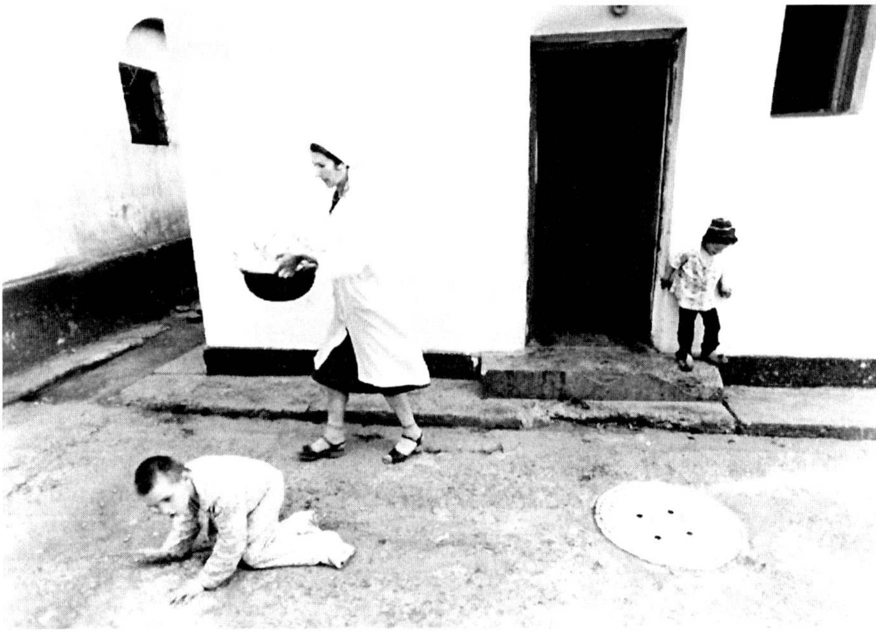

TEENAGE BOY BEHIND BARBED WIRE

Photo, published August 21, 1990, shows one of the one hundred orphans who stayed at their home in Vulturesti, Romania, as teenagers, because there was no other place they couldgo. The barbed wire indicated the conditions under which the orphans had to live. There was not enough money to hire more employees to look after them.

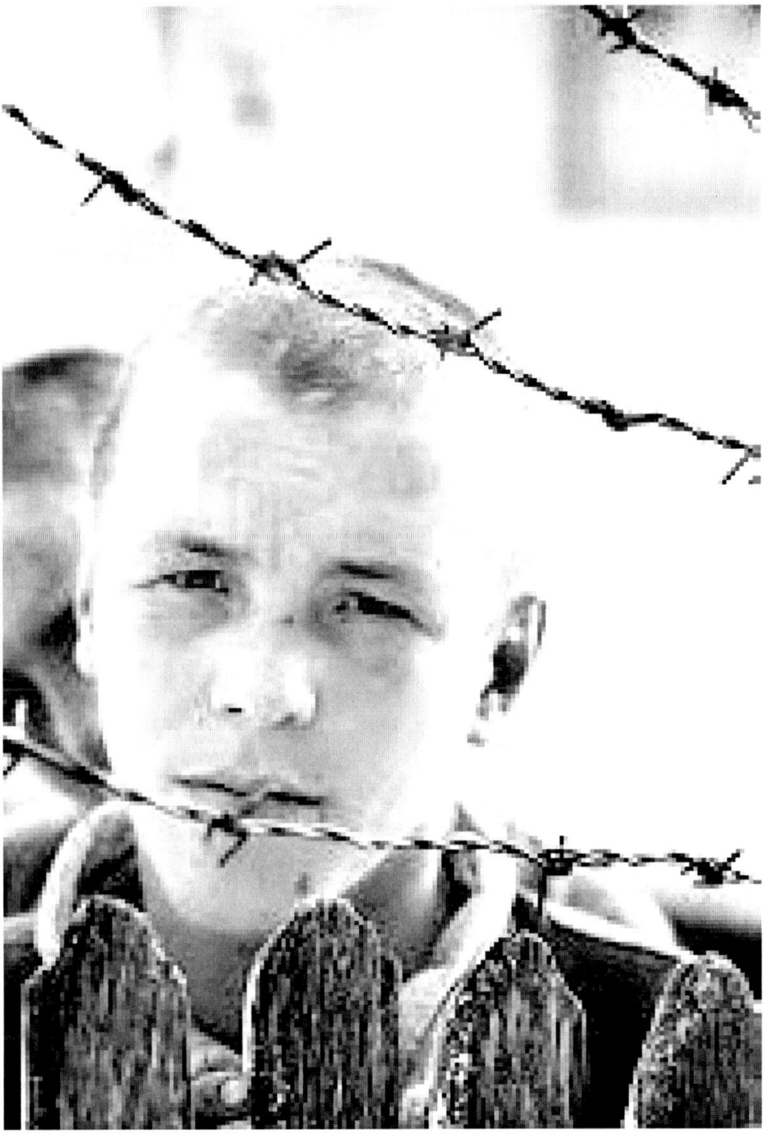

1992 AWARD

THE LIFESTYLES OF TWENTY-ONE-YEAR-OLDS ACROSS THE U.S. IN 1991

by JOHN KAPLAN, *Block Newspapers*

In the opening passage of their report the jurors of 1992 mentioned the entry by JohnKaplan of the *Monterey Herald* who had „vividly told the story of seven individuals across the nation in an extraordinary series, 'Age Twenty-One in Our Culture.' Both the concept for the feature series and its execution were exceptional. Kaplan's photography is riveting, capturing the essence of life." Paul Kuroda of the *Orange County Register* had sent in an exhibit about „illegal immigration across the U.S.-Mexican Border", whereas Charles W. Snead of the *Washington Post* was selected for his „portfolio from the Kurdish refugee camps." The Board decided in favor of John Kaplan of the *Monterey Herald*, although in its official announcement of the winner it did not cite the newspaper itself, but rather the newspaper group to which the *Monterey Herald* belonged, Block Newspapers of Toledo, Ohio.

Kaplan had got the idea for the series when he photographed a 21-year-old murder suspect in Pittsburgh, and he decided to photograph a diverse group of 21-year-olds, „people who were cultural icons, people who we might fantasize being when we grow up... and people who had been left behind," f.e. a female model, a heavy-metal singer, a football player or a male prostitute.„No matter what their circumstances", Kaplan remembered, „people see it as a compliment that you're interested in finding out who they are." His work reflected the notion that „in America we have a variety of choices, but those choices are limited by background, environment, individual talents and today's wide polarization of American society," Kaplan remarked. His goal was „to let the viewer make his or her own conclusions about the variety of lifestyles in our culture."

John Kaplan, born on August 21, 1959, in Wilmington, De., studied at Ohio University from which he graduated with a journalism degree cum laude in1982. The following year Kaplan was engaged by the *Spokane Review/ Chronicle*, Wa., where he stayed for one year. The photojournalist then switched to the *Pittsburgh Press*, Pa. In 1990 Kaplan left the *Pittsburgh Press* to join the *Pittsburgh Post-Gazette*. From 1991 on he also worked as a Special Correspondent for *Block Newspapers*.

BAND MEMBER WITH HIS PET BOA

Photo,published November 10, 1991, portrays rock musician Phil Anselmo with his pet boa. He had been touring with his Texas-based metal band Pantera for the whole year trying to find fans for their debut album, 'Cowboys from Hell.'

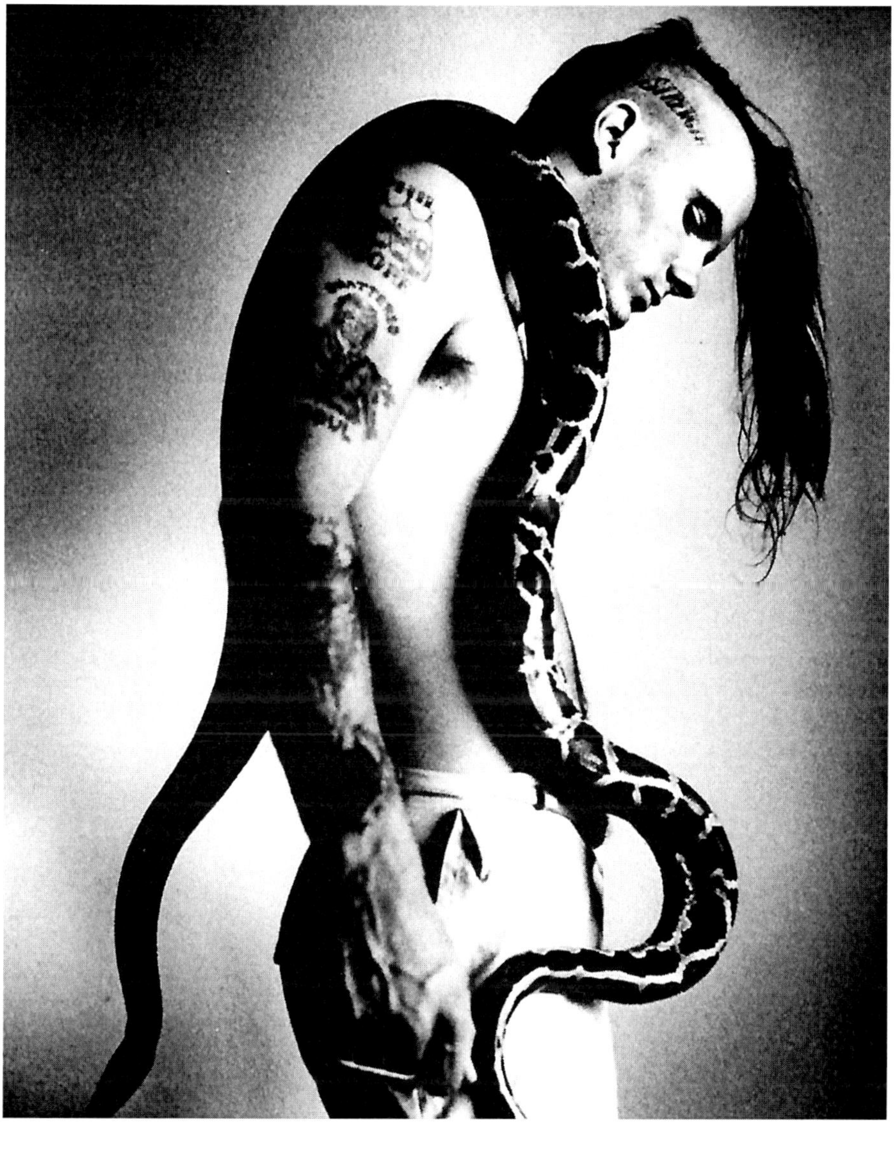

HARVARD STUDENT IN HER DORM ROOM

Photo, published December 23, 1991, portrays Malli Marshall, a senior at Harvard Medical School, dozing off while studying for one of her five classes. At the same time, she was juggling a part time job and a long-distance relationship, which was taking its toll.

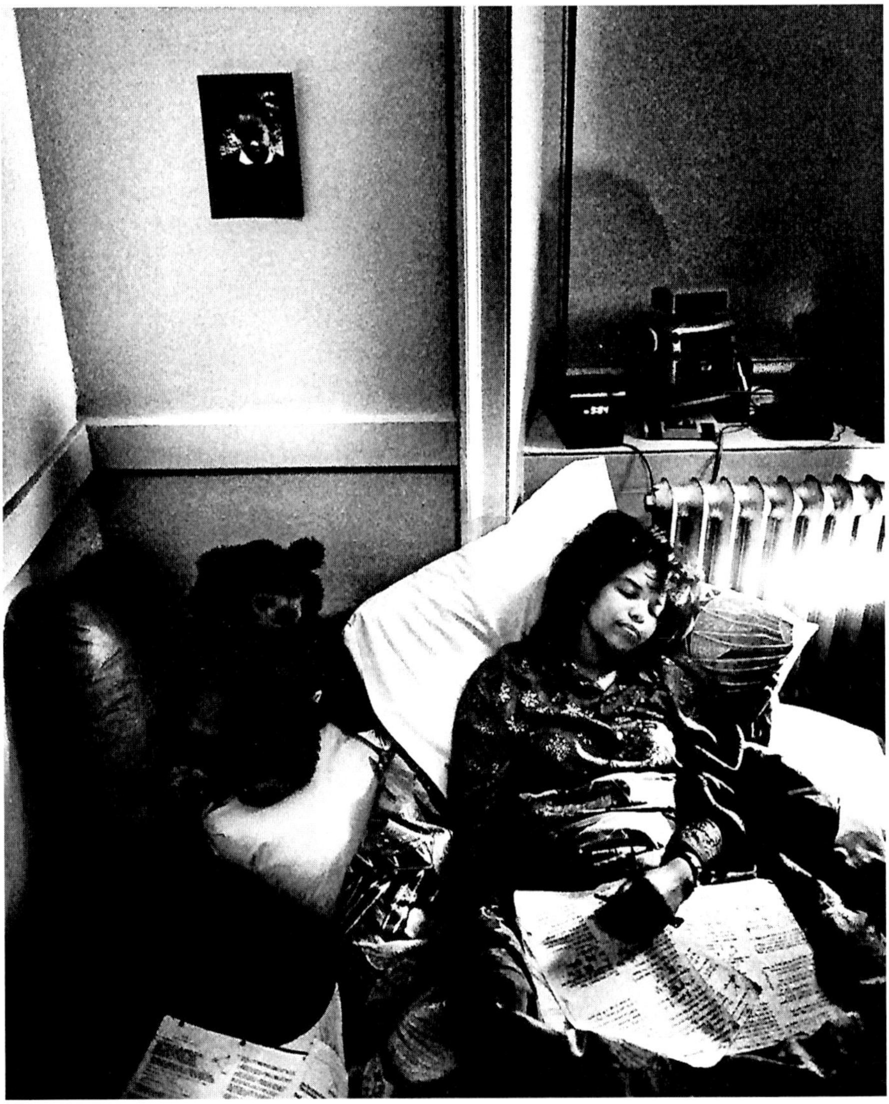

BOY DISPLAYS HIMSELF ON THE STREET

Photo, published December 31, 1991, depicts Brian, a male prostitute who did not want to reveal his last name, trying to attract clients. He had been living of the street for three years,selling sex in order to finance his addiction to drugs. He refered to meeting a client as „going on a date." Brian originally came from an upper-middle class family in Missouri.

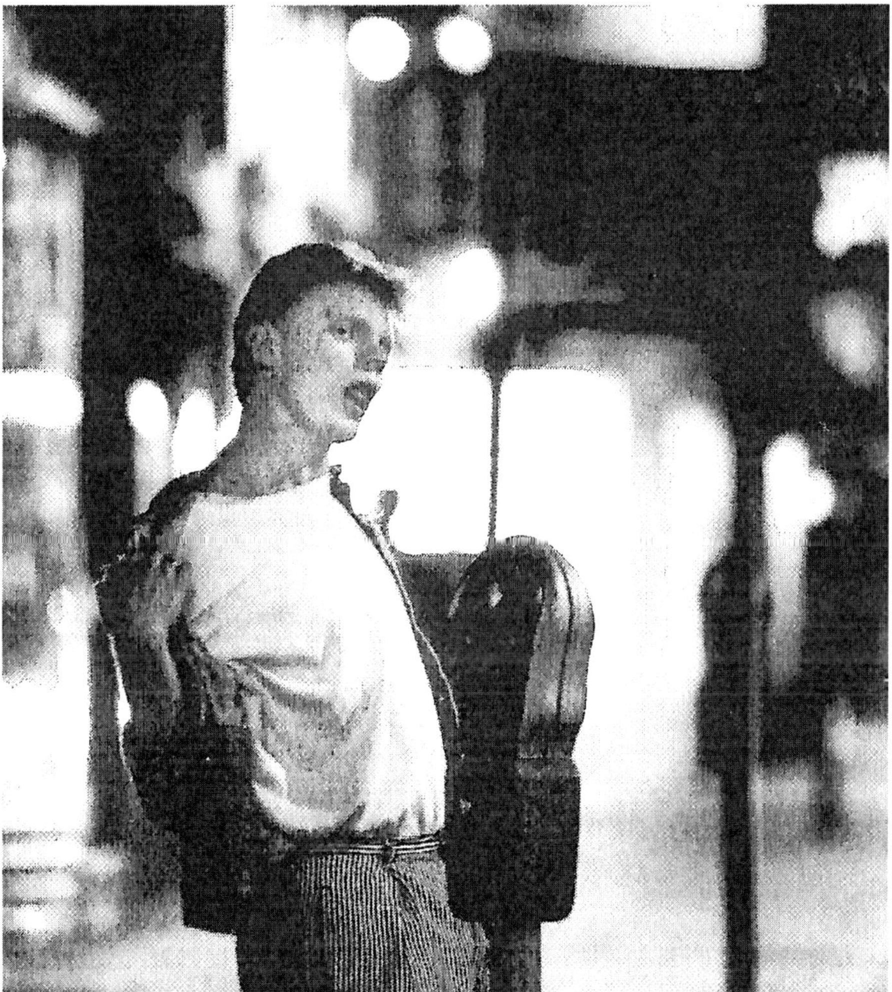

1993 Award

SOME IMPRESSIONS OF BILL CLINTON'S PRESIDENTIAL CAMPAIGN IN 1992

by GREG GIBSON ET AL., *Associated Press*

Three staff entries found their ways on the jury's 1993 shortlist, two of them from the *Associated Press*. One *AP* exhibit, in the words of the jurors, had „covered the hell out of the 1992 presidential campaign... The emotional and spontaneous reflections of the candidates and their families, the sincere interaction with voters and children along the campaign trails, all were captured with experience and expertise by the *AP* photographers.“ The second group entry from the *Associated Press* had presented „outstanding, sustained coverage of Somalia's desperate plight. Each picture tells a story of individuals struggling to survive. Together, the pictures comprise a complex portrait of a nations' will to live.“ Yunghi Kim of the *Boston Globe* also had covered the Somalia tragedy in a twelve-picture portfolio. The Board voted for one of the two *AP* entries which earned the Pulitzer Prize „for its portfolio of images drawn from the 1992 presidential campaign.“

One of the *AP* senior photographers from the award-winning team and some of his colleagues had followed the campaign of Bill Clinton in New England. They took pictures from Clinton press conferences, at debates, with his family, while he played saxophone. Everywhere they went, there were hordes of potential voters, campaign workers and journalists. „It was just a typical campaign day“, Gibson remembered, „when Clinton was kind of hopscotching around New Hampshire. He was real big on shaking everybody's hand. I'll bet he shook every hand in the state twice... There was so much press and so much interest in him, it was difficult to find something different to shoot.“One day, Gibson took pictures during a campaign stop at a shopping center, and he saw a „little boy leaning on the counter and he had his head in his hands and I just knew Clinton was going to stop there. Sure enough he did, and he was talking to the boy and pretty soon Clinton had his chin in his hand like the boy.“

Greg Gibson shared the Pulitzer Prize with these nine colleagues: J. Scott Applewhite, Richard Drew, David Longstretch, Doug Mills, Marcy Nighswander, Amy Sancetta, Stephan Savola, Reed Saxon and Lynne Sladky.

SMALL TALK IN NEW HAMPSHIRE

Photo, published February 15, 1992, shows contestant for the presidential candidacy Bill Clinton talking with three-year-old Josh LaBarra of Salem, New Hampshire. The conversation took place at the counter of an ice cream shop in Salem. The primary in New Hampshire was taking place just three days later. The primary in that state was decisive as it was traditionally one of the first in the country and thus gave the first impression of who was a serious contestant for the presidential office in the respective party.

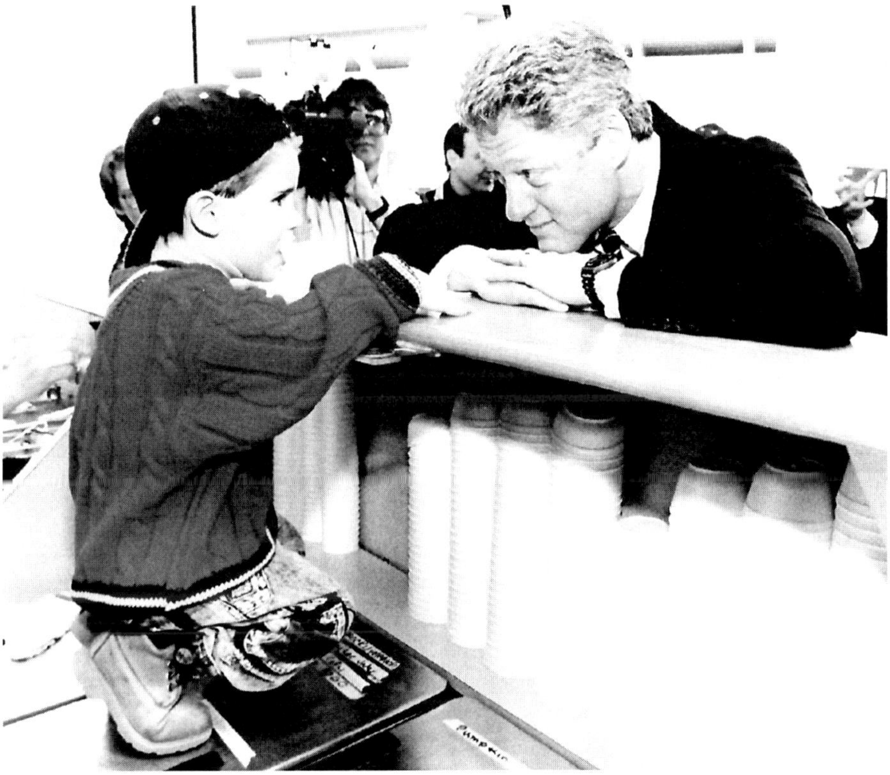

EARLY BIRD SPEECH IN TEXAS

Photo, published October 29, 1992, shows Democratic presidential candidate Bill Clinton giving a speech early in the morning in downtown Houston, Texas. For the elections, it was important to win over the large states such as Texas or California because of the proportionally high number of electoral votes that these states had. Clinton thus focused his last efforts on Texas, giving a speech in Houston only four days before the presidential elections were being held.

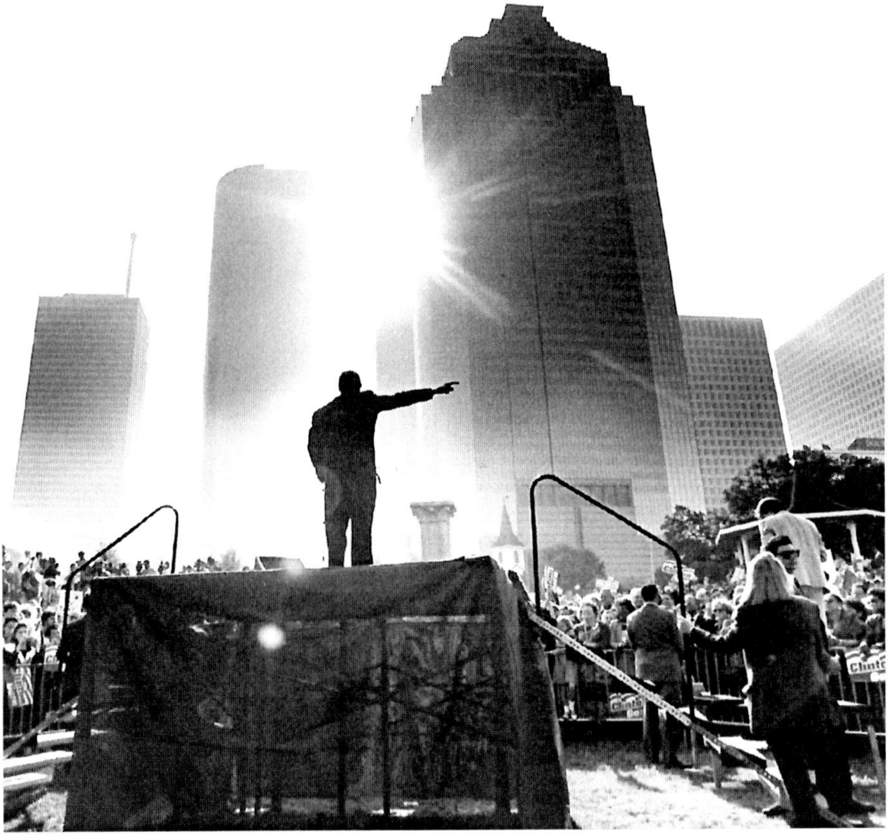

SAXOPHONE PLAYER IN GEORGIA

Photo, published November 24, 1992, shows Bill Clinton as a face in the band with the Sugar Bear marching band of Central High School at City Hall in Macon, Georgia. He was already elected next President of the United States, but the inauguration was still to come. For publicity reasons, the candidate of the Democratic Party had also played the instrument on other occasions, such as the 'Arsenio Hall' show, a night talk show. This contributed to establishing an image of Clinton as a more energetic and innovative politician than his contestants.

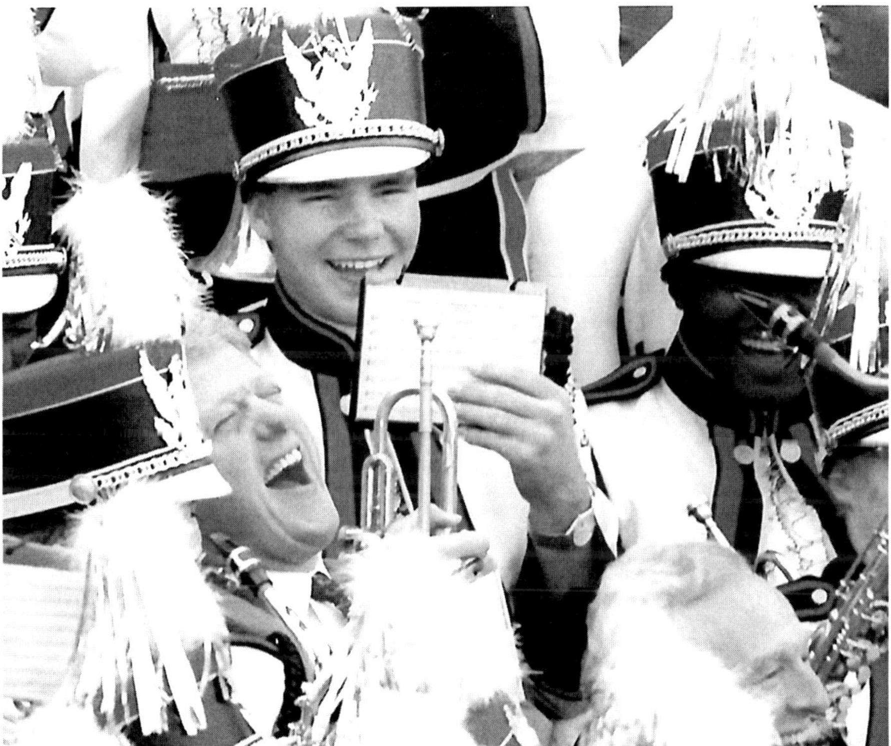

1994 Award

A COLLAPSED SUDANESE GIRL ON HER WAY TO A FEEDING CENTER IN 1993

by KEVIN CARTER, *New York Times*

The jury members of 1994 had the following three finalists on their list: Stan Grossfeld of the *Boston Globe* for his ecologic series of pictures on „The Exhausted Earth,“ April Saul of the *Philadelphia Inquirer* for a series of photos called „American Dreamers“, and the *Associated Press* staff for motifs of the „Conflict in the Middle East.“ Grossfeld's pictures, in the eyes of the jury, had made „the abstract concept of global-environmental depletion... real and moving.“ The photographer Saul had „made extraordinary pictures out of ordinary events.“ The *Associated Press* photographers had „put human faces on a baffling and age-old political problem.“ But in the end, none of the three finalists made it, as the award went to Kevin Carter, who originally was on the shortlist in the spot news photography category, „for a picture, first published in the *New York Times*, of a starving Sudanese girl who collapsed on her way to a feeding center while a vulture waited nearby.“

Carter had traveled to the Sudan to cover the relentless East African famine. At a feeding station at Ayod, he found people so weakened by hunger that they were dying at the rate of an hour. As he photographed their hollow eyes and bloated bellies, he heard a soft whimpering in the bush. Investigating he found a tiny girl trying to make her way to the feeding center while a vulturelanded nearby. Carter took his photo and chased the bird away. Afterwards, he sat under a tree and cried. This shocking photograph ran in newspapers world-wide and many people asked: Why didn't he pickup the child? But journalists in the Sudan had been told not to touch famine victims.

Kevin Carter, born on September 13, 1960, in Johannesburg, South Africa, began working as a sports and news photographer for the *Sunday Express* in 1983. The following year he switched to the *South Africa Star*. In 1988 Carter worked for the *Associated Press*, then for the Johannesburg *Sunday Tribune*, before he joined the *Rand South Africa Daily Mail*. He switched to the *Mail and Guardian* and he also worked for *Reuters* and the *New York Times*. But the controversy about his confession that he did not help the photographed child overwhelmed him, and in July 1994, at the age of 33, he took his own life, - several weeks after winning the Pulitzer Prize.

AN ICON OF STARVATION

Photo, published March 26, 1993, shows a Sudanese girl on her way to a feeding center. She collapsed from hunger and dehydration. The vulture in the background was apparently waiting for her to pass out. However, she only rested and proceeded on her way to the food center in Ayod in the South of the country after the photographer had chased away the vulture. But it is not known whether she ever reached her destination. There were several reasons for the scarcity of food supplies in Sudan: Under the military al-Bashir regime, many ethnic minorities were forced to leave their villages.

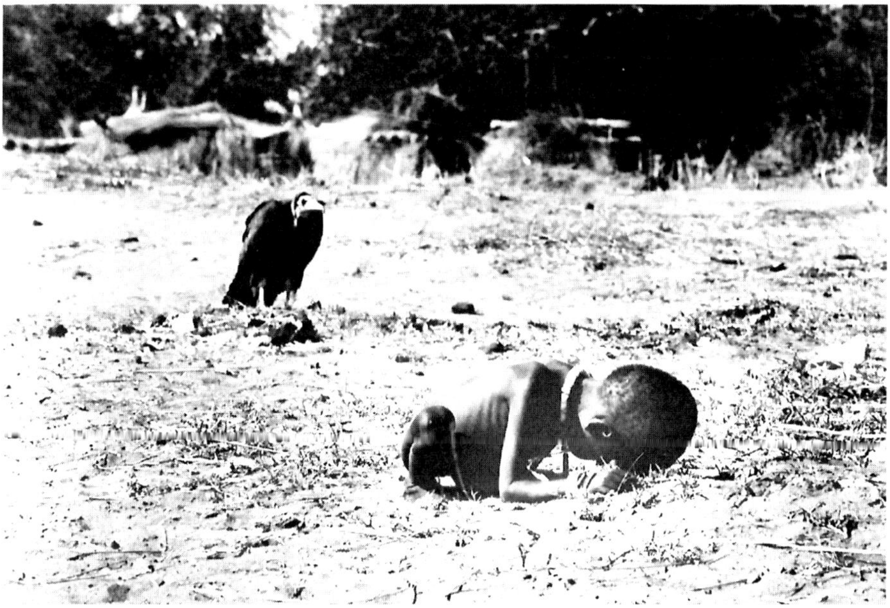

1995 Award

THE FLIGHT OF RWANDANS TO OVERCROWDED ZAIRE CAMPS IN 1994

by KARSTEN THIELKER ET AL., *Associated Press*

The first prize-worthy entry on the jury's 1995 shortlist was a series of photos taken by several staff members of the *Associated Press*. With regard to this submission the jurors stated: „We were struck by the consistent excellence of this entry. Few could look at these photographs and not feel the humanity of the men, women and children of subsaharan Africa. With great skill and variety, the *AP* photographers conveyed the crushing emotion of this devastation with both momentous and subtle images." Staff photographers of the *Long Beach Press-Telegram* had sent in pictures „of the everyday lives of the community's residents. The moments captured are small and mundane - and enormously human... The energy and freshness of these photographs present ordinary lives in a way that any newspaper would be proud to emulate." The third proposal on that list was Carl Bower of the *Newhouse News Service*, selected for his photos of a woman and her „battle with breast cancer..., a story of courage and empowerment in the face of illness and disfigurement."

The Board members decided to give the Pulitzer Prize to the *Associated Press* staff „for its portfolio of photographs chronicling the horror and devastation in Rwanda." Four AP photographers had covered the devastating violence and its terrible aftermath, all of them confronted with ethical problems. One of them later expressed his feelings when taking photos in that African country: „I didn't want to sent pictures of bones in dirty bloody clothes..., of the rotting bodies in the middle of the street..., of these hundreds of dead, lying together as if they were still afraid to die." Another one said: „As I was photographing, my eye would routinely linger in the frame to see if the person I was photographing was breathing." A third one of the award-winning photographers remembered: „In a field of dead people, you must concentrate on taking pictures, trying to forget the smell... The smell of rotting human flesh was absolutely everywhere... The camps were a mess, swarms of Hutus and tens of thousands of kids. The lucky ones with their parents, the others just trying to survive..."

The small group of four AP photographers included Jacqueline Artz, Javier Bauluz, Jean-Marc Bouju and Karsten Thielker, the first German-born photography winner after the double-laureat Horst Faas several decades ago.

HUNDREDS OF REFUGEES IN NEED

Photo by Karsten Thielker, taken May 17, 1994, shows groups of Refugees carrying water containers on their heads making their way back to their huts at the Benaco Refugee Camp in Tanzania, near the Rwandan border, East Africa. Benaco, with a population surpassing 300,000, was the largest refugee settlement in the world by that time. Aid Agencies had difficulty feeding, doctoring and sheltering the refugees who were fleeing the ethnic bloodbath in neighboring Rwanda.

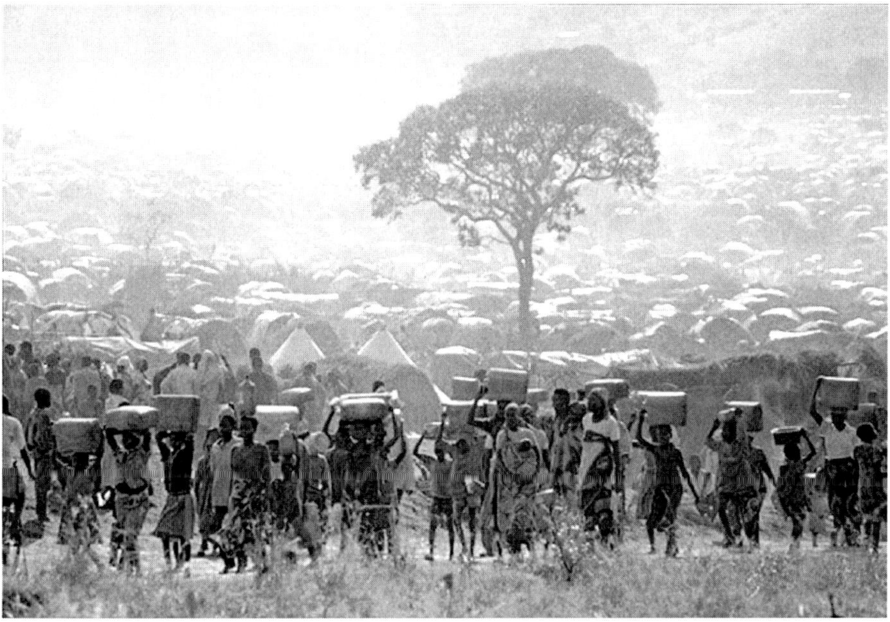

CHILD TOO WEAK TO STAND IN VACCINATION LINE

Photo by Jacqueline Artz, published July 29, 1994, shows a small Rwandan child who was about to get vaccinated against the diseases that were spreading in the refugee camps. However, the child who was in the SOS village orphanage in Ndosho, near Goma, in Zaire, was already too weak to keep standing up in line. In the village, there were 3,000 Rwandan children who had lost their parents in the turmoil of fleeing. Apart from this, in every refugee camp there were groups of children who were taking care of each other.

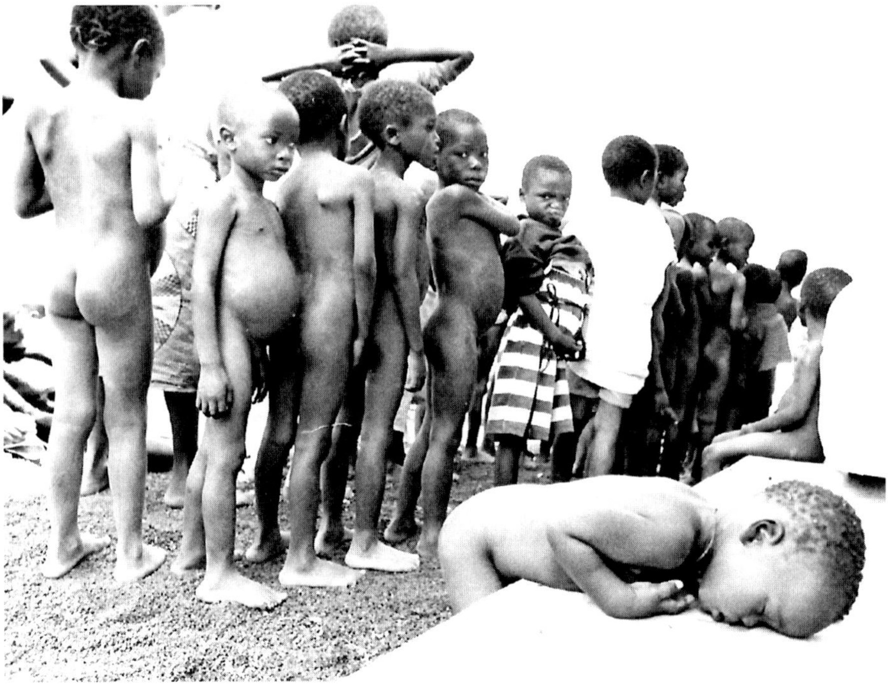

REFUGEE CHILDREN SEPARATED FROM THEIR FAMILIES

Photo by Jean-Marc Bouju, published August 21, 1994, documents the desperation of several Rwandan boys who got separated from their mother. She had just passed the bridge to Zaire when Zairean soldiers had closed the bridge. An estimated 10,000 Hutus were waiting to flee into Zaire at that border point as they were terrified of Tutsi soldiers. U.N. officials tried to convince the Zairean government to reopen the border. Roughly 300,000 refugees had already fled to Zaire by that time.

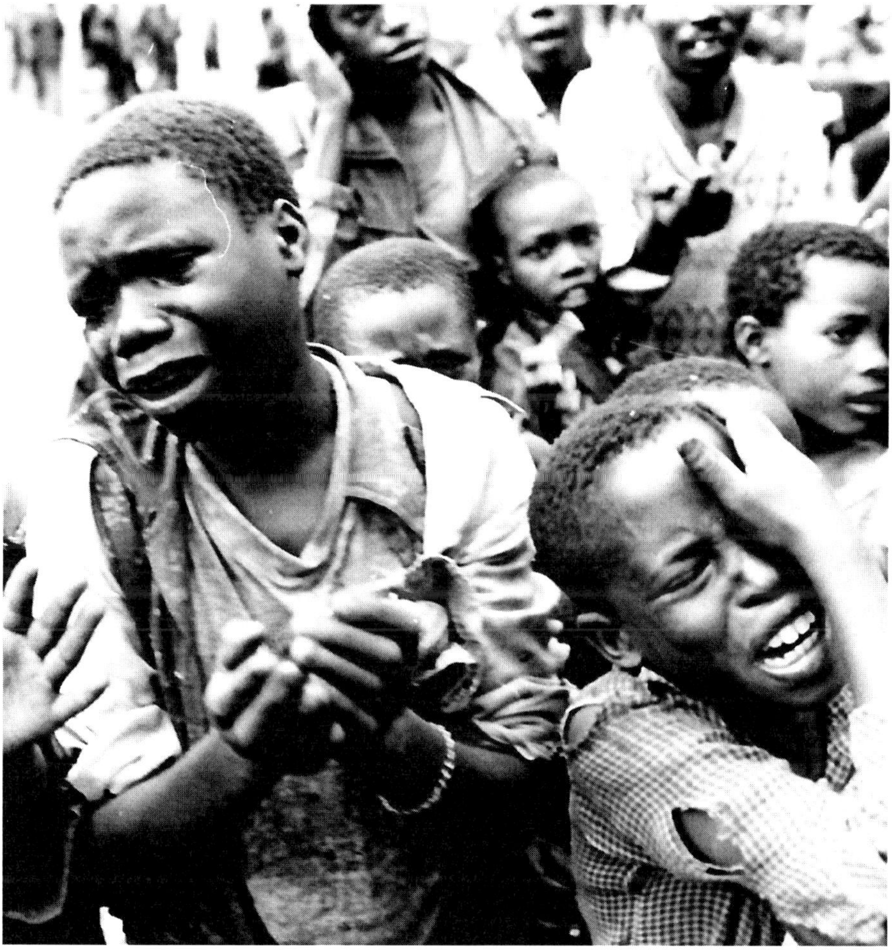

1996 Award

A KENYAN GIRL SUFFERING FROM A SHOCKING CIRCUMCISION RITE IN 1995

by STEPHANIE WELSH, *Newhouse News Service*

Right at the beginning of the 1996 jury report, Stan Grossfeld of the *Boston Globe* was praised for „a gritty realism... documenting kids having kids. The photographer had shrewdly captured the triangulation of three generations caught in an overwhelming cycle... We found this photo story and its individual pictures rich, complex and rewarding, it is documentary photography at its best.“ David Turnley of the *Detroit Free-Press* and his photographs of the civil war in Bosnia also had made it onto the jury's shortlist, where can be read that his „remarkable work breathes life into this terrible conflict and shows that war is about people, not about soldiers and bullets alone... The photos have a timelessness, a classic feeling... Through his lens, Turnley makes us care.“ Furthermore, the jurors were completely overwhelmed by the work of Stephanie Welsh of the *Newhouse News Service*, because, as they put it, „the raw power of this disturbing yet provocative set of photographs is almost indescribable.“ What exactly was meant with this description was made more explicit by the official announcement of this winning entry. It explained that Stephanie Welsh received the Pulitzer Prize „for her shocking sequence of photos... of a female circumcision rite in Kenya.“

The photographer was an intern on an English-language newspaper in Nairobi, Kenya, when she learned about ritual circumcision. After months of searching, Welsh located 16-year-old Seita Lengila, whose family agreed to allow Welsh to photograph the ritual. „The family was somewhat honored that I wanted to be there,“ she remembered, „bacause it's the most significant moment in her life. It's a celebration. Sita, since she had been to school, was afraid. She knew it was painful and it was dangerous. And that's something nobody else in the tribe ever talks about... When they started cutting, Seita screamed. I was shaking so terribly,“ Welsh confessed, „I could hardly focus.“

Stephanie Welsh, born on June 27, 1973, in Quantico, Va., graduated from Syracuse University. She began working for *Syracuse Newspapers* before she moved to Kenya, Africa, where Welsh joined the *Nairobi Daily Nation* in 1994. Two years later she came back to the U.S.A. and was engaged by the *Palm Beach Post*, Fl., where she got the post of a staff photographer.

BEFORE THE CUTTING

Photo, published September 17, 1995, depicts a girl, Seita Lengila from Kenya, before being circumcised. The ceremony during which her labia and clitoris were cut away marked her step into adulthood. It was also supposed to make her more desirable to potential husbands. She was not allowed to express pain or fear. The mutilation was undertaken solely with an ordinary razor blade.

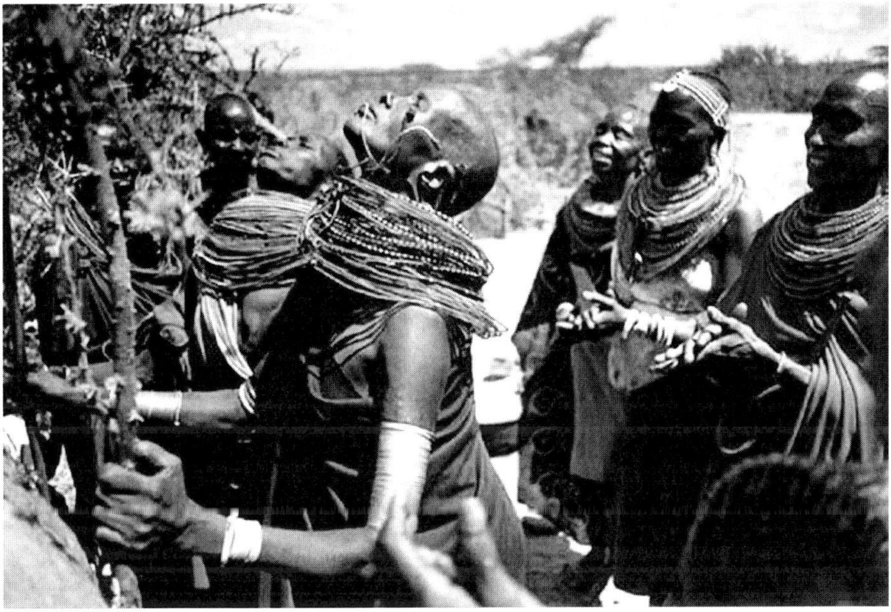

AFTER THE MARTYRIUM

Photo, published September 17, 1995, shows Seita Lengila after she had been circumcised. Her god-mother was comforting her. Other girls who already had been circumcised had spent the night before the ceremony with Seita, calming her and reassuring her that it would not be painful. In preparation for the ceremony, her head had been shorn and she had been painted in bright colors. The numerous rings around her neck had also been a part of the decoration.

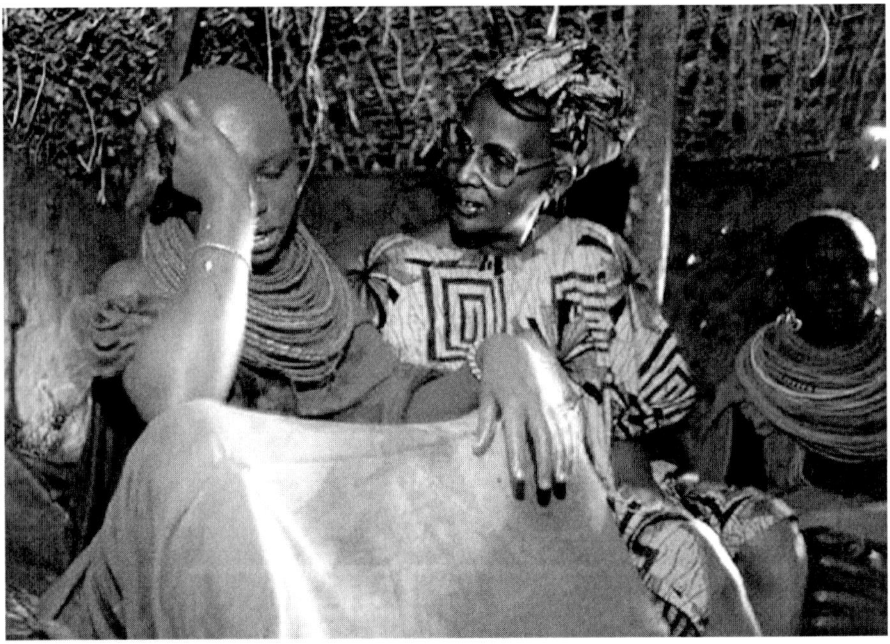

DOUBTS AND FEARS

Photo, published September 17, 1995, depicts Seita a few hours after her circumcision. When the bleeding had stopped she went to check if the midwife who had performed the cutting had done a good job. For if she had left out parts of Seita's genitals, the girl would have had to be operated once more.

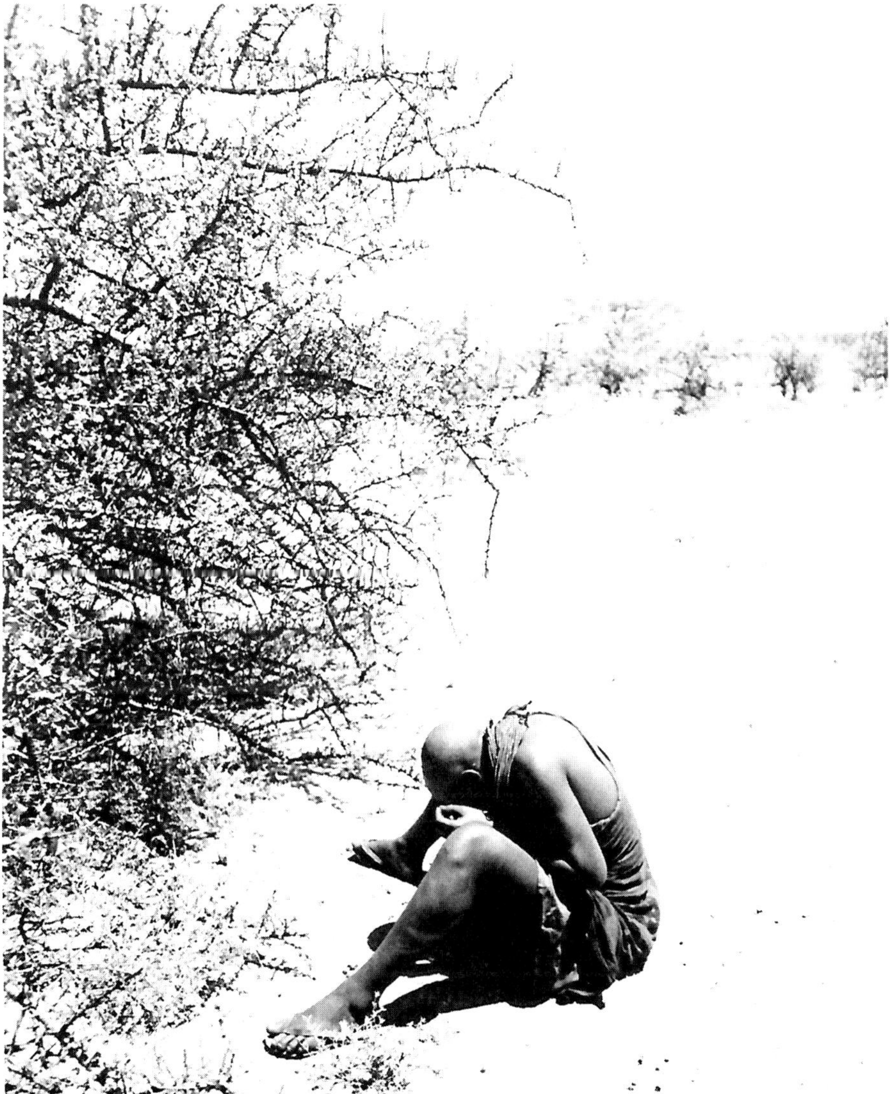

1997 Award

RUSSIAN PRESIDENT YELTSIN AT A ROCK CONCERT IN ROSTOV IN 1996

by ALEXANDER V. ZEMLIANICHENKO, *Associated Press*

The jurors in their 1997 report placed first photos by Jeffrey L. Brown of the *Joliet Herald-News*. He had presented a „step-by-step picture coverage of the underground travels of a Mexican immigrant to the United States, a remarkable photographic record of a common but seldom shown odyssey... It is an enlightening insight into one of America's most pressing social and econo-mic issues." Jon Kral of the *Miami Herald* had done photos about prisons in Venezuela, „a grotesque horror,... the terrifying conditions make U.S. prisons look like a country club. Kral's pictures were produced by an artistic eye, a journalistic mind, and an outraged heart." Third on the list was Michele McDonald of the *Boston Globe* for pictures of a woman's fight against cancer. „The photos captured a wide range of emotions", the jurors stated.

But the Board accepted none of the above and chose one of the finalists in the spot news category instead, thus bestowing the prize on Alexander Zemlianichenko of the *Associated Press* „for his photograph of Russian president Boris Yeltsin dancing at a rock concert during his campaign for re-election." Yeltsin's economic reforms had failed to produce results, and he was recovering from two heart attacks he suffered the year before. So he tried to demonstrate his energy at the rock concert in Rostow where *AP* photographer Alexander Zemlianichenko found him dancing on stage. „I feel like I ought to share the prize with Yeltsin," the photographer expressed after earning the Pulitzer award, „if he didn't dance I wouldn't have gotten the photo."

Alexander V. Zemlianichenko, born on May 7, 1950, in Saratov, Russia, attended Saratov Technical Institute and the Juilliard School of Music in New York. Zemlianichenko started to work as a photographer for the *Komsomolskaya Pravda* newspaper in Moscow in 1980. Four years later he switched to the *Soviet Union Magazine*. The photographer then joined the *Motherland Magazine* in 1988 where he stayed for two years. During this time he also worked as a string correspondent for the *Associated Press*. In 1990 Zemlianichenko joined the *AP* staff in Moscow. He was part of the group that won the 1992 Pulitzer Prize in the spot news photography category. His second award followed five years later, this time in the feature category.

DANCING BORIS YELTSIN

Photo, published June 11, 1996, depicts the President of Russia, Boris N. Yeltsin, promoting his reelection. He was dancing at a rock concert in Rostov to prove that he was in good health. His contestant, Communist Gennady A. Zyuganov, had been ahead of Yeltsin in the polls so far but Yeltsin managed to break even with him by means of two strategies: first, by doing publicity stunts such as the rock concert. He also played along traditional games at another festival in Tatarstan to be perceived more in tune with the people of Russia. And secondly, by introducing popular legislation.

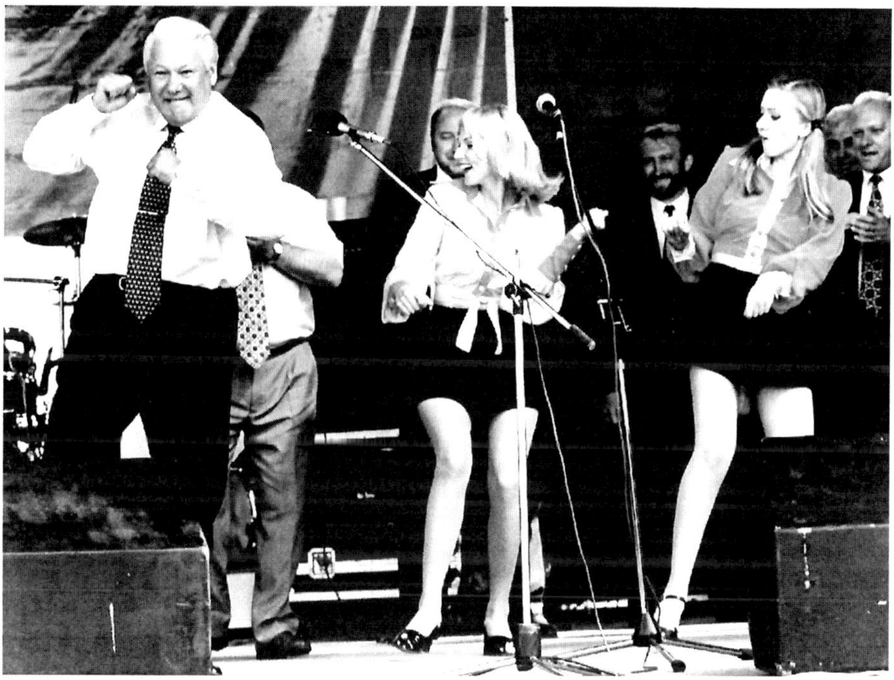

1998 Award

YOUNG CHILDREN OF ALCOHOL AND DRUG ABUSING ADULTS IN 1997

by CLARENCE J. WILLIAMS III, *Los Angeles Times*

Judging the 1998 entries in this category, the members of the jury favored pictures of completely different subject matters. Allan Detrich of the *Block Newspaper Alliance* had captured „an intricate underground railroad of spouses and children of abusive families." Detrich's coverage, the jury report continues, „focused on the children of the underground and the families in 'safe houses' who offer them shelter... Detrich's compassionate photos showed every step an abused child or spouse took on their way to a safe house." Joseph Stefanchik of the *Dallas Morning-News* on the other hand dealt with „the human toll taken by land mines" in Angola, „the photos show a country crippled by war", victims carrying artificial limbs. And Clarence Williams of the *Los Angeles Times* had submitted „images of drug addiction". He received praise because, as the jurors emphasized, his „documentary photographes go beyond the stereotypes of yet another scarred junkie shooting up."

The Board was of the same opinion and annonced that Clarence Williams would be honored with the Pulitzer Prize „for his powerful images documenting the plight of young children with parents addicted to alcohol and drugs." Several of his award-winning pictures showed a drug-addict mother and her three-years-old little daughter. The photographer spent many weeks to cover the interactions between these two persons for a story about „orphans of addiction". „They would wake up in the morning", Williams later remembered, „and I would be sitting on their front steps, I would stay there until they went to bed." He photographed reveal harsh ugliness, and occasional joys for the mother and her child. After the story ran in the newspaper, the mother was arrested for child endangerment, and the daughter was taken into protective care.

Clarence J. Williams III, born on January 22, 1967, in Philadelphia, Pa., studied mass communications at Temple University, Pa., and graduated with a B.A. degree in 1992. He received a photography internship with the *Philadelphia Tribune* from 1992 to 1993 and furthermore a summer internship with the *York Daily Record*, Pa. In the same year Williams joined the *Reston Times Community Newspapers*, Va., as a staff photographer. Since 1996 Williams was engaged as a staff photographer at the *Los Angeles Times*.

ALCOHOLIC FATHER AND HIS SON

Photo, published November 16, 1997, shows under which circumstances eight-year-old Kevin Bryan and his ten-year-old sister had to live: Kevin watched as his father, Calvin Hollornan, a speed addict and alcoholic, tossed back a beer. Kevin called the addicts who frequented their small apartment „the bad people."

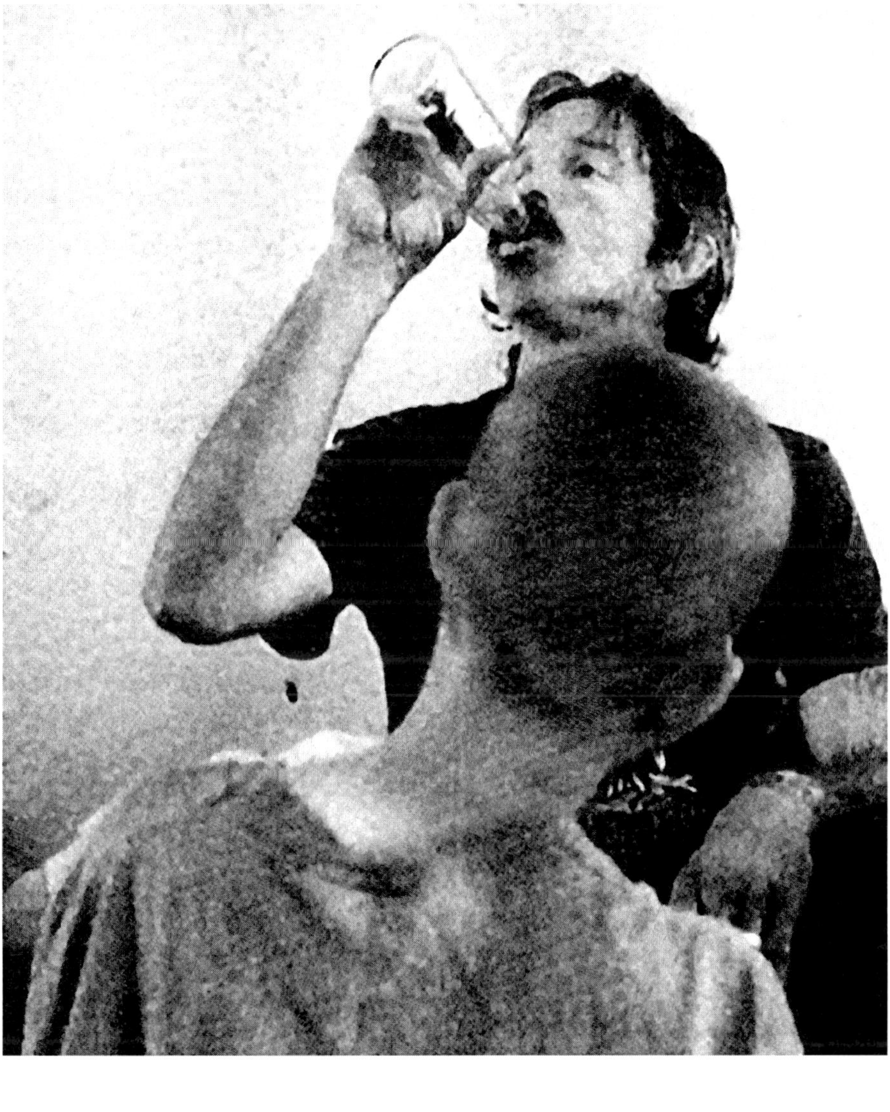

WOMAN SCREAMING AT YOUNG BOY

Photo, published November 16, 1997, depicts how Kevin Bryan was turning away from Rita Green, his father's girlfriend, who was screaming at him. Both Rita and Kevin's father, Calvin Holloman, were addicted to drugs. Their one-bedroom apartment in Long Beach, California, was also a hangout for other drug-addicts.

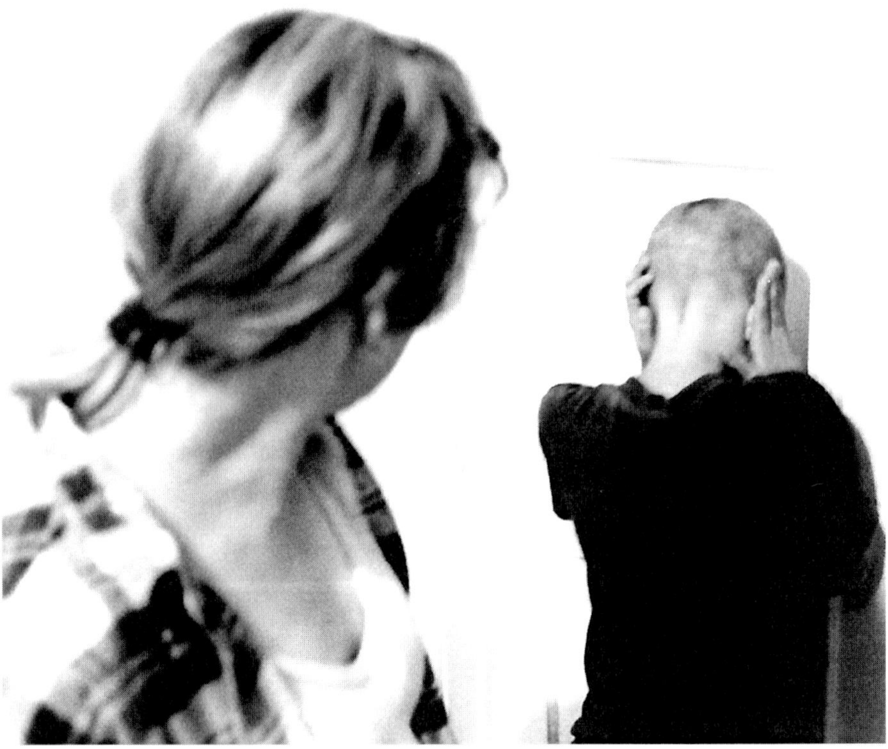

BOY DIGS THROUGH GARBAGE CONTAINER

Photo, published November 16, 1997, shows Kevin Bryan, 8, trying to find new clothes for his ten-year-old sister, Ashley, who had been wearing the same clothes for a week. Their father had spent all his money on drugs and alcohol. While his father watched, Kevin found a pair of canvas tennis shoes. Unfortunately, they were too small for Ashley so that Kevin's search had to continue at another place.

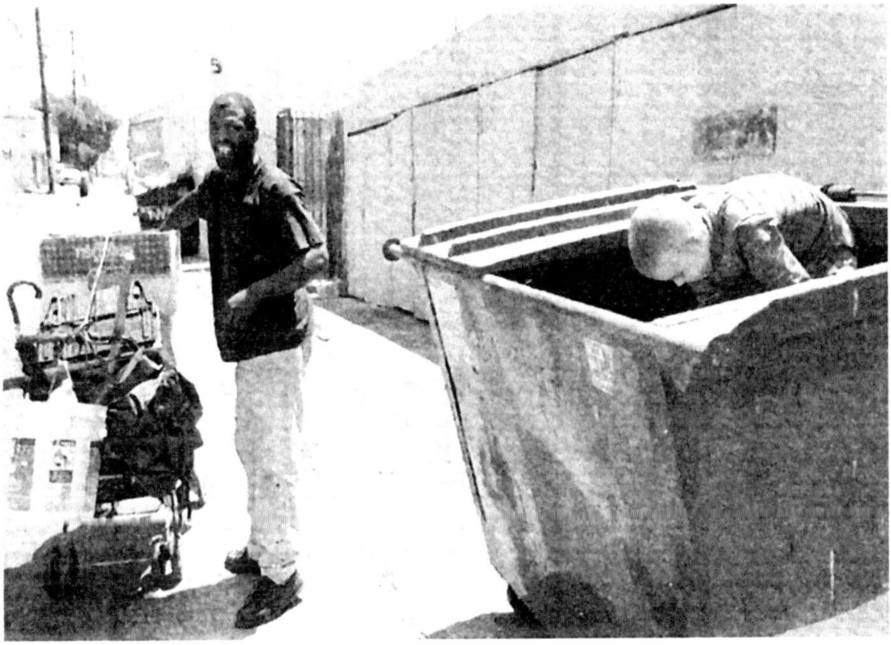

1999 AWARD

PRESIDENT BILL CLINTON'S IMPEACHMENT AND THE FOLLOWING-UP IN 1998

by DOUG MILLS ET. AL., *Associated Press*

First finalist mentioned by the 1999 jury was Bill Greene of the *Boston Globe* „for his inspirational images that traced the work of... a descendent of slaves who helped the residents of poor Southern communities assume civic responsibility and improve their lives." Next on the jury's list was a group entry by the *Associated Press* photo staff, called „Presidency in Peril." These photographs „captured the story of an unprecedented political drama that engulfed the nation in 1998: the impeachment of President Bill Clinton. The photographs portray the significant characters and moments of the mesmerizing event - and show them in signature emotional context. Every picture documents a new and often surprising chapter of a developing story... The images carry more than the gravity of this historic event - they also convey the enormously tragic quality of what began as an illicit sexual affair between the president and a White House intern. The jury felt," the report stated, „that the photographic work by the *Associated Press* staff was riveting in composition, news value and clarity." Third finalist was Daniel A. Anderson of the *Orange County Register* „for his skillful and moving portraits of local children growing up in decaying residential motels."

For the Board it was no question that the *AP* staff should earn the prize „for its striking collection of photographs of the key players and events stemming from President Clinton's affair with Monica Lewinsky and the ensuing impeachment hearings." Doug Mills, one of the *AP* photographers, called the pictures „a huge historical event, you had to keep perspective that every image that you took will be looked at again in ten, twenty years down the road." Another *AP* man, Dan Loh, intended to get a photo of Monica Lewinsky, and he got his shot in Philadelphia. And Susan Walsh was at the White House when Clinton thanked the Democratic members of the House who voted against impeachment.

The successful *AP* photo staff consisted of fifteen photographers: J. Scott Applewhite, Roberto Borea, Khue Bui, Robert F. Bukaty, Ruth Fremson, Greg Gibson, Ron Heflin, Charles Krupa, Wilfredo Lee, Dan Loh, Joe Marcuette, Doug Mills, Pablo M. Monsivais, Stephen Savoia and Susan Walsh.

PRESIDENT IN EMOTIONAL CONDITION

Photo, published December 19, 1998, shows President Bill Clinton wiping his eyes after sharing a laugh with Vice President Al Gore and First Lady Hillary Rodham Clinton as he prepares to speak with House Democrats outside the Oval Office at the White House following the historic impeachment vote by the House of Representatives.

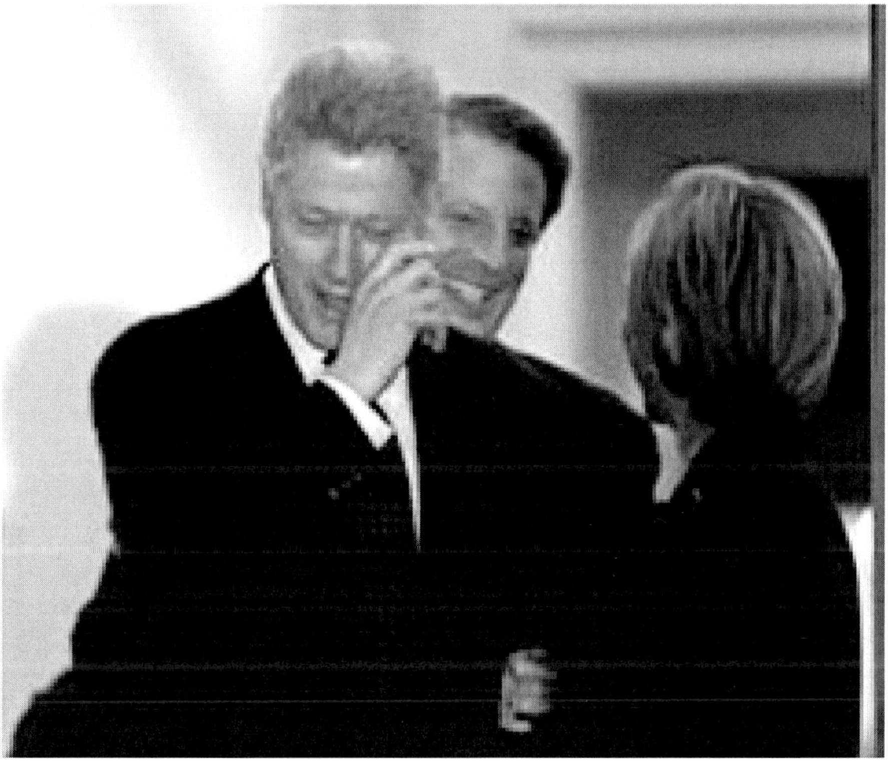

PRESIDENT SPEAKING TO FOLLOWERS

Photo, published December 19, 1998, depicts President Clinton thanking Democratic members of the House of Representatives who voted against impeachment, as First Lady Hillary Clinton looks on, outside the White House.

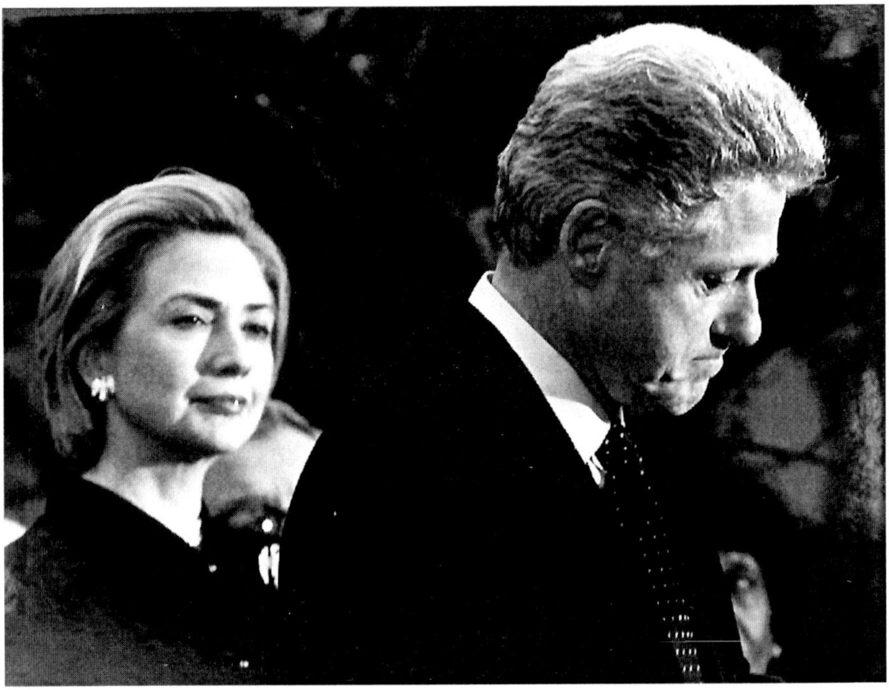

PRESIDENT AND FAMILY DEPART

Photo, published December 19, 1989, shows President Bill Clinton, his daughter Chelsea, center, and wife Hillary walk with their dog, Buddy, from the White House toward a helicopter as they depart for their vacation on Martha's Vineyard.

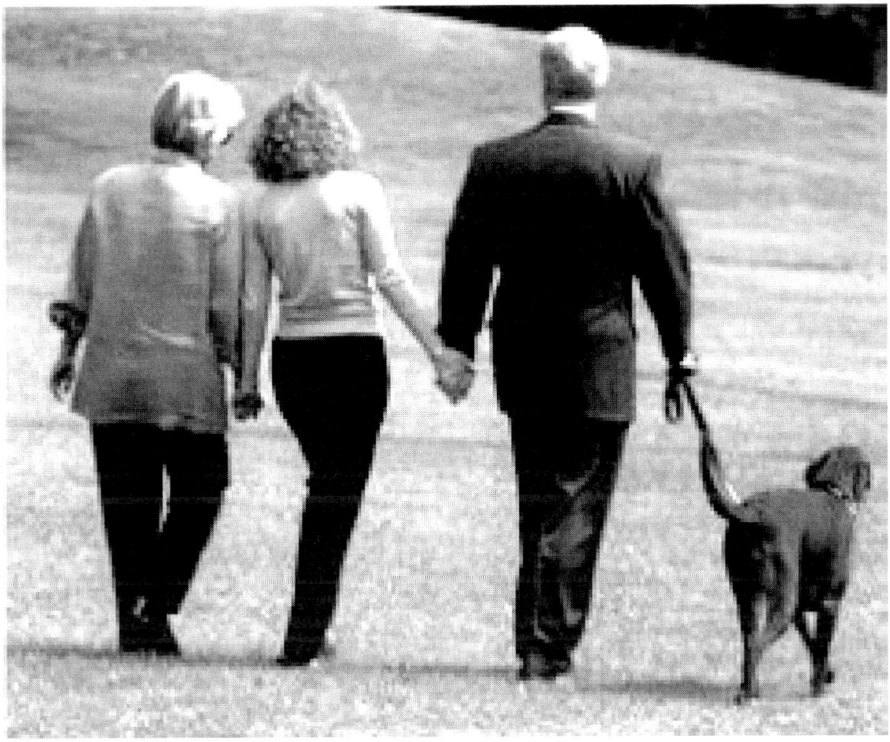

2000 Award

PICTURES OF THE TRAGIC FATE OF REFUGEES FROM KOSOVO IN 1999

by CAROL GUZY, ET AL., *Washington Post*

In the eyes of the 2000 jurors, two photographers of the *Miami Herald*, Candice Barbot and Nuri Vallbona, made it on the list of finalists „for their photographs of Liberty City, a neighborhood crippled by drugs and violence, which detail the community's effort to reclaim the area.“ The photo staff of the *Worcester Telegram & Gazette* from Massachusetts was praised „for its moving photographs of the grief and devastation that followed a local fire that killed six firefighters.“ Three photographers of the *Washington Post*, Carol Guzy, Lucian Perkins and Michael Williamson, had presented to the jury „an intimate, unique look at the impact of the Serbs' ethnic cleansing campaign in Kosovo... Every photograph is journalistically and artistically powerful.“

The Board members selected the *Washington Post* exhibit and gave the prize to Guzy, Perkins and Williamson „for their intimate and poignant images depicting the plight of the Kosovo refugees.“ Carol Guzy later remembered that „no still picture could possibly convey their tears and pain or the hell from which they had come“. Perkins had taken pictures in a no man's lang where he photographed sorrow and desperation. Williamson met a man in a burned-out house who thaught the photographer was a war crimes investigator there to document the deaths of his cousins.“

Carol Guzy, born on March 7, 1956, in Bethlehem, Pennsylvania, started her journalism career at the *Miami Herald*, where she became a co-winner of the Spot News Photography Pulitzer Prize in 1986 and after switching to the *Washington Post* she earned a second one in 1995 in the same award category. Five years later, she received her third Pulitzer Prize.

Lucian Perkins, born on December 2, 1952, in Fort Worth, Texas, was hired full-time by the *Washington Post* in 1979. In 1995 he earned his first Pulitzer Prize in the Explanatory Journalism category, his second one followed five years later.

Michael Williamson, born on June 8, 1957, in Washington, started his journalism career at the *Sacramento Bee* in 1975 and became a Co-Pulitzer Prize winner in 1990 as a book author in the General Non-Fiction category. Williamson joined the *Washington Post* in 1993 and earned his photojournalism Pulitzer award seven years later.

HOMELESS REFUGEE

Photo, published April 17, 1999, shows Velina, a Gypsy woman, pondering the future near the Kosovo City of Pec. She said her home was burned by Ethnic Albanian refugees returning home.

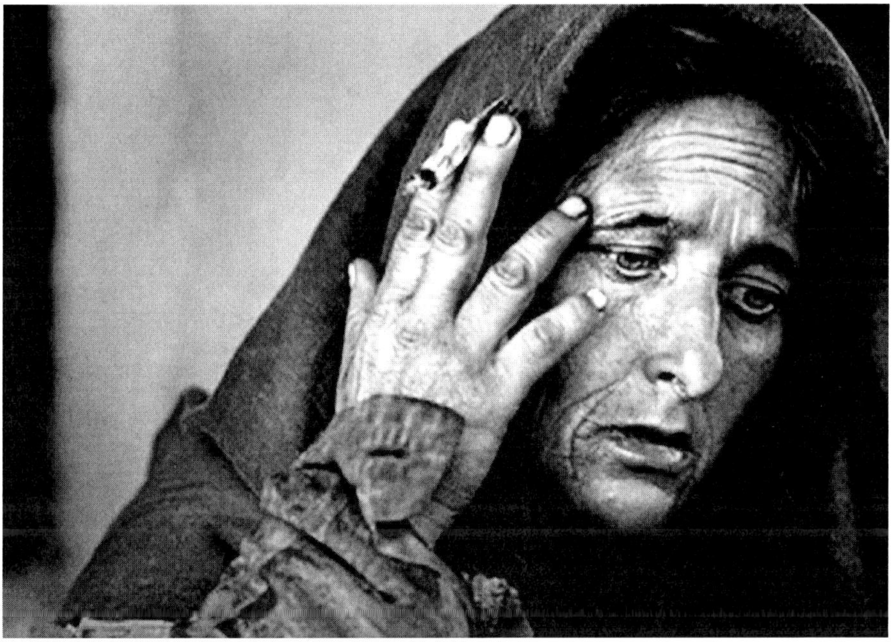

FAMILY REUNITED

Photo, published May 14, 1999, shows Kosovar refugee Agim Shala, 2 years old, being passed through the barbed wire fence into the hands of family members at a camp in Kukes, Albania.

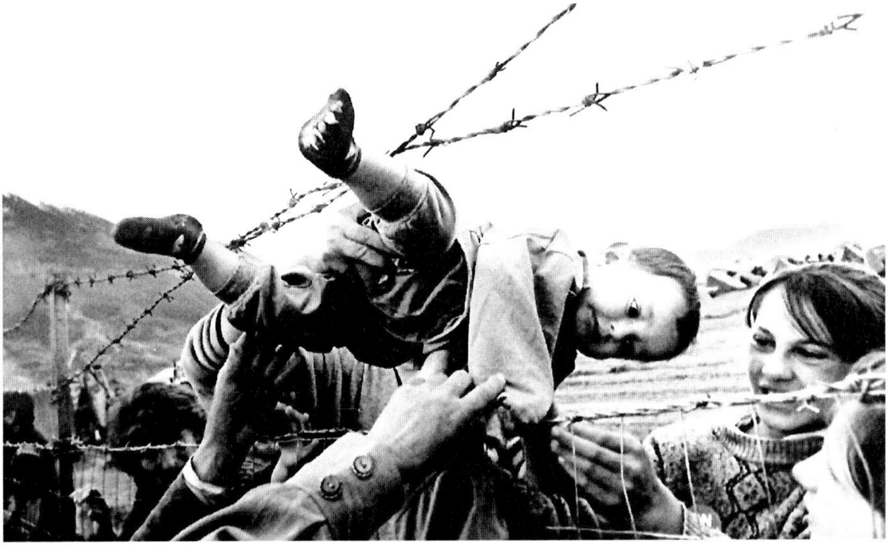

WAITING REFUGEES

Photo, published June 12, 1999, depicts refugees waiting for their bus to be unloaded in the Senokos refugee camp in Macedonia, after a journey from the border.

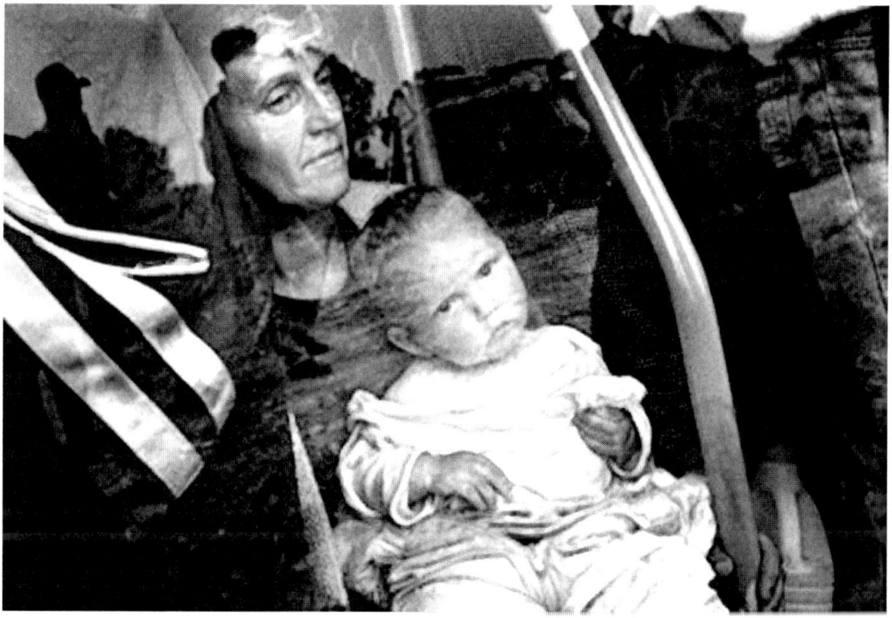

2001 AWARD

TWO OF SEVERAL STUDENT VICTIMS AFTER A DORMITORY FIRE IN 2000

by MATT RAINEY, *Newark Star-Ledger*

First on their 2001 list, the jurors nominated *Associated Press* photographer David Guttenfelder. His photos told „the remarkable story of a 'A Journey of Hope', the journeys of North and South Koreans to visit relatives they had not seen for half a century. Sometimes under the close surveillance of North Korean officials, Guttenfelder captured not only what was staged in public arenas but also the intense emotion of private moments for the families." Marc Picotty of the *Denver Rocky Mountain News* was praised „for his illuminating images of suburban high school students facing adulthood." Matt Rainey of the *Newark Star-Ledger* was the third finalist, for he and his newspaper had set „an extraordinary standard for feature photography with 'After the Fire', the off-the event, news-focused feature coverage of a horrible tragedy in New Jersey."Matt Rainey had worked this story from all angles, exploring the personal lives and struggles of two of four students who were critically burned during a dormitory fire at Seton Hall University.

The Pulitzer Prize went to Matt Rainey of the *Newark Star-Ledger* „for his emotional photographs that illustrate the care and recovery of two students critically burned..." Three people died in the dorm fire, fifty-eight others were injured. Shawn Simons and Alvaro Llanos, the two victims, were crawling for their lives when the fire had reached their third-floor room. Simons found an exit, turned downstairs, his hands smoking. Llanos made it into the lobby so badly burned his girlfriend did not recognize him. After ten days in a morphine-inducted coma, Simon waked up in the hospital, Llanos' coma lasted nearly three months. The families allowed Rainey to spend eight months chronicling the pair's fight for life. For Rainey the visits were more than a job. „I spent seven days a week," he said, „usually 10 to 12 hours a day with the families; shot about 500 rolls of film." When Rainey celebrated news of his Pulitzer Prize, first into his arms with congratulations were Simons and Llanos.

Matt Rainey, born on August 14, 1966, in Denville, New Jersey, started as a photojournalist in 1988, straight out of Rutgers University. He toured five New Jersey daylies, running the photo departments at two of them, before settling in at the *Newark Star-Ledger* in 1995. He became a staff photographer in January, 2000.

COMA PATIENT

Photo, published April 15, 2000, shows Alvaro Llanos, one of the most seriously injured students, enduring a several months lasting coma on an operating room table as he awaits a skin grafting on his chin and neck.

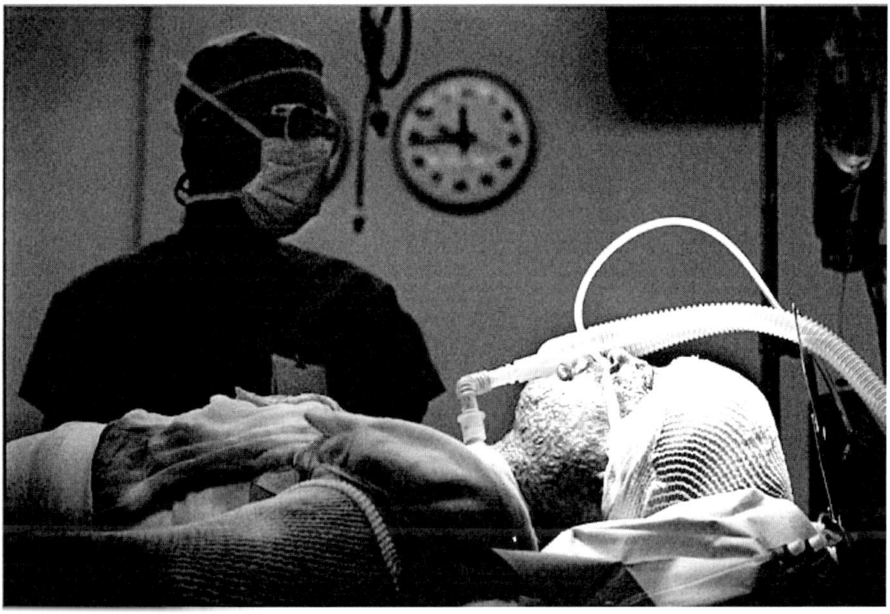

BURNED HAND

Photo, published April 17, 2000, decipts the other student in the hospital's Burn Center. While Alvaro Llanos continues to linger in a coma, his roommate, Shawn Simons, sees his burned hand for the first time.

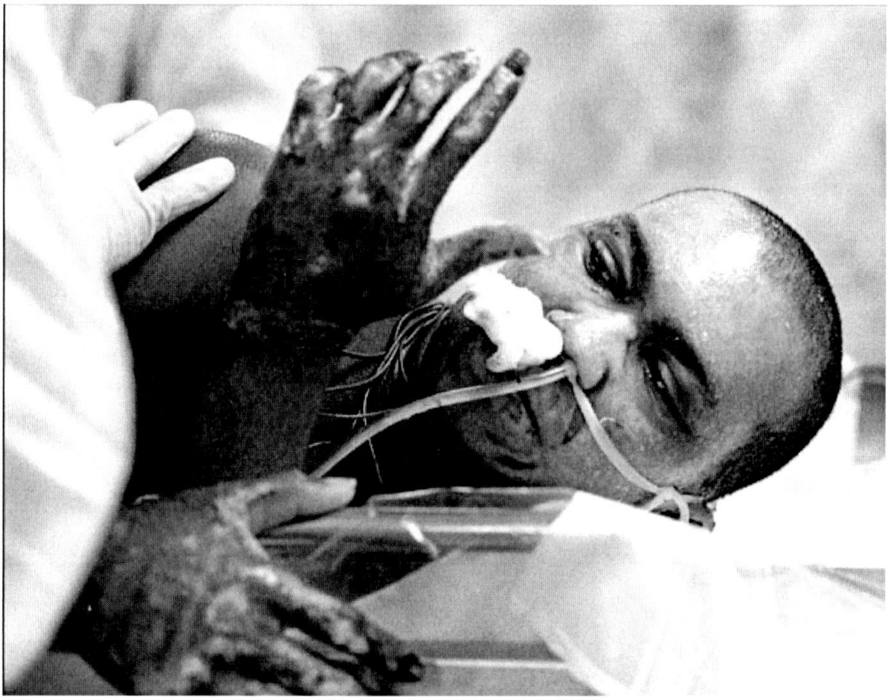

FIRST STEPS

Photo, published April 28, 2000, shows Alvaro taking his first steps since the fire three months ago. He is shaky, and he needs support from a burn technician and a therapist. This first day he walked five steps, the next day he took already 88 steps.

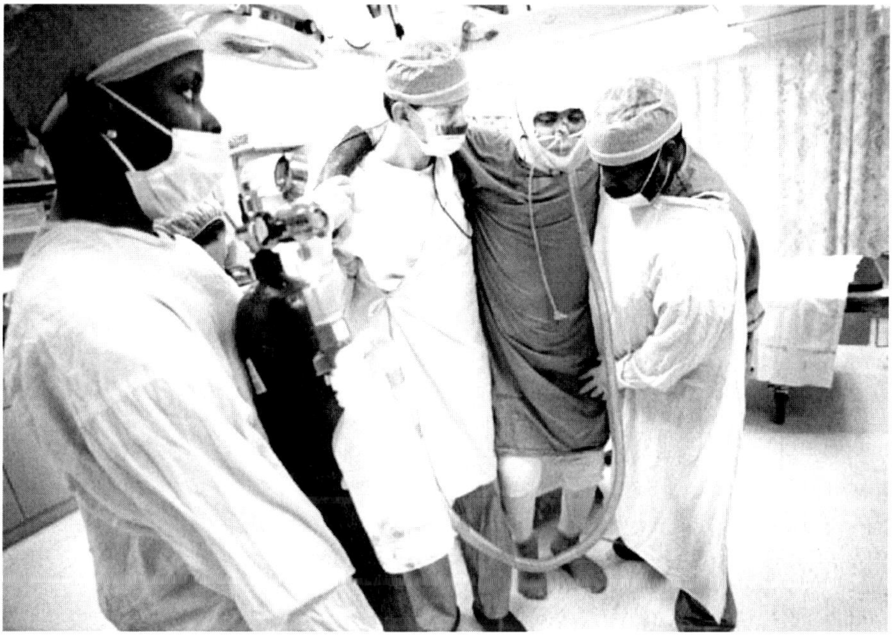

2002 Award

VARIOUS ASPECTS OF CIVIL LIFE IN WAR-TORN AFGHANISTAN IN 2001

by STEVE COWLEY, ET AL., *New York Times*

In the eyes of the 2002 jury, *Miami Herald* photographer J. Albert Diaz „had succeeded in illustrating an important American story that does not easily lend itself to photography, - the sprawl and the values of South Florida... From a drive-in-wedding, to development advancing on the Everglades, the remarkable work of J. Albert Diaz on this difficult and significant story deserves recognition.“ Another Florida newspaper, the *Fort Lauderdale Sun-Sentinel*, had sent in pictures by three of its photographers, Hilda M. Perez, Mike Stocker and A. Enrique Valentin. They had „documented the stark reality of the AIDS epidemic in this hemisphere“, the jury report stated. „Working in Haiti, the Dominican Republic, Jamaica, Puerto Rico and Cuba, these photographers comprehensively depicted the causes and consequences of this disease that infects some 390,000 people in the Caribbean, but which also reaches into the communities of South Florida.“ Third entry on the list was by a group of *New York Times* photographers. They had „succeeded in documenting the spirit of a people enduring protracted conflict. Poignant moments photographed with talent, enterprise and sensitivity depict both the pain and perseverance of people in Pakistan and Afghanistan.“

The *New York Times* staff entry earned the Pulitzer Prize, so that in that year the newspaper not only won the breaking news photography award but also the one for feature photography. It was given „for its photographs chronicling the pain and the perseverance of people enduring protracted conflicts in Afghanistan and Pakistan.“ One of the photographers, James Hill, was in the legendary city of Mazar-i-Sharif where people visited the Shrine of the prophet Mohammed's son and came to feed the doves as goodwill toward appeasing Allah. Another *New York Times* photographer, Vincent Laforet, looked for Afghan refugees in Pakistan. In one picture, he documented the death of a 13-year-old boy who was killed during an anti-American demonstration by Pakistani police officers.

The five *New York Times* staff photographers who earned the Pulitzer Prize included: Steve Crowley, Ruth Fremson, James Hill, Vincent Laforet and Chang Lee.

FEEDING DOVES

Photo, published September 9, 2001, shows the place at the shrine of Agrat Ali in Mazar-i-Sharif, home to the spirit of the son of the prophet Muhammad, where a man is feeding thousands of doves.

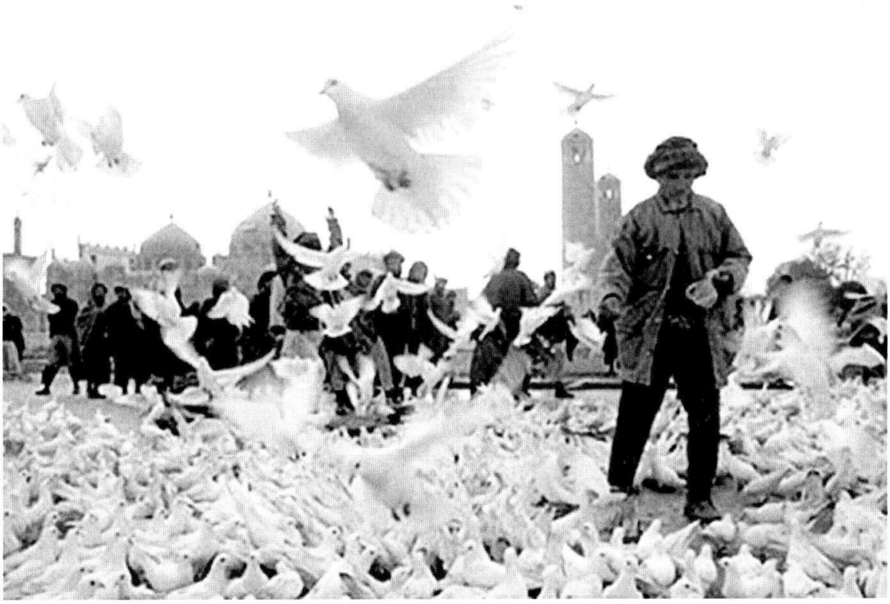

RIDING HORSES

Photo, published September 17, 2001, shows the Buzkashy race to catch a small cow riding horses at Charman Babrak in Shah Shahid town near Afghanistan's capital Kabul.

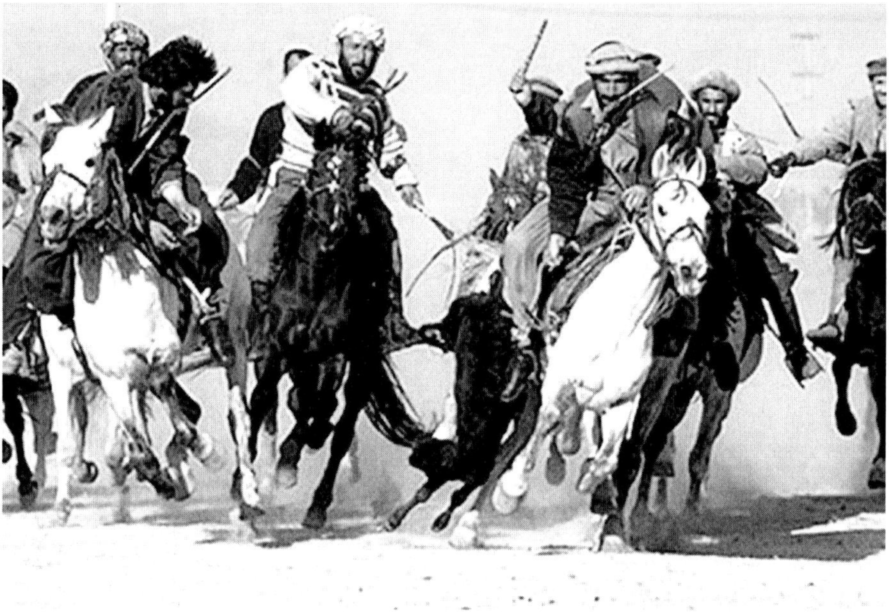

PLAYING CHILDREN

Photo, published October 2, 2001, depicts Afghan children, while relatives watched, rode an improvised carousel that had been made from artillery shell casings Nazar-i-Sharif.

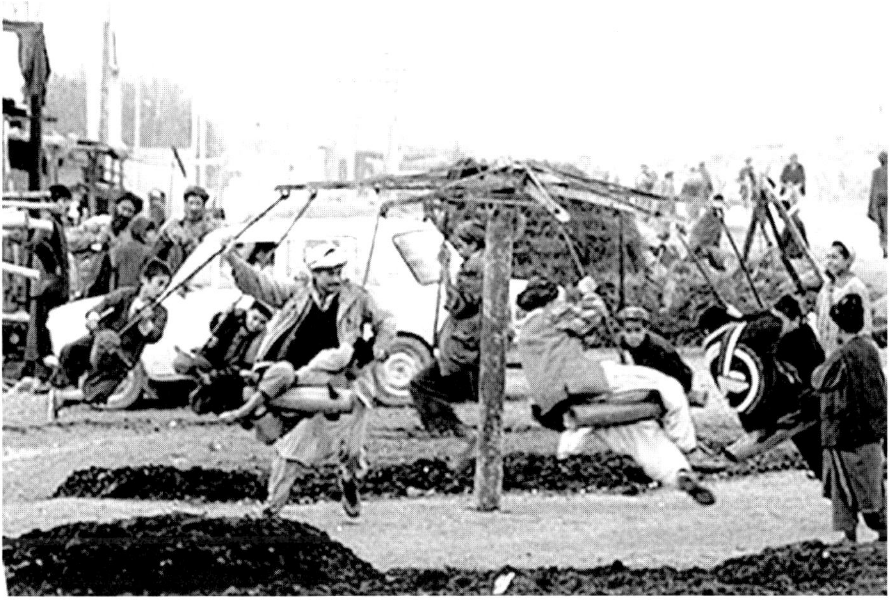

2003 Award

JOURNEY THROUGH HELL FOR COUNTLESS CENTRAL AMERICAN TEENAGERS, TOWARDS THE U.S. IN 2002

by DON BARTLETTI, *Los Angeles Times*

The jury of 2003 selected the following three finalists: Bradley Clift of the *Hartford Courant*, Don Bartletti of the *Los Angeles Times* and Matt Black, a freelancer, also working for the *L.A. Times*. Black's pictures, in the eyes of the jurors, „documented a little known legacy of the black sharecroppers who migrated from the Depression-era Dust Bowl to the San Joaquin Valley of California... Black's photographs present their lives in a striking documentary style that borders on art." Don Bartletti had told „the story of a young boy who traveled for 57 days, more than 8,400 miles, from Honduras in search of his immigrant mother somewhere in the U.S.A. No collection of photos could better illustrate the ambitions of feature photography." Bradley Clift's entry, called „Heroin Town", also had told a big story. „As America struggles with the reemerging problem of domestic heroin abuse," the jury stated, „Bradley Clift's remarkable photographs document the struggle of middle-class victims of a town in denial. His telling photographs show heroin addiction in a way words can't describe and probe the motives of city fathers' attempts to deny accountability."

The Pulitzer Prize went to Don Bartletti of the *Los Angeles Times* „for this memorable portrayal of how undocumented Central American youths, often facing deadly danger, travel north to the United States." The photographer had told a personal story of a boy, but also the story of thousands or tens of thousands of Central Americans trying to make new lives it the U.S. Bartletti walked with him, rode on the tops of rail cars through Central American jungles, snuck past Mexican borders guards and waded rivers. As they moved North, Bartletti produced photographs that are artistic and technically perfect in spite of difficult, uncontrolled and often overtly dangerous circumstances. He and writer Sonia Nazario, both authors of the Pulitzer Prize-winning article series „El Norte Bound", took remarkable risks to photograph and report the story.

Don Bartletti, born on December 29, 1947, in Philadelphia, Pa., is a graduate of Palomar College in San Marcos, California. He worked as a photographer at the California newspapers *Vista Press, Oceanside Blade-Tribune* and *San Diego Union* before he joined the *Los Angeles Times* in 1992 to work for its Orange County Edition.

VERY DANGEROUS JOURNEY FROM HONDURAS

Photo, published September 29, 2002, shows Enrique, a teenager, who rode a freight train from Honduras through Mexico to the United States in search for his mother, Lourdes. She had left him eleven years ago, moved to the U.S. and never returned to their home in the outskirts of Tegucigalpa, Honduras. Virtually unnoticed, Enrique became one of the estimated 48,000 children who enter the United States from Central America and Mexico each year, illegally and without either of their parents.

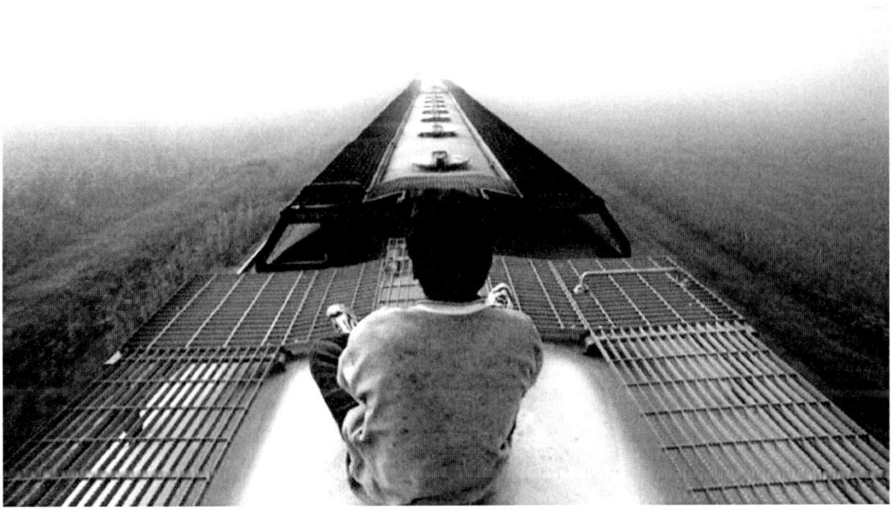

RISKY TRAVEL CONDITIONS FROM GUATEMALA

Photo, published September 28, 2002, shows Guatemalans ride through a mountain tunnel en route to Mexico City. Migrants become more hopeful once they have conquered „the beast," the brutal ride through Mexico's southern states. They are nearing the halfway point in their 1,500 mile journey through Mexico.

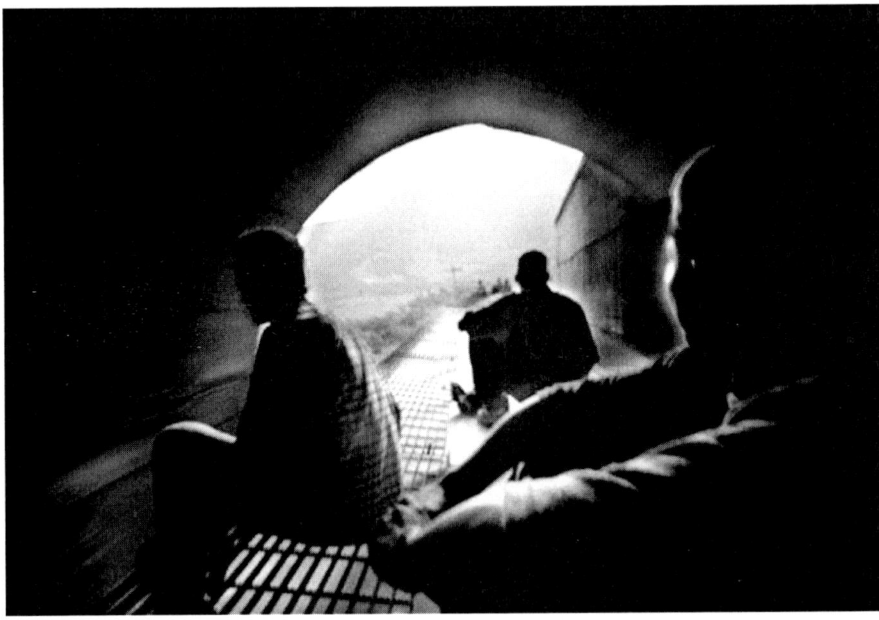

TERRIFYING FREIGHT TRAINS FROM MEXICO

Photo published September 30, 2002, decipts how undocumented Central Americans crowd the tops of Freight train cars in Mexico. They will be treated as lawbreaking foreigners if caught, but cargo rail lines have become a major passageway north to the U.S. border.

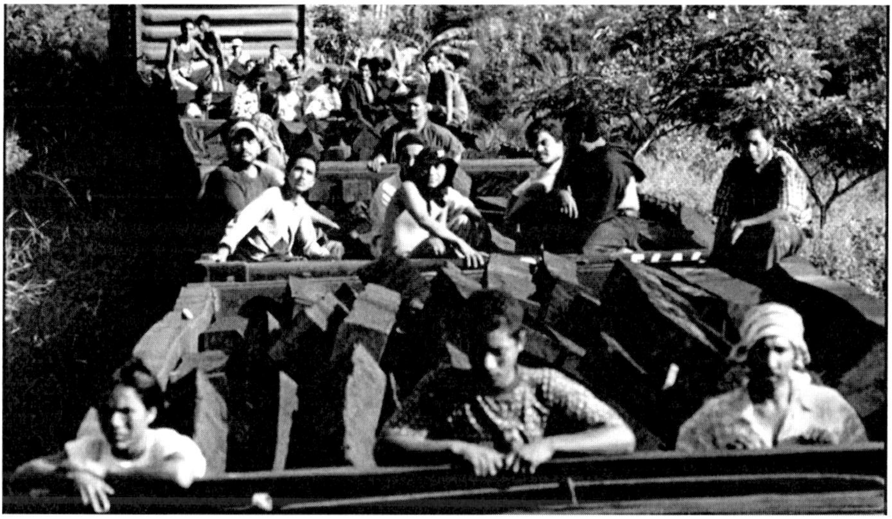

2004 Award

ASPECTS AND PERSONAL DESTINY OF PEOPLE DURING THE CIVIL WAR IN LIBERIA OF 2003

by CAROLYN COLE, *Los Angeles Times*

Similar to the 2004 situation in the breaking news group, two of the three feature finalists had presented war-related pictures. Carolyn Cole of the *Los Angeles Times* was praised by the jury for „a cohensive, behind-the-scenes look at the effects of the civil war in Monrovia. Haunting, shocking images illustrated the pain, suffering and rage of the people of the Liberian capital. Thousands of men with guns dragged their people through barbarity... The collection re-minded us that the ravages of war claimed victims in places other than Iraq.“ Three photographers of the *San Jose Mercury-News*, Pauline Lubens, Dai Sugano and Patrick Tehan, had covered „an unprecedented political crisis“ about a voter recall of a California Governor „with originality and sophisticated humor.“ Damir Sagolj of *Reuters*, third on the jury list, had delivered an entry called „Medic,“ a scene from the Iraq war.

The Pulitzer Prize was given to Carolyn Cole of the *Los Angeles Times* for her pictures from „civil war in Liberia, with special attention to innocent citizens caught in the conflict.“ The photographer was on assignment in Baghdad when the call came, and two days later she was stepping off an airplane in Monrovia. Rebel forces had laid siege to the Liberian capital, and President Charles Taylor was refusing to cede power. A humanitarian crisis was unfolding in the West African nation that would soon overshadow its 14-year civil war. From the start, Carolyn Cole's images of the conflict were distinct, clear and unambiguous, and within a month she had created an important document of the fights. She made extraordinary photographs that captured the whirlwind of death, anxiety and terror filling the streets of Monrovia. With thousands of Liberians fleeing, Cole found herself transfixed by their daily lives: grieving for their dead, lining up for food, bathing in cold water.

Carolyn Cole, born on April 24, 1961, in Boulder, Colorado, is a University of Texas graduate at Austin with a degree in photojournalism. She started her journalistic career at the *El Paso Herald-Post* in 1986, moved to the *San Francisco Examiner* two years later, worked as a freelance photographer for a couple of years and came to the *Sacramento Bee* in 1992. Two years later, she got the position as a staff photographer at the *Los Angeles Times*.

CIVIL WAR UNDERFOOT

Photo published August 7, 2002, shows how bullet casings carpet a street in Liberia's capital Monrovia, at the heart of the battlefied between government and rebel soldiers, while Nigerian troops secure the airport.

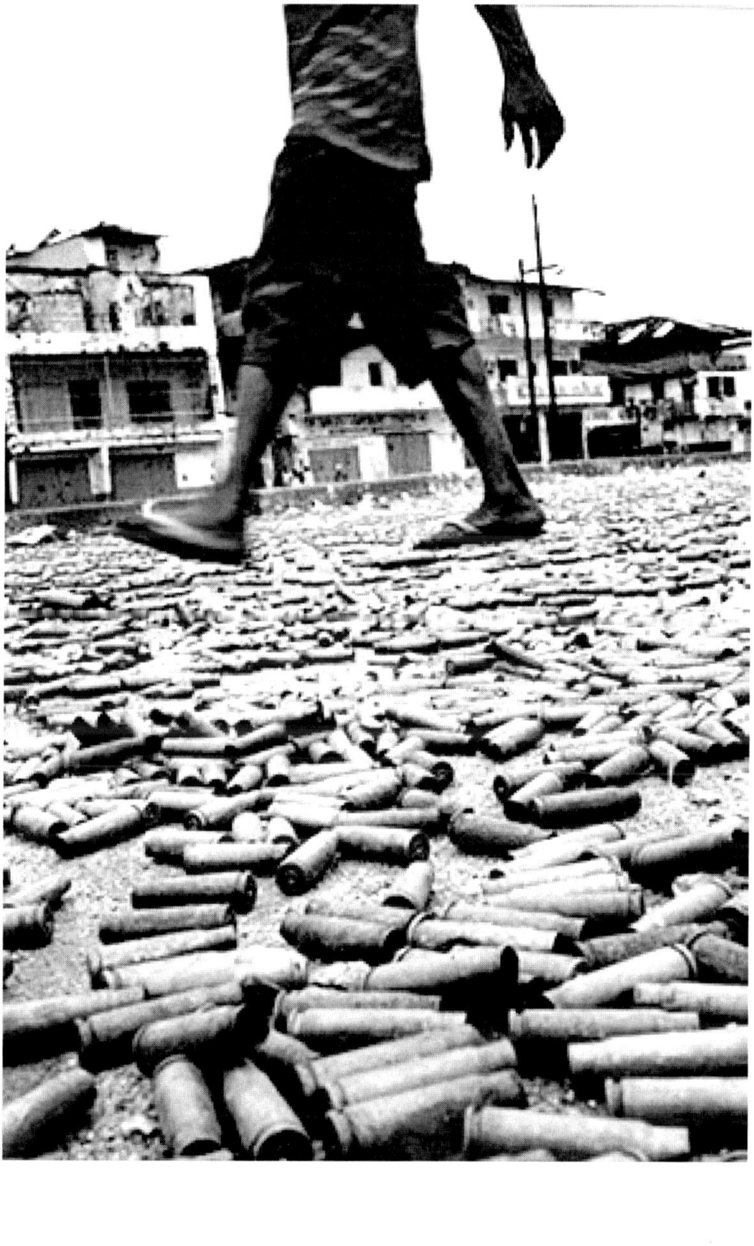

IT IS TOO LATE

Photo published August 8, 2003, shows a soldier crying for his comrade who died in his arms after a frontline offensive on August second, as government soldiers fought to take back territory lost to rebel forces.

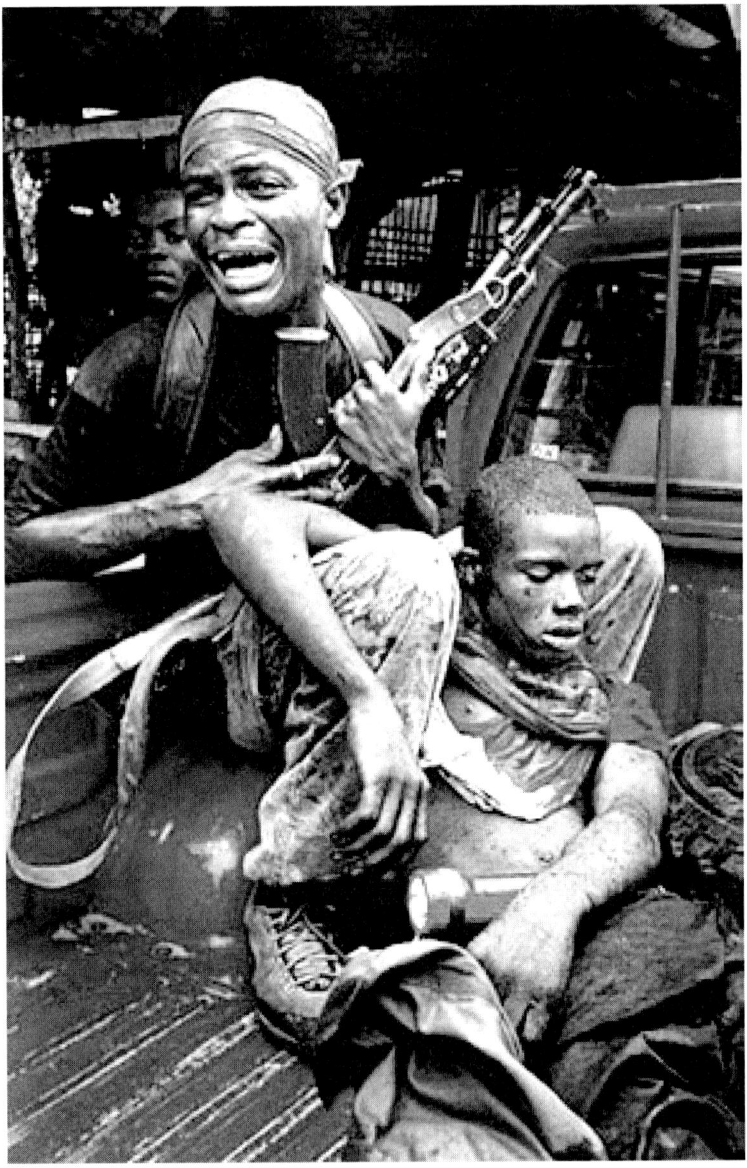

AMID THE THRONG

Photo published August 9, 2003, shows a girl standing in the center of a rain-drenched stadium field where more than 30,000 people had taken refuge. Rebels had been at war with President Charles Taylor, a former warlord, since 1989.

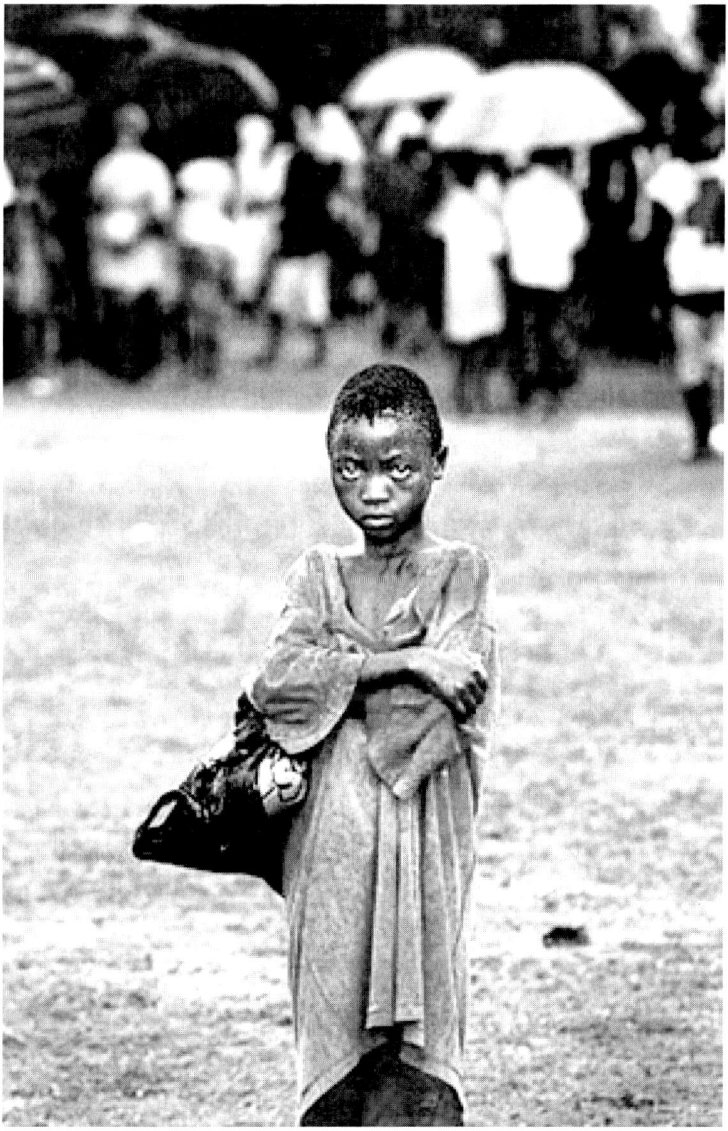

2005 Award

OPERATION LION HEART OF AN IRAQI BOY IN AN U.S. HOSPITAL AT OAKLAND IN 2004

by DEANNE FITZMAURICE, *San Francisco Chronicle*

All three 2005 finalists had covered different aspects from the war in Iraq. First was Deanne Fitzmaurice of the *San Francisco Chronicle*. Her „series of telling moments lay out a tale of the near-death of a young Iraqi boy, who was horribly injured by an improvised explosive device, to his triumphal recovery in the United States. It is a story of courage and compassion, of small miracles, of the ties that bind families and the people of nations.“ Second among the finalists was Jim Gehrz of the *Minneapolis Star-Tribune* for a series called „Back From Iraq.“ „These pictures“, the jurors stated, „bring the war home by taking us inside the day-to-day struggles of a woman soldier wounded when an explosion blasted shrapnel into her head.“ Luis Sinco of the *Los Angeles Times*, third on the list, had presented to the jury a picture entitled „Face of Battle“. The photo showed a „young Marine, taking a cigarette break from battle... If there is one picture that depicts the emotional and physical toll of the Iraq war on the U.S. fighting forces, this is it... This is a picture that will be remembered,“ the jurors said.

But the Board did not think so and declared Deanne Maurice of the *San Francisco Examiner* the Pulitzer Prize-winner „for her sensitive photo essay on an Oakland hospital's effort to mend an Iraqi boy nearly killed by an explosion.“ The photographer first saw Saleh Khalaf in November, 2003, in a children's hospital in Oakland, California, and she recalled: „I didn't know if he was going to survive.“ Over the next 13 months, Deanne Fitzmaurice recorded Saleh's story in a way that did justice to his ordeal and to his remarkable spirit, which earned him the nickname 'Lion Heart'. „He simply refused to die,“ Fitzmaurice remembered, „everyone who came in contact with him saw his strength of spirit and wanted to help him. He came into our lives and brought the war to us on such a personal level.“

Deanne Fitzmaurice, born on July 6, 1957, in Melrose, Massachusetts, is a graduate of the Academy of Art College in San Francisco, where she earned a degree in photography. She published her photos in magazines like *Time, Newsweek, U.S. News & World Report, Sports Illustrated* and *People*, before she came to the *San Francisco Chronicle* in 1989.

AFTER THE EXPLOSION

Photo. published July 13, 2004, shows Iraqi boy Saleh undergoing medical treatment at the Children's Hospital in Oakland. An explosion in Iraq had ripped open Saleh's abdomen, torn off his right hand and most fingers on his left, blown out his left eye and killed his older brother.

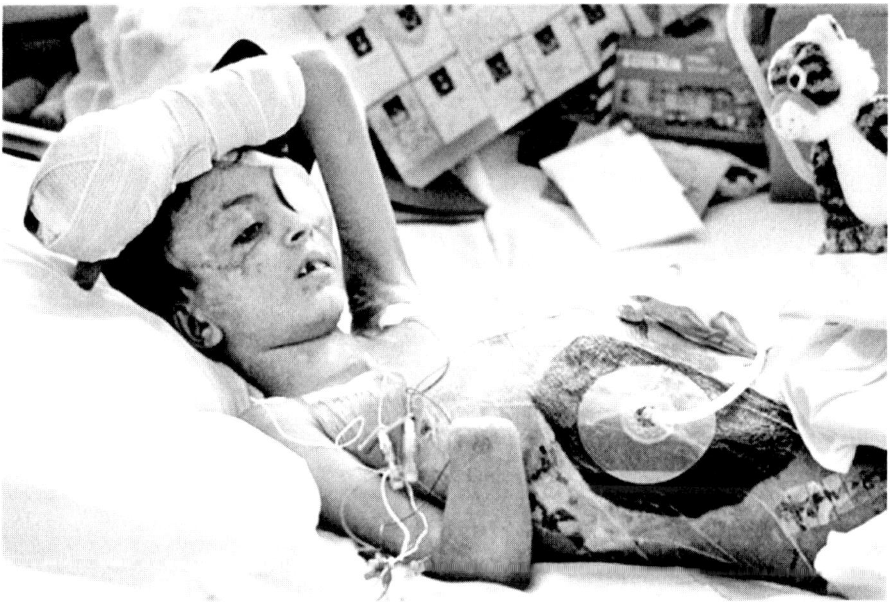

OUTSIDE THE HOSPITAL

Photo, published August 30, 2004, shows Saleh as he ventured more often outside the hospital. He used to wear sunglasses to hide his scars. On this trip to a grocery store, he forgot them and drew the stares of other customers.

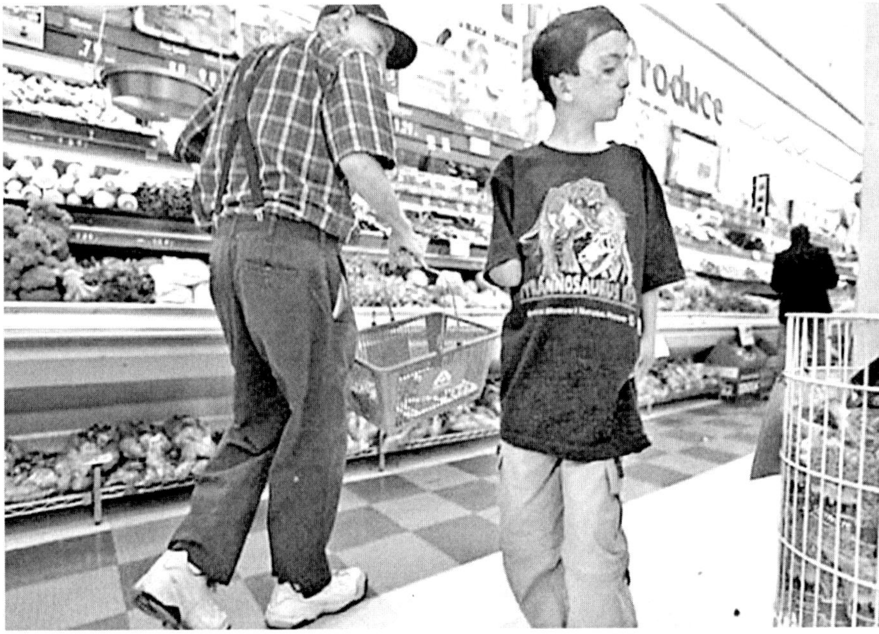

BEFORE THE RECOVERING

Photo, published September 13, 2004, shows that Saleh's recovery went better than anyone expected. One night at Children's Hospital, he and a custodian played soccer in the hallway until a nurse caught them and sent Saleh back to bed.

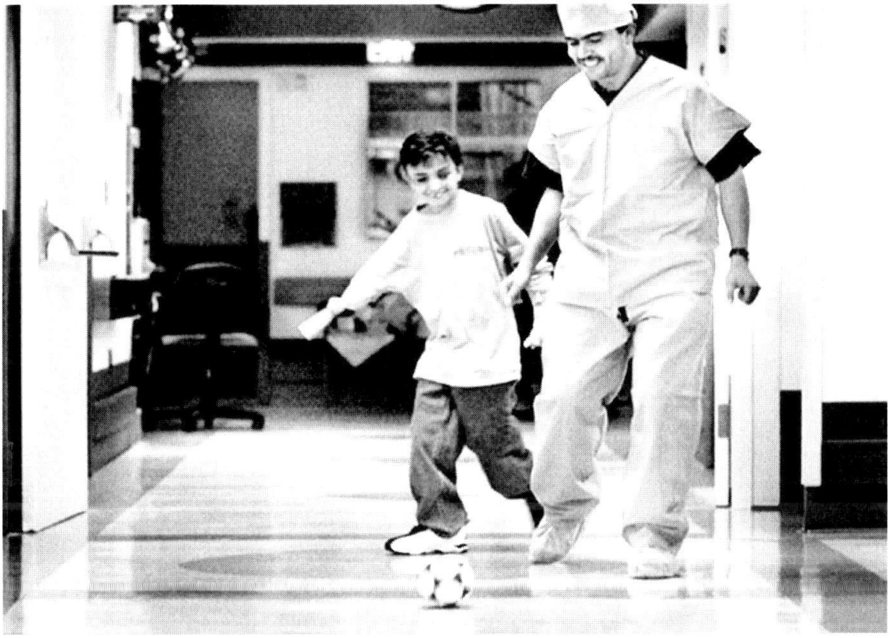

2006 Award

FINAL SALUTE FOR AMERICAN MARINES COMING HOME FROM IRAQ IN CASCETS IN 2005

by TODD HEISLER, *Denver Rocky Mountain-News*

„Every juror shed tears over this project", the 2006 report stated about the exhibit „Final Salute" by Todd Heisler of the *Denver Rocky Mountain-News*, telling the story of killed Marines on their ways home in caskets. „The jurors are wellversed in images on the topic of military funerals", they confessed, „but this narrative was conceived and developed by the photographer in a way that is fresh, searing and memorable. Every picture is a chapter, each has a clear purpose... The viewer can feel the impact and emotional toll on the honor guard members who carry out this heartbreaking duty, a new dimension of a familiar story of soldier deaths... It was a complete package that stood out among all entries." Damon Winter of the *Los Angeles Times*, next on the shortlist, had presented a story called „Missionary's Dark Legacy." In the words of the jury, „it is an unexpected offshoot of a national story of sexual abuse by Catholic priests." Third contender on the list was Mike Stocker of the *South Florida Sun-Sentinel* for „his imaginative exploration of Holocaust survivors as Judaism faces a new century."

The Board members shared the jury's high praise for Todd Heisler's entry of the *Denver Rocky Mountain-News* and gave him the prize „for his haunting, behind-the-scene look at funerals for Colorado Marines who return from Iraq in caskets." Before Heisler had gotten permission to do this job, he had to meet several times with a Major of the Marines, since the Marines were responsible in that region. Heisler's photos showed the cost of war, the impact of the loss of a single life and the caring spirit of the Marine Corps. In one picture, stunned faces peered out the oval windows of a passenger jet as Marines in dress blues board the cargo hold to unload the casket of one of their fallen comrades. In another frame, a widow lies on a bed before her husband's casket on the night before his funeral, listening to the music of her Wedding celebration, her face lit by the glow of her laptop screen.

Todd Heisler, born on January 4, 1972, in Arlington Heights, Illinois, is a 1994 graduate of Illinois State University. Heisler worked for a number of community newspapers in Suburban Chicago where he grew up. In 2001 he joined the *Denver Rocky Mountain-News* as a staff photographer.

UNLOADING OF A CASCET

Photo, published November 3, 2005, shows the arrival of a Marine's casket at Denver International Airport, described by a Major with these words: „See the people in the windows? They sit right there in the plane, watching those Marines, knowing that they are on the plane that brought one Marine home.“

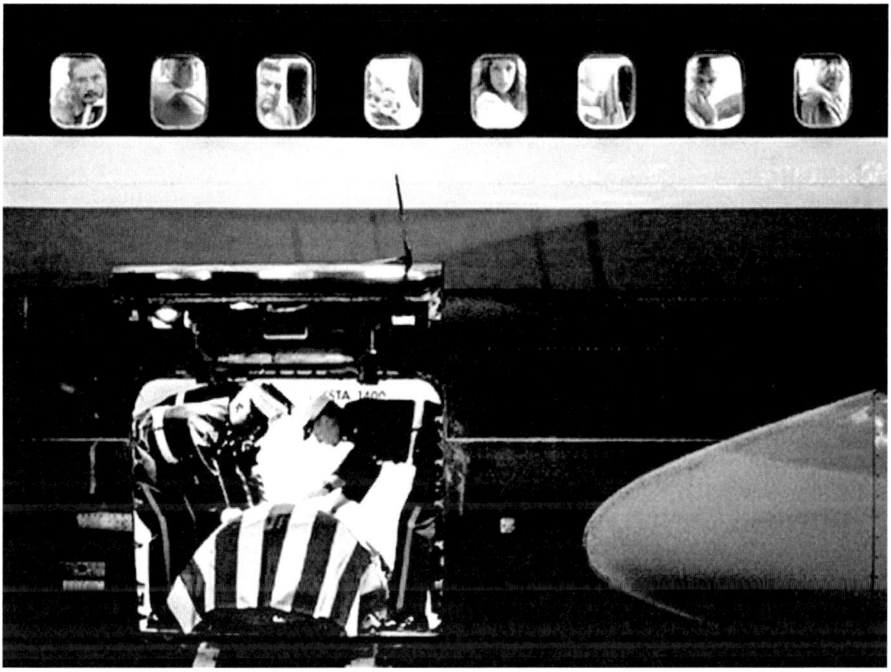

INSPECTION OF A BODY

Photo, published November 8, 2005, shows an Marine Major preparing for the final inspection of a Marine's body, only days after notifying his wife of the Marine's death in Iraq. When the wars began in Afghanistan and Iraq, the Marine Major expected to find himself overseas, but he never thought he would be the one arranging funerals for his fallen comrades.

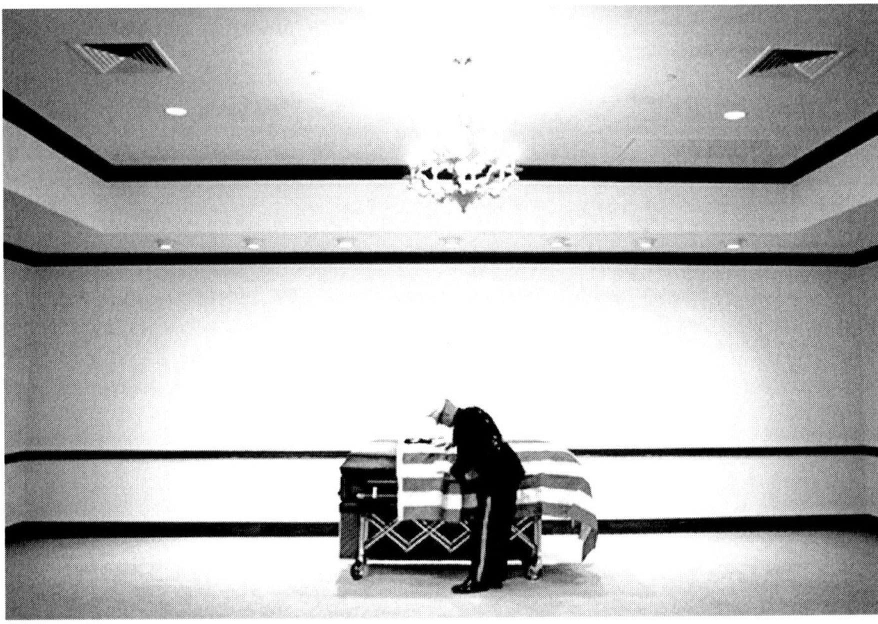

NIGHT BEFORE A BURIAL

Photo, published November 11, 2005, shows the widow of a killed Marine in Iraq the night before her husband's burial. She refused to leave his casket, and she slept next to him all time. The Marines had gathered for her sheets and an air mattress, setting up a make-like bed for her. Before she fell asleep, she opened her laptop and played the songs they had enjoyed at their wedding.

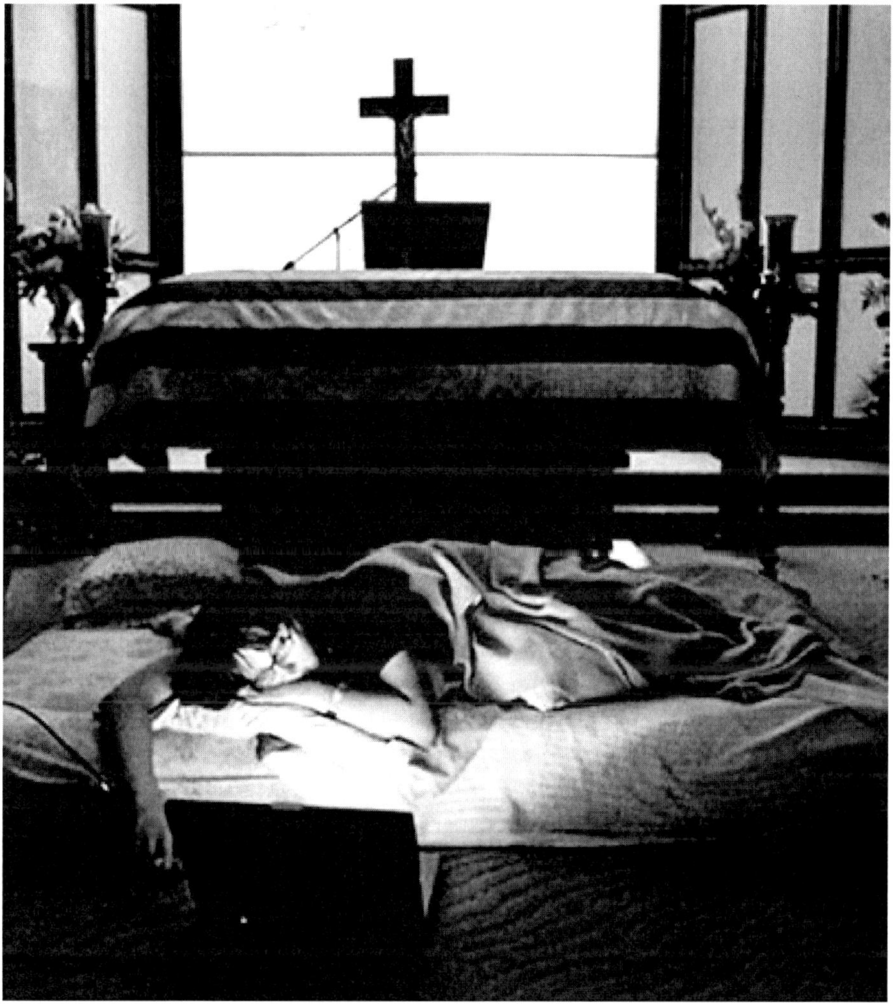

2007 Award

TWO BRAVE WARRIORS WHO FOUGHT A LOOSING HEALTH BATTLE IN CALIFORNIA IN 2006

by RENEE C. BYER, *Sacramento Bee*

The 2007 jurors placed first on their shortlist an entry by Mary F. Calvert of the *Washington Times* entitled „Ethiopia's Trail of Tears", praised as „an amazing example of photojournalism. It takes a painful topic not known to many and brings it to life. The photographer uses mesmerizing compositions that command attention... From despair to hope, there is a range of emotion to this entry that gives it depth and sophistication. This is a startlingly intimate portrayal of the unknown." Next on the jury list was Gary Coronado of the *Palm Beach Post*. His entry „Desperate Journey" was called „a masterful collection of photos on the familiar topic of immigration, executed to perfection. The photographer has a unique ability to bring a refreshing approach to a familiar story. There is no way to view this superior collection of images and not be moved by them... Coronado explored new angles by delving into the lives of those who failed to successfully make the crossing" to the U.S. Third finalist was Renee Byer of the *Sacramento Bee* for her exhibit „A mother's journey," called by the jury „an intensely personal look at a child's battle with cancer told through an extraordinary collection of uncommonly intimate images... These images avoid the routine by not fixating on the mother's tears... This is a celebration of life."

For the Board it was no question that Renée Byer of the *Sacramento Bee* should earn the prize „for her intimate portrayal of a single mother and her young son as he loses his battle with cancer." The photographer had initiated this yearlong documentary project after she met the mother and got her permission. Byer told that story by showing the power, fortitude and determination of a mother and son's bond as cancer takes over, published in a four-part series of the *Sacramento Bee*. Her pictures showed the emotional impact on finances, job loss and the complex relationship between mother and son.

Renée C. Byer, born on June 11, 1958, in Yonkers, New York, is a longtime photographer with over twenty years of experience in the media industry. She has worked around the United States at a number of top dailies. When she was at the *Seattle Post-Intelligencer*, she received an offer of the *Sacramento Bee* as a staff photographer and accepted it.

HAPPY MOMENTS

Photo, published June 21, 2005, documents the single mother Cyndie French and her son Derek Madsen's fight with neuroblastoma, a rare childhood cancer. The picture shows Derek in gleeful exultation as a worried Cyndie races his wheelchair through the hospital hallways.

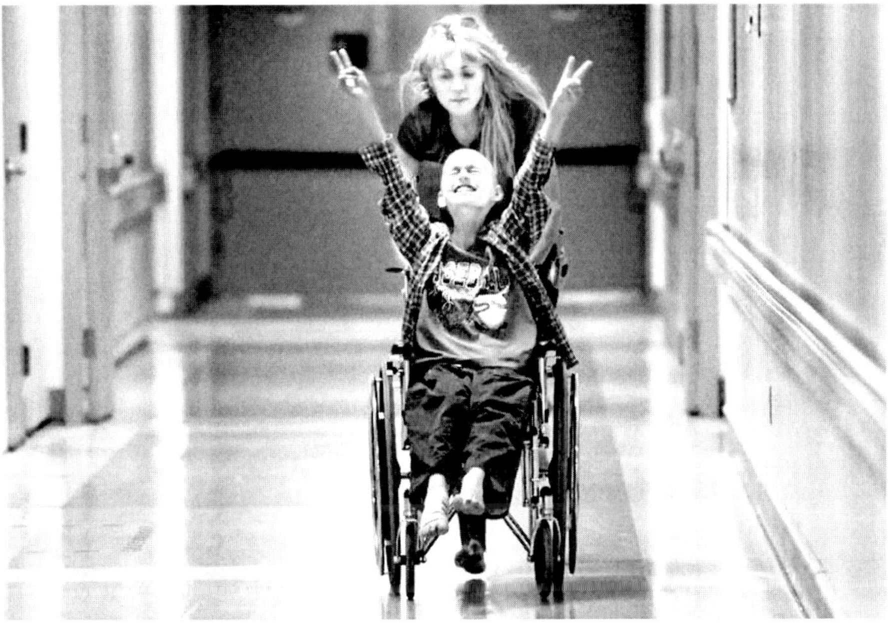

TERRIBLE PAINS

Photo, published April 26, 2006, shows Derek as he had a final burst of energy after days of Cyndie keeping vigil at his bedside. She helps her anguished son walk. A cancerous tumor has distended Derek's stomach so far that his pants no longer fit. Another tumor in his brain impairs his eyesight making navigation difficult inside their rental home.

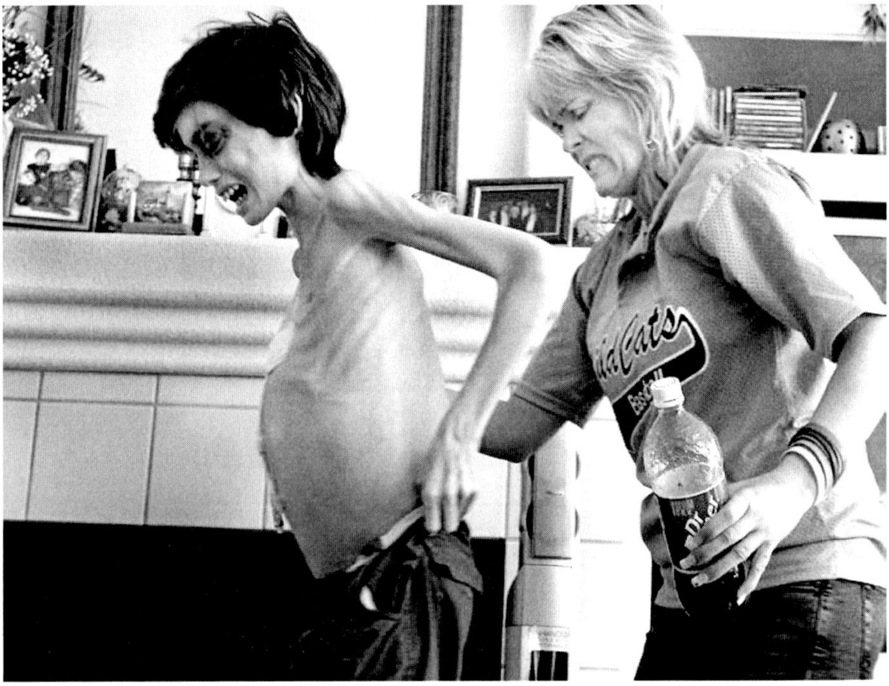

LAST DESTINATION

Photo, published May 19, 2006, shows Cyndie leading Derek's casket to burial with assistance from her two other sons as well as several friends. „I will forever carry your memory in my heart and remind others to give of their time, energy and support to other families like ours," Cyndie says at the funeral. Derek was buried in Mount Vernon Memorial Park in Fair Oaks, California.

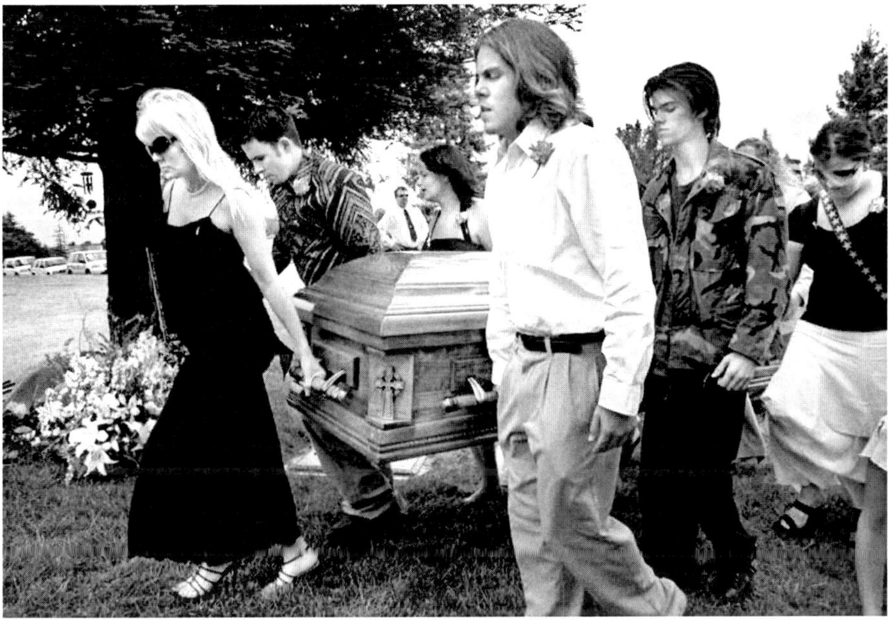

2008 Award

LAST PHASE OF A TERMINALLY ILL CANCER PATIENT FROM NEW HAMPSHIRE IN 2007

by PRESTON GANNAWAY, *Concord Monitor*

After completing their selection process, the jurors of 2008 presented three proposals to the Board, all of them from single photographers. First mentioned on the shortlist was Preston Gannaway of the *Concord Monitor* from New Hampshire, telling a story about a death in a family. „In only 19 images", the jury said, „the photographer skillfully conveys the emotions of every member of the family and the efforts to work through their pain. The series is shot with compassion and sensitivity and is photographically outstanding. It is intimate without being voyeuristic or intrusive. Each image stands on its own and links smoothly into the others without redundancy." David Guttenfelder of the *Associated Press* came on the list „for his harrowing portfolio of Vietnamese children afflicted by the toxic legacy of Agent Orange, three decades after the Vietnam War ended." Third on the shortlist was Mona Reeder of the *Dallas Morning-News* „for her memorable pictures of disadvantaged Texans hidden amid the state's economic abundance."

Preston Gannaway of the *Concord Monitor* became the winner „for her intimate chronicle of a family coping with a parent's terminal illness." The photographer had stayed with the story for 19 months. Gannaway saw the family's experience as a way to tell a story that was both universal and unique - a family facing death while struggling to maintain its balance. Over the course of the project, Gannaway stayed in touch with the family almost daily. She photographed the family through various treatments, hospital stays, family holidays, and the emotions of coping with the disease as the patient's condition worsened. In the woman's final weeks, Gannaway spent most days at the family's home. She was there for Carolynne's final hours and her death.

Preston Gannaway, born on December 14, 1977, in Charlotte, North Carolina, earned her Bachelor of Arts in fine art photography at Virginia Intermont College. She began her career at the *Coalfield Progress* in rural southwest Virginia and interned at the *Santa Fe New Mexican* and the *Bangor Daily News* of Maine. Gannaway became a photojournalist for the *Concord Monitor* in New Hampshire in 2003 and won several awards.

PATIENT AND DAUGHTERS

Photo, taken January 13, 2007, depicts Carolynne St. Pierre, stricken with terminal liver cancer, surrounded by family members. For nearly three years, the 44-year old mother of three childen had fought the aggressive illness with constant support of her husband and other loved ones. A month ago, doctors at the hospital had told her there were no treatment options left.

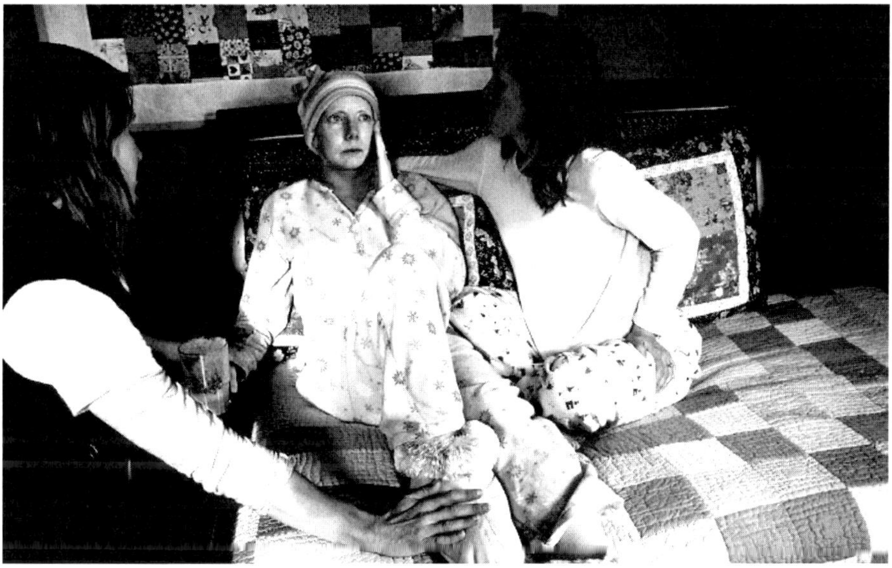

PATIENT AND HUSBAND

Photo, taken January 13, 2007, shows Carolynne's husband Rick who takes a moment to rest beside Carolynne at Concord Hospital. She was admitted in early January because of an infection in her salivary gland.

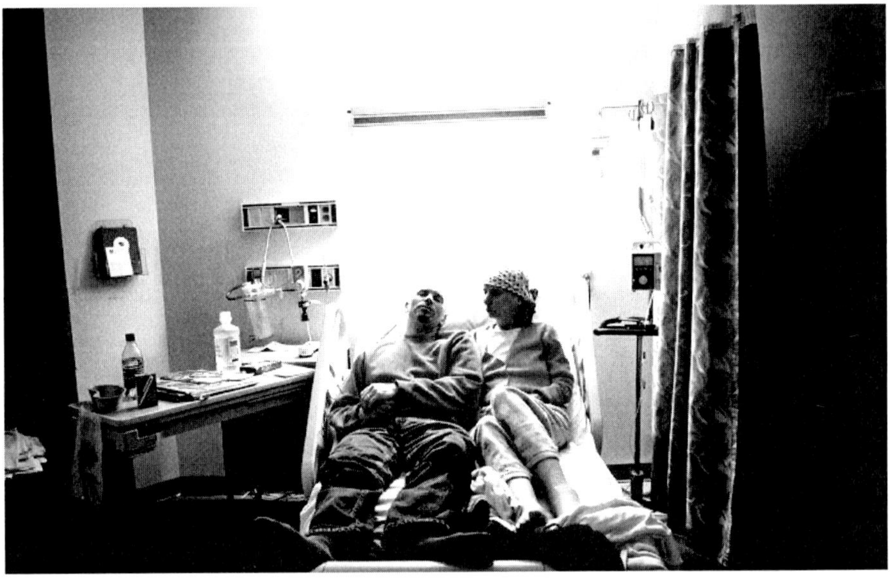

PATIENT JUST DIES

Photo, taken February 13, 2007, shows Rich kissing his wife Carolynne the moment she passes away. Her family comforted her and held her during her final moments, as she hoped for.

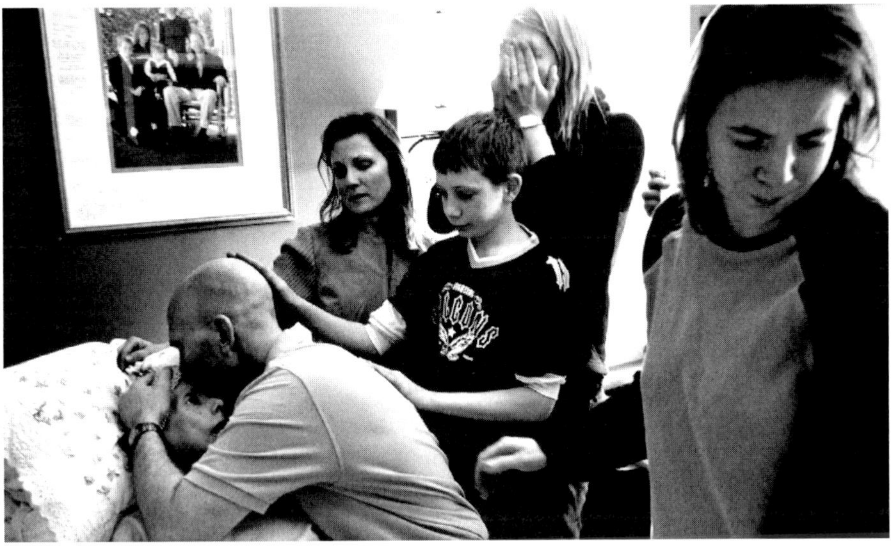

2009 Award

PRESIDENTIAL CANDIDATE OBAMA IN VARIED CONTEXT DURING HIS RALLY IN 2008

by DAMON WINTER, *New York Times*

Carol Guzy of the *Washington Post* came on the jury's shortlist of 2009 for an essay called „Birth and Death." It takes us „to a gruesome place," the report stated, „the epicenter of maternal mortality in Sierra Leone... Guzy is sometimes inches away from her subjects, filling her frame with texture and intensity. The photos have heart, and show great compassion and courage." A similar subject, photographed by Sonya Hebert of the *Dallas Morning-News*, made it on the jury's list, „Hebert takes on a subject few in our culture want to confront", the jurors expressed, „our own mortality... Each person's dying experience is a story unto itself and so is each individual picture." Damon Winter of the *New York Times* had presented to the jury a quite different subject, the mechanics of the presidential campaign, like several other entries in the competition. „Winter went beyond the obvious to capture the essence of Obama as an iconic figure and the mesmerizing impact the candidate had on his followers," the jurors said, „Winter's photographs combine a sophisticated use of light with unusual vantage points and raw emotion."

Damon Winter became the winner „for his memorable array of pictures deftly capturing multiple facets of Barack Obama's presidential campaign." This election was Winter's first deep immersion in campaign coverage. „You always knew", Winter remembered, „that you were watching history." Bill Keller, Executive Editor of the *New York Times*, who had sponsored the Winter exhibit, pointed out: „He let us see the candidate, through the eyes of others: The workers inside a Texas ticket booth; children writing out 'Obama' in the infield dirt in Sarasota; six workers in the Deli Den in Fort Lauderdale, their faces sweaty and smiles electric... Damon Winter, refreshingly new to the campaign trail, rose to the challenge with photos that spoke to the moment and to history."

Damon Winter, born on December 24, 1974, in Elmira, N.Y., grew up in St. Thomas in the United States Virgin Islands and earned a bachelor's degree in environmental science from Columbia University. Before he joined the photo staff of the *New York Times* in 2007, he had worked at the *Los Angeles Times*, the *Dallas Morning-News*, *the Indianapolis Star, the Ventura County Star* as well as for *Newsweek* and *Magnum*.

SPEAKING IN PENNSYLVANIA

Photo, taken October 28, 2008, shows Barack Obama speaking to a crowd in Chester, Pennsylvania, during a chilly rain storm, about a week before election day.

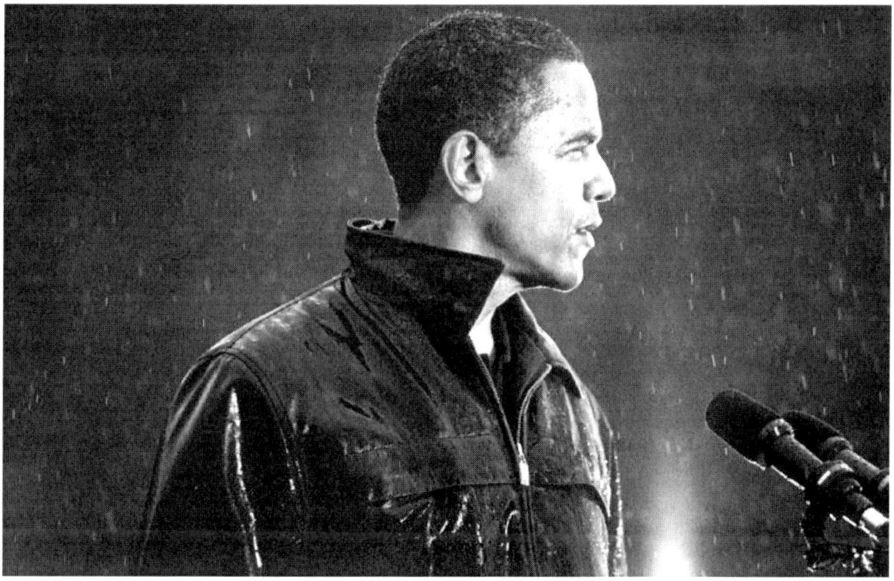

GREETING IN MISSOURI

Photo, taken November 1, 2008, shows Senator Barack Obama and daughters Sasha and Malia at a campaign rally in Springfield, Missouri, three days before election day.

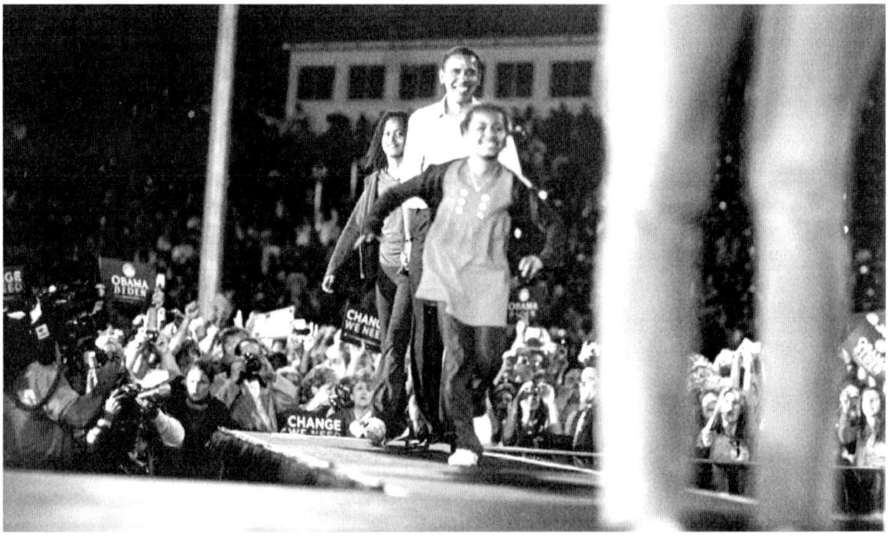

LAUGHING IN FLORIDA

Photo, taken on November 3, 2608, during the Barack Obama Rally in Jacksonville, Florida, the day before election day.

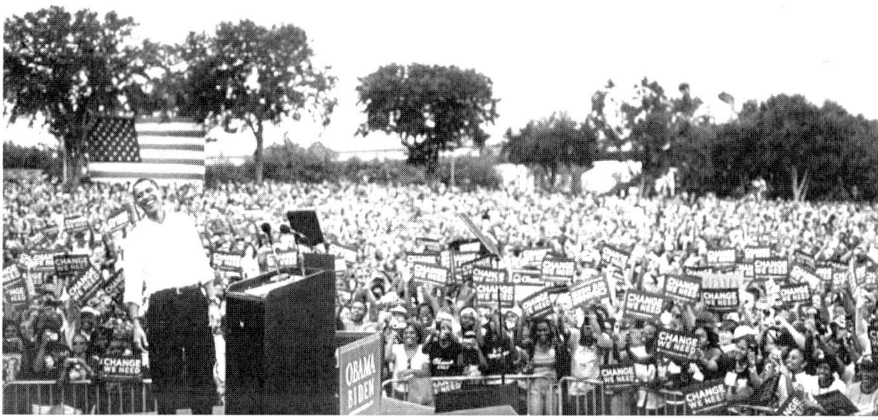

2010 Award

AN AVERAGE YOUNG AMERICAN CONFRONTED WITH MILITARY SERVICE IN THE IRAQ WAR IN 2009

by CRAIG F. WALKER, *Denver Post*

Mary F. Calvert of the *Washington Times*, in the eyes of the 2010 jury, had „told an amazing story in very risky circumstances. In the Democratic Republic of the Congo rape has become a tool of war destroying families and the social fabric of the country. This body of work shows a photographer rising to a great challenge, showing the cultural repercussions of acts of violence against women and the continuing menacing nature of men in the armed forces and society.“ Robert Cohen of the *St. Louis Post-Dispatch*, another finalist, had taken „a heartbreaking contemporary look at one of the central issues in America today, people losing their homes as the economy worsens and they lose their jobs. This story is happening in every city and town in the country... Cohen captured intimate and stressful moments between husbands and wives facing eviction from the last place they have to go. He was engaged and captured the emotional intensity of the situation.“ Craig F. Walker of the *Denver Post*, third on the shortlist, had „captured moments of insight and humor presenting the 27-month journey“ of a young man „as he sought his place in the world. The wide range of emotions seen as a teen tried to become a man, joining the Army and searching for a mate... This story immediately stood out from among a number of exceptional entries“, the jury report said.

So thought the Board and gave the prize to Craig Walker „for his intimate portrait of a teenager who joins the Army at the height of insurgent violence in Iraq, poignantly searching for meaning and manhood.“ The young man, 18-year-old Ian Fisher, was photographed at home and in uniform. The photographer recounted his civilian life that wouldn't lose its grip and the political realities of a war that, upon his arrival at the army, bore no resemblance to the violent conflict he both feared and craved. In short, the photographs captured the story of countless young men who find themselves moved to the military by some combination of patriotism and personal inertia.

Craig F Walker, born on July 14, 1966, in Shreveport, Louisiana, is a graduate of the Rhode Island School of Photography. He began his career in Massachusetts at the *Marlborough Enterprise* and then moved to the *Berkshire Eagle* in Pittsfield, Ma. Walker came to the *Denver Post* in 1998.

ON THE KNEES

Photo, taken July 13, 2008, showes a Reverend laying a hand on Ian Fisher during a babtism ceremony in Denver on his mother's birthday. She said the greatest gift she could ask for was to see her son baptized before he deployed to Iraq.

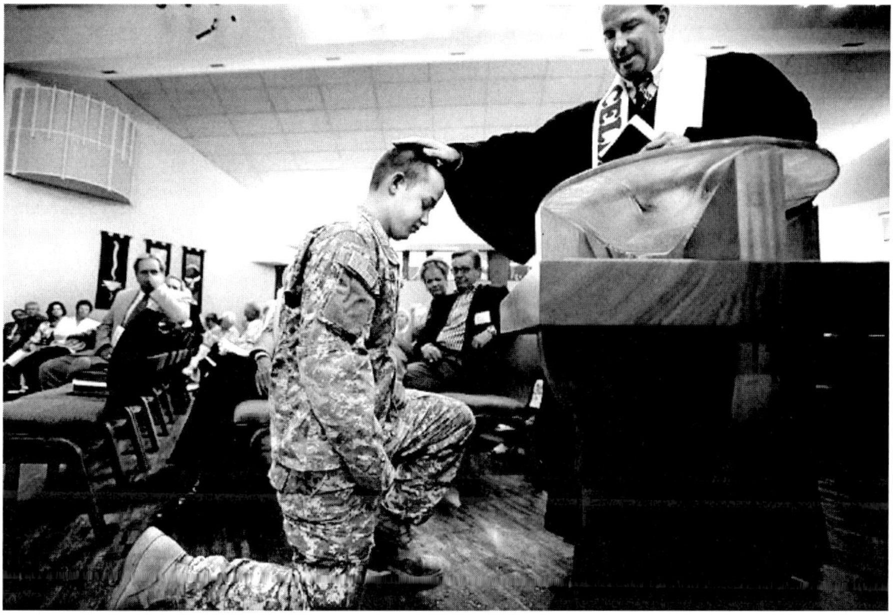

IN THE WAR

Photo, taken November 28, 2008, shows Ian Fisher smoking during his Iraq time. The Iraq by that time was bothing like the Iraq that Ian had envisioned upon enlisting. With violence down, Fisher questioned his purpose.

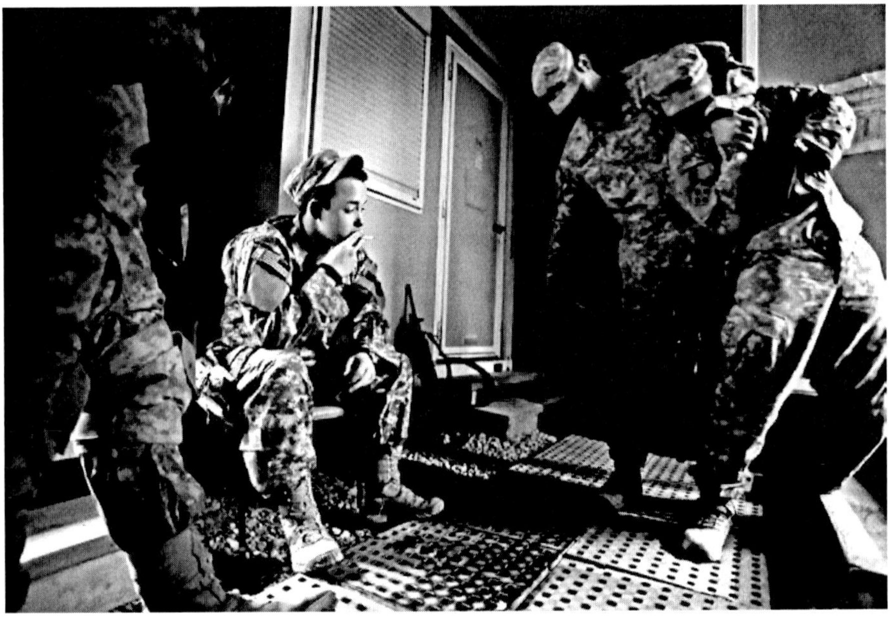

BEFORE THE MARRIAGE

Photo, taken August 24, 2009, shows Ian Fisher and his girlfriend Devin three days after Ian's return from Iraq. They applied for a marriage license at the Jefferson County, Colorado, clerk's office and were married an hour later in a quiet courtroom.

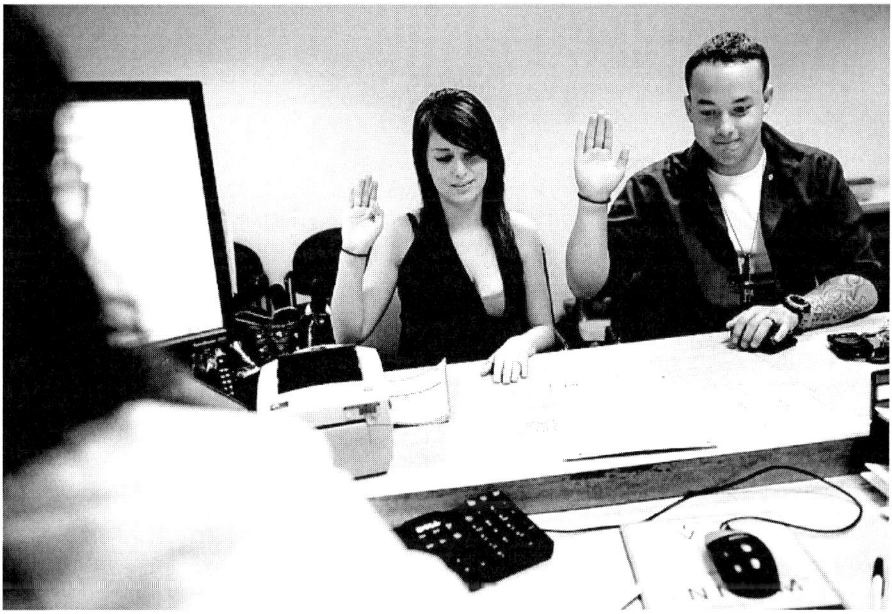

2011 Award

MANY INNOCENT VICTIMS OF GANG VIOLENCE IN THE LOS ANGELES AREA IN 2010

by BARBARA DAVIDSON, *Los Angeles Times*

When the Pulitzer Prize jurors met in March, 2011, they made the following statements about three finalists, mentioning them in alphabetical order by names. Barbara Davidson of the *Los Angeles Times* was praised „for an intimate story of the innocent victims of gang violence in the Los Angeles area. The work is testament to her persevance in telling the story of a comnunity easily overlooked and often misunderstood - a community truly 'Caught in the Crossfire.'" Todd Heisler of the *New York Times* had made it on the shortlist „for the unadorned simplicity of photographs that capture the unique condition of an ill-faced Columbian family born with a high probability of carrying a mutation that causes early-onset Alzheimers."

Greg Kahn of the *Naples Daily News* had impressed the jurors and was placed on the list of finalists „for a comprehensive body of work that chronicles the struggles of professionals out of work, families coping with foreclosure and savvy businessmen who profit from the misfortune of others. His work put a human face on the financial devastation that still ravages the country." The Pulitzer Prize Board was in favor of the work by Barbara Davidson so that she earned the Pulitzer Feature Photography award „for her intimate story of innocent victims trapped in the city's crossfire of deadly gang violence."

Barbara Davidson was born and raised in Montreal, Canada, and holds both Irish and Canadian citizenship. She graduated from Concordia University with a Bachelor of Arts degree in Photography and Film Studies. She started her journalistic career at *The Record* in Ontario, Canada, then she moved to the *Washington Times* and afterwards to the *Dallas Morning News* before she became a staff photographer for the *Los Angeles Times*. She became co-winner of the 2006 Pulitzer Prize for Breaking News Photography with seven fellow staff members for their body of work depicting the pain and chaos after Hurricane Katrina. In 1911, Davidson earned her personal Pulitzer Prize for Feature Photography.

TEN-YEARS-OLD-VICTIM

Photo, published December 29, 2010, depicts ten-year-old Erica Miranda who was shot three times in the back, knee and hip while playing basketball outside her home, now waiting for her bandage to be changed. A young man had walked up to the crowded street corner and started firing a handgun in what police believe was a gang assault.

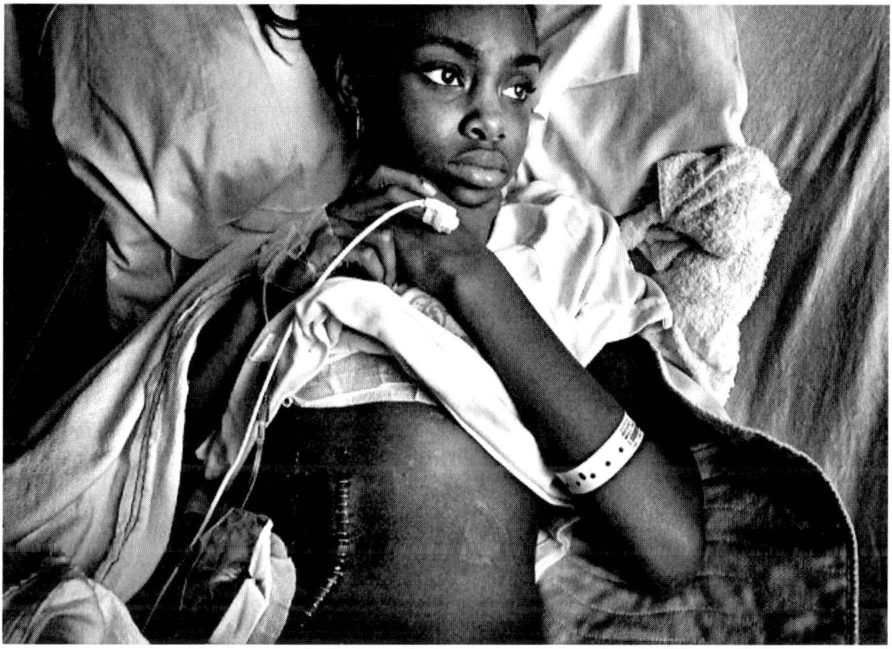

FIVE-YEARS-OLD-VICTIM

Photo, published December 29, 2010, shows a dove released at the memorial service for five-year-old Aaron Jerel Shannon Jr., who died after he was shot in the head by a stray bullet on Halloween. Shannon had been modeling his new Spiderman-costume in the backyard of his South Los Angeles home.

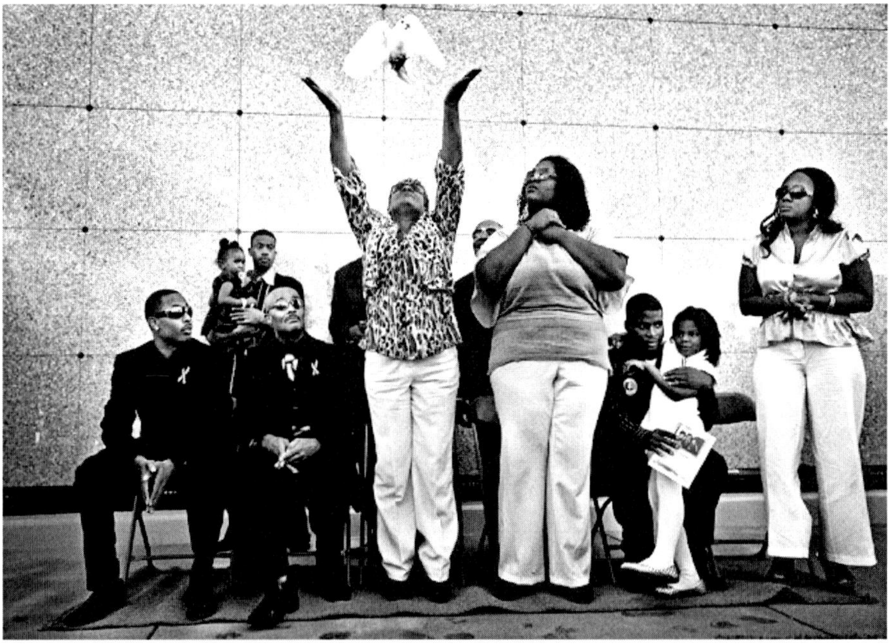

TEN-YEARS-OLD-VICTIM

Photo, published December 29, 2010, shows Jamiel Shaw Sr. kneeling before his ten-years-old son's coffin during funeral services and said: „To see my son lying there dead in a casket to be shot, slaughtered like a dog it makes you want to go out there and just round up everybody that is in a gang and makes you want to be a crime fighter."

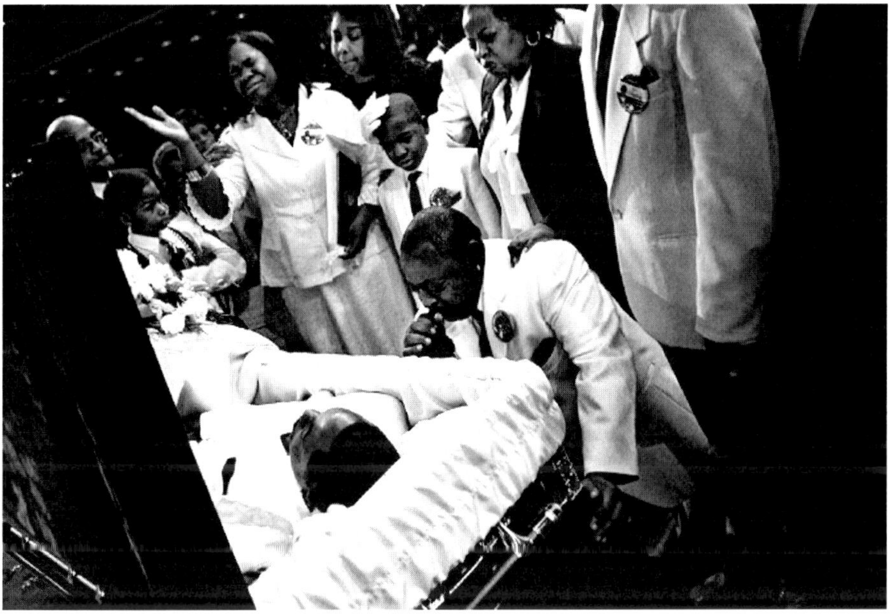

2012 Award

AN EX MARINENE SUFFERING FROM HIS TRAUMATIC EXPERIENCES DURING THE IRAQ WAR IN 2011

by CRAIG F. WALKER, *Denver Post*

First name on the Pulitzer Prize Photography Jury Report of March 2012 was that of Francine Orr of the *Los Angeles Times* „for a poignant and compassionate portrait of the suffering endured by desperate families and misunderstood children who live day-to-day with autism. The great strength in the body of work comes from the photojournalist not exploiting the subjects, but instead using her skills to uncover tiny truths in the lives documented and form a searing and heart rendering depiction of their existence.“ Next on the jury's list had made an *Associated Press* entry by David Guttenfelder, Ng Han Guan and Rafael Wober, called „A View into North Korea - Inside a closed Society.“ In the opinion of the jurors, „this body of work is admirably able to shine a spotlight on what has been and continues to be an obscure and nebulous world not often penetrated by the lens of a free and democratic press.“

Craig F. Walker of the *Denver Post* was represented on the jury's shortlist with a portrait of Scott Ostrum who tried to make peace with his role in the war in Iraq and returned home to the U.S. with a severe case of PTSD. „This extraordinarily intense and intimate work,“ the jury report reads, „captures the profound and personal upheaval of one veteran and gives voice to a significant issue that is facing the men and women of America as they return from far-flung wars with wounds not readily visible. The photojournalist was able to expose these scars of war in fashion that does not demean the subject, but instead enables the reader to share in the rawest of emotions while gaining a deeper understanding of this critical national issue.“ The Board made Walker the Pulitzer Prize winner.

Craig F. Walker, born on July 14, 1966, in Shreveport, Louisiana, grew up in York, Pennsylvania, attended the Rhode Island School of Photography, graduating in 1986. He worked for the *Marlboro Enterprise* and the *Berkshire Eagle* prior to taking a position with the *Denver Post* in 1998. For his portrait of an American teenager in his transition from high school student to soldier Walker earned the 2010 Pulitzer Feature Prize. Only two years later, in April 2012, he won the same award again.

PANIC ATTAC

Photo, published December 29, 2011, shows Brian Scott Ostrom who cups his hand over his mouth as he tries to calm a panic attack at his apartment in Boulder, Colorado. Scott says it has been hard to find meaning in his life since 2007, when he was honorably discharged from the United States Marine Corps.

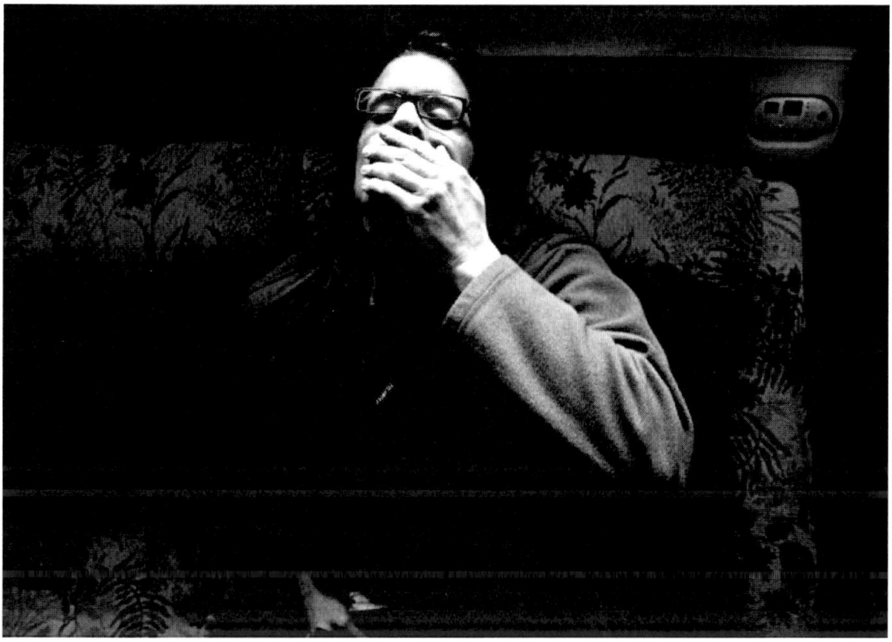

DAILY ATTACS

Photo, published December 29, 2011, shows Scott standing tensely in the kitchen, where his day starts with a panic attack. He said that the day before was „ one long panic attack“ and that this day was starting similarly.

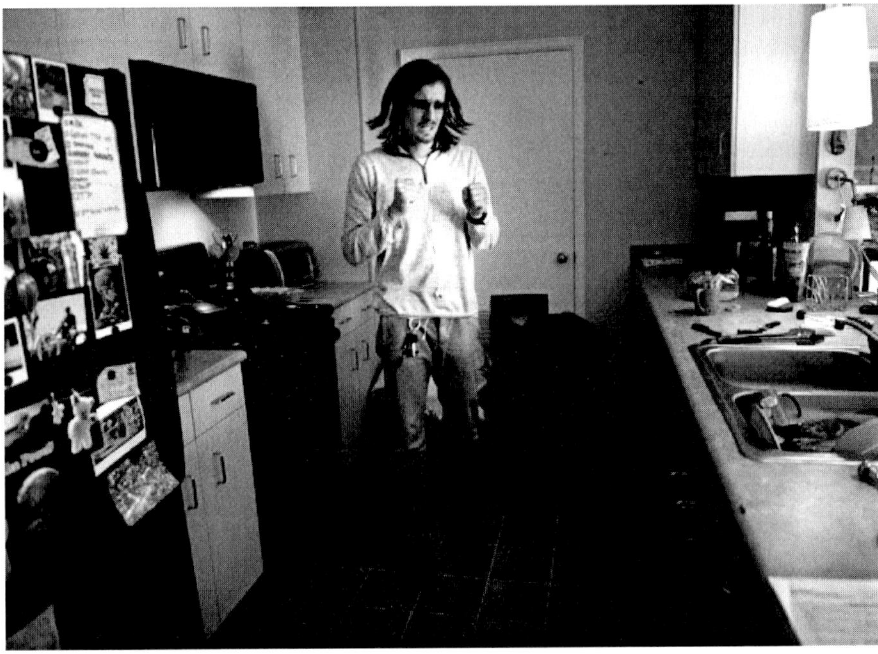

ATTAC RELIEF

Photo, published December 29, 2011, shows Scott waiting outside the pharmacy at the VA Medical Center in Denver. After seeing Scott's mental state, a doctor gave him a prescription for an antipsychotic medication.

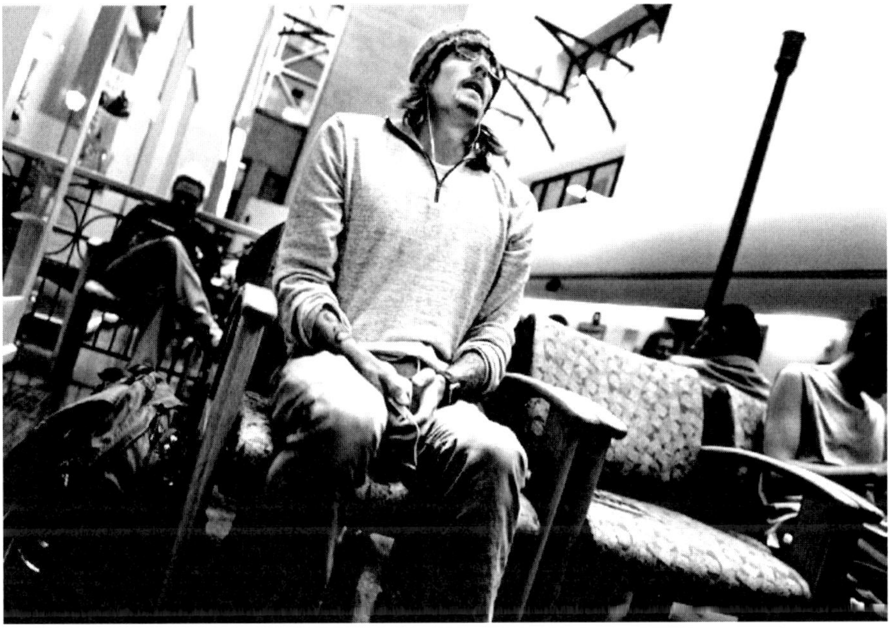

2013 Award

VERY EXCEPTIONAL SNAPSHOT FROM A BATTLE AREA OF SYRIA IN 2012

by JAVIER MANZANO, *Agence France Press*

One of the three finalists placed on the jury's shortlist of March 2013 was Liz C. Baylen of the *Los Angeles Times*. She had learned that millions of Americans were addicted to prescription drugs and she documented this epidemic and its tragic, often fatal, consequences. „This powerful, as well as masterfully executed essay," the jury report states, „shows great commitment by the photographer to telling this story at the highest of levels. She takes the viewers into the most intimate locations, whether it be to a young man's bedroom while his mother changes his diaper after he suffered profound brain damage from a prescription drug overdose."

Renee C. Byer of the *Sacramento Bee*, another finalist, portrayed a grandfather's sorrows, following his daughter's violent death and raising his three grandchildren. „The photographer", the jury report says, „expertly gives the viewer an intimate look into the lives of this family brougt closer together by intense personal tragedy as they struggle through their grief and exhaustion." The third exhibit mentioned on the jury's report only contained one single photo shot by Javier Manzano of *Agence France Press*. „This image", the jurors stated, „made by a single photographer in the harshest and most stressful of situations, perfectly defines what separates the professionals from the amateurs... It is a truly haunting and beautiful image and could easily be considered one of the iconic scenes from the Syrian civil war." For the Board it was no question that this single photo by Javier Manzano should earn the prize.

Javier Manzano was born in 1975 in Mexico but moved to the United States with his family when he was eighteen years old. He worked as a journalist and photographer for advertising agencies and the *Rocky Mountain News* until the newspaper closed its doors in 2009.Afterwards he began working as a freelance photographer for the *Associated Press, Foreign Policy* and other news outlets before he moved to *Agence France Press* where he earned his Pulitzer Prize.

MULTIPLE LIGHTENINGS

Photo, taken October 18, 2012, was shot when two rebel soldiers in Syria guard their position in the Karmel Jabl neighborhood of Aleppo as light streams through more than a dozen holes made by bullets and shrapnel in the tin wall behind them. The dust from more than one hundred days of shelling, bombing and firefights hung in the air. Karmel Jabl is strategically important because of its proximity to the main road that separates several of the main battlegrounds in the city.

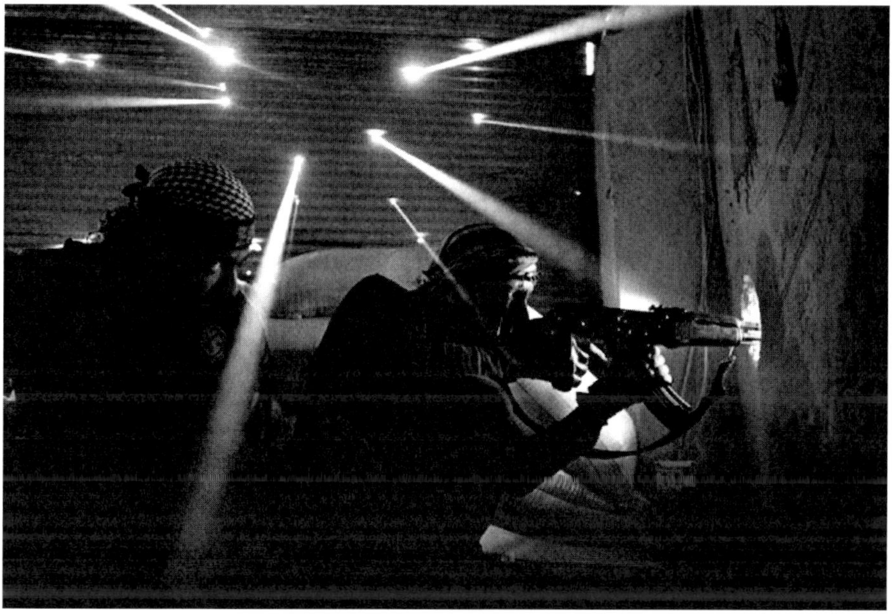

2014 Award

ONE OF MANY VICTIMS OF THE BOSTON MARATHON BOMBINGS IN 2013

by JOSH HANER, *New York Times*

„The complicated story of an Oakland, Calif., school desperate to reverse a tragic statistic," it can be read in the jury report of March, 2014, „is deliberately and artfully told through photographer Lacy Atkins' photos" from the *San Francisco Chronicle*. Josh Haner's photographs from the *New York Times*, in the words of the jurors, „show the incredible efforts by Jeff Bauman to overcome the loss of both his legs. The image of Bauman being rushed from the scene of the (Boston) Marathan bombing became a symbol of the carnage that was seen round the world. Haner had to earn the trust of Bauman and his very protective family before he could start to tell his story of the quiet, isolated and painful struggle of rebuilding his life... The images move you through the heartwarming support of his girlfriend, mother, the Boston community and the fellowship of beer drinking with buddies."

Third on the jury's shortlist was the work by Michael Williamson of the *Washington Post*. According to the jury report he „took on the daunting challenge of visualizing the effects of government politicies on the nation's 47 million food stamp recipients. Williamson illustrated his broad issue with subjects who weren' just on the extremes of society, but were people viewers could identify with ...His year-long journey yielded images that decipt the dual scourge of hunger and obesity, against a backdrop of American visual culture that is both garish and beautiful." The Board voted in favor of Josh Haner and declared him Pulitzer Prize winner.

Josh Haner grew up in San Francisco and graduated from Stanford University in 2002, with a B.S. degree in Symbolic Systems and a B.A. in Studio Art. Working as a photographer, his pictures appeared in magazines like *Fortune, Newsweek, Time* and *Rolling Stones*. After coming to the *New York Times* in 2006, Haner moved up to several photography-related positions and finally became the newspaper's Senior Editor for Photo Technology. He won numerous awards and received the 2014 Pulitzer Prize for Feature Photography.

AMPUTATED LEGS

Photo, taken May 8, 2015, shows Jeff Bauman resting during occupational therapy at Spaulding Rehabilitation Hospital less than a month after having his lower legs blown off in the first of two pressure cooker bombs that exploded at the Boston Marathon.

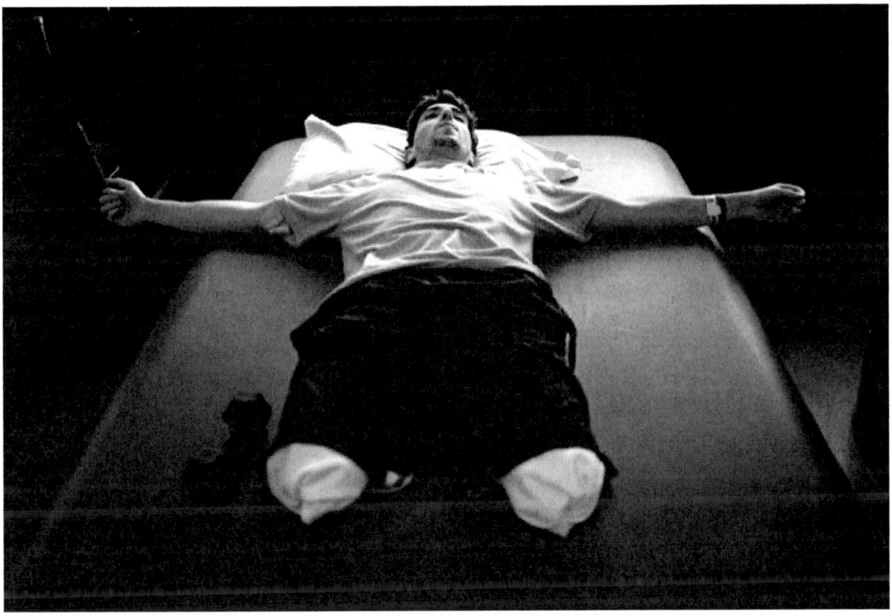

PROTHETIC LEGS

Photo, taken May 31, 2015, shows Bauman at a final fitting for his prothetic legs. He walked on his own for the first time since the day of the marathon. His girlfriend Erin, looked at him and said, 'I love that you're standing right now,' before coming around to steady him and kiss him.

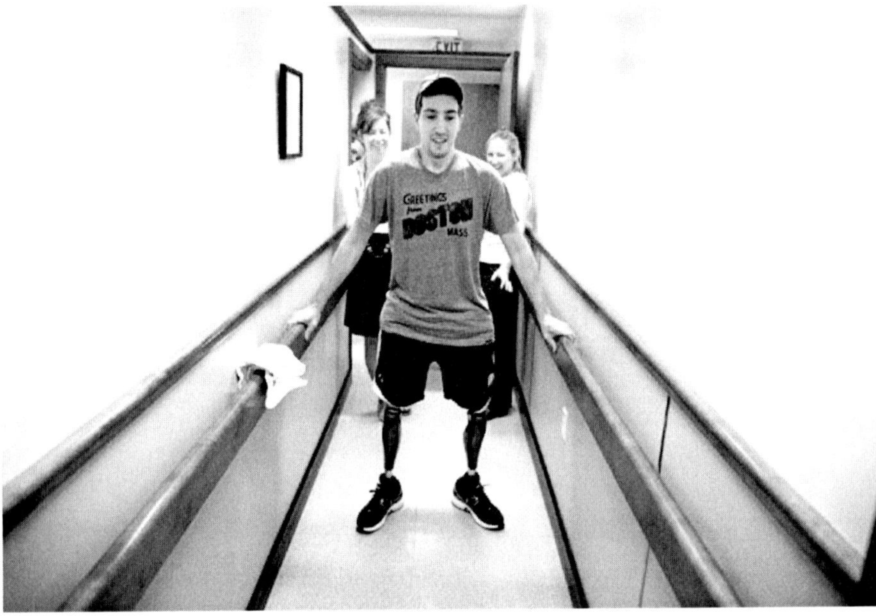

STANDING UPRIGHT

Photo, taken June 24, 2013, shows Bauman when invited by the icehockey team Boston Bruins to appear before Game 6 of the Stanley Cup finals. Jeff did not want to appear, but his mother encouraged him and eventually convinced him.

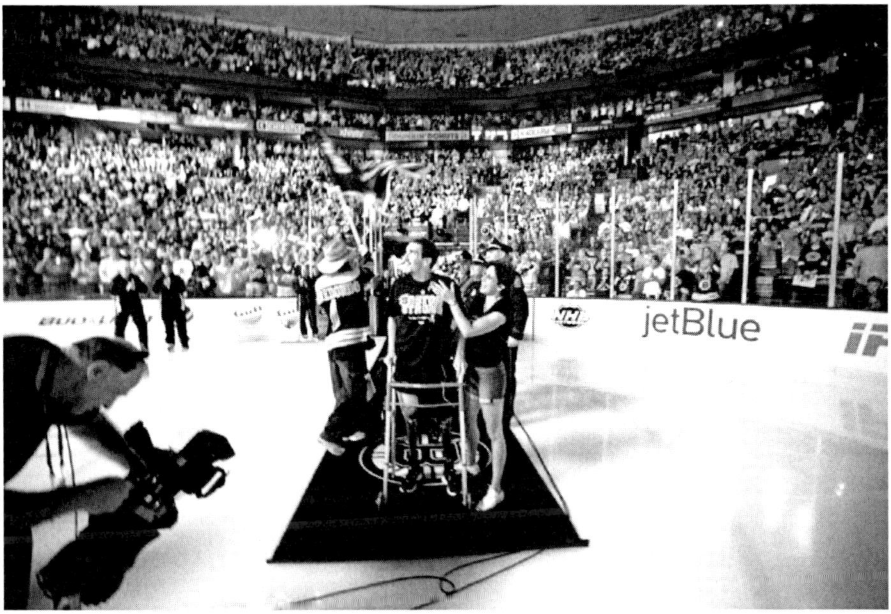

2015 Award

VICTIMS OF THE HIGHLY INFECTIOUS DEADLY EBOLA DISEASE ACROSS WESTERN AFRICA IN 2014

by DANIEL BEREHULAK, *New York Times*

Bulent Kilic of *Agence France Press* was mentioned first on the jury's shortlist of March 2015, stating his merits in these words: „As ISIS stormed the small Kurdish towns on the Syrian/Turkish border, people were on the run. Bulent Kilic's photographs of the exodus paint an intimate picture of the Kurds fleeing for their lives. He not only tells the broader story from the refugee perspective but also documents a country dealing with a war on its border. Kilic's pictures persuade the viewer to care about individual lives... He confronts the unimaginable and captures the unimaginable. You cannot turn away."

Next on the jury's list was the work by Daniel Berehulak of the *New York Times*. „To make intimate photographs and carry the reader into the world of Ebola," the jurors said, „Daniel Berehulak had to get close to the crisis raging around him... His images tell a gripping story of forgotten people who languished mostly alone. His photography, taken with selfless disregard for personal dangers, shed light on an infectious deadly disease spreading across Western Africa and spilling out into the world. Each of Berehulak's photographs transports the viewer into the crippling world of Ebola - one that few journalists volunteered to cover."

Third on the shortlist came an exhibit by Bob Owen, Jerry Lara and Lisa Krantz of the *San Antonio Express-News*. With the imigration crisis boiling over", the jurors explained, „and an upsurge of undocumented women and children flowing into Texas. The photographer... chose to go to the root of the issue, where story begins - Central America... For some of the subjects, the journey ends before that dream is realized... Each photograph has a immensely touching story." Finally, Daniel Berehulak won the award.

Daniel Berehulak was born in 1975 in Sydney, Australia, the son of Ukrainian immigrants. After studying history at the University of New South Wales, he turned to photography in 2000 and visited more than 60 countries covering history-shaping events. He won the 2015 Pulitzer Prize for Feature Photography, and in 2017 followed his second Pulitzer decoration, this time in the Breaking News Photography award ctegory.

SUSPECTED VICTIM

Photo, taken September 5, 2014, shows James Dorbor, 8, suspected of being infected with Ebola. He is carried by medical staff to an Ebola treatment center in Monrovia. The boy, who was brought in by his father, lay outside the center for at least six hours before being seen.

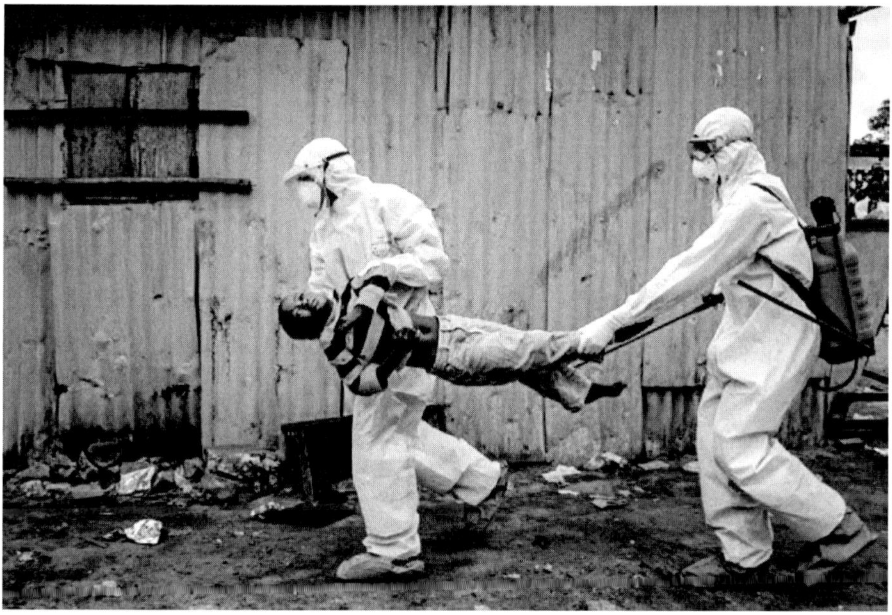

WEEPING BOY

Photo, taken September 18, 2014, shows Eric Gweah, 25, weeping as a burial team removes the body of his 62-year-old father, who died at home, arms thrashing and blood spewing from his mouth, in front of his sons after being turned away at the treatment centers in Monrovia, Liberia.

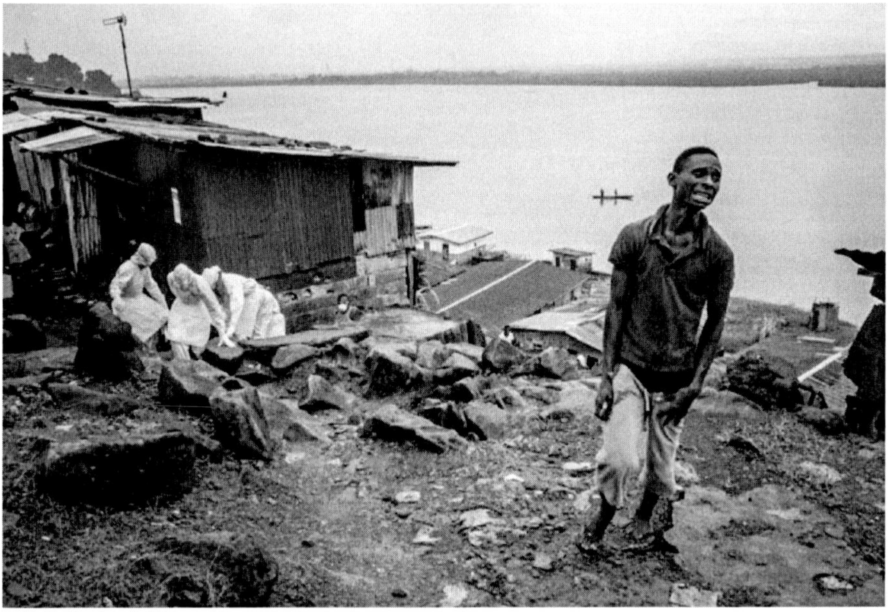

BURIAL TEAM

Photo, taken October 5, 2014, shows a burial team transfering Mama Flomo, a 37-year-old mother of three who died before she reached a center that would treat her, to her grave adjacent to the Bong County unit. She died while giving birth prematurely.

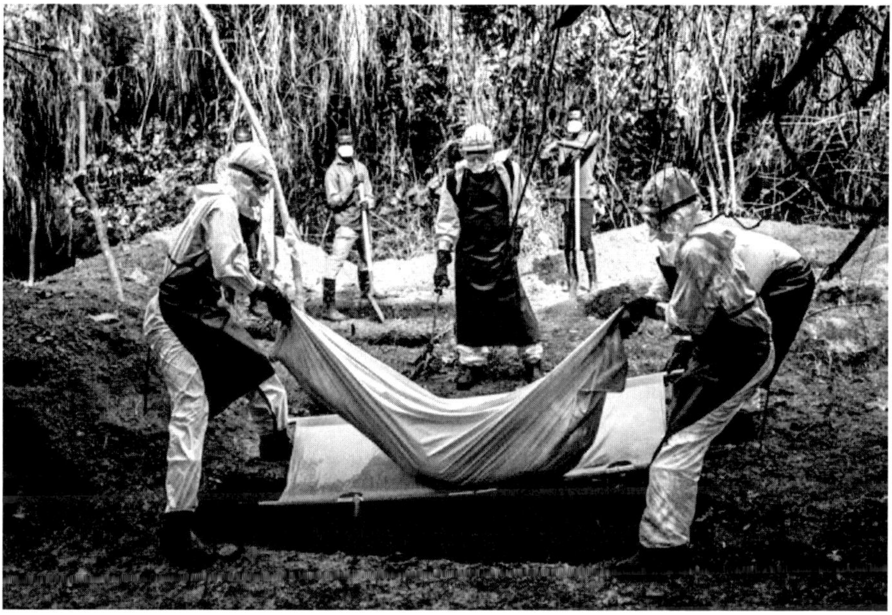

2016 Award

THE FATE OF AN ABUSED POOR YOUNG BOY FROM A PART OF RURAL MAINE IN 2015

by JESSICA RINALDI, *Boston Globe*

When the jurors, according to their report of March 2016, had finished their selection process, the result was very uncommon and had never before occurred in the close to fifty years history in any pohotography category: two different entries by Jessica Rinaldi of the *Boston Globe* had made it on the list of three finalists. Her first exhibit dealt with Opioids that had devastated Massachusetts families, killing an estimated 1,200 people within one year. „Opioids are an epidemic on a national scale," the jury report reads, „but *Boston Globe* photographer Jessica Rinaldi humanizes the Plight of the addict in this powerful story."

The other Jessica Rinaldi entry dealt with a boy who was abused as a child in a poor part of rural Maine. „Unfortunately," the jury report states, „poverty and abuse are an ongoing subject in need of attention. *Boston Globe* photographer Jessica Rinaldi quietly encapsulates the humanity of one boy... who struggles to find his feet after abuse at the hands of those he trusted. He's a boy surrounded by darkness, making light of his situation. This is a story of life - raw and revealing, one boy's story reflects the horrors faced by so many young people across the nation."

Third finalist on the jury's shortlist was an exhibit by the Photography Staff of the *Post and Courier* from Charleston, South Carolina, „for photographs that tell from many angles the story of a racially motivated church shooting and its sorrowful but sometimes also heartening aftermath. The breadth of these images takes us through the aftermath of the tragic murders and provides a comprehensive account of the events that ultimately changed history for one state." The Board decided in favor of one of the Rinaldi entries and gave her the award for the child-abuse story.

Jessica Rinaldi was born in Waterbury, Connecticut, and graduated from Boston University in 2004 with a B.S. in Journalism. She spent ten years as a contract photographer for *Reuters* based in Boston, Dallas and New York City. After she joined the *Boston Globe* in 2010, Rinaldi was named the 2014 Boston Press Photographer of the Year. She earned multiple other prizes before she received the 2016 Pulitzer decoration.

UNHAPPY YOUNGSTER

Photo, published November 8, 2015, shows Strider Wolf who was born poor in rural Maine. When he was two, his mother's raging boyfriend beat him nearly to death. He managed to pull through, ending up in the care of his grandparents who became homeless trying to provide for Strider and his younger brother, Gallagher. In the chaos and deprivation, Strider had a simple and abiding wish: to be loved.

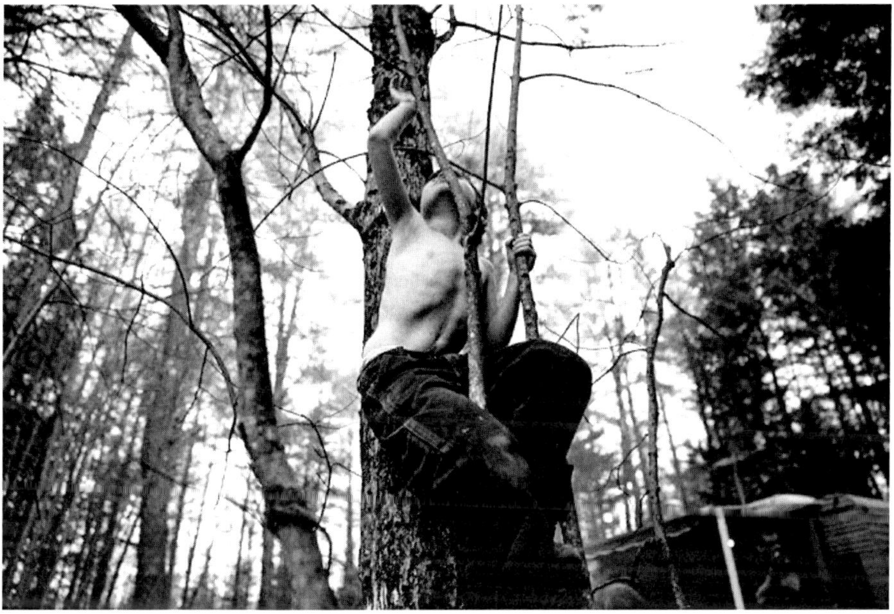

CARRYING WATER

Photo, published November 8, 2015, shows Strider carrying gallons of water filled from a spigot at a campground where his grandparents settled. His grand mother will heat the water on a small stove to do dishes and bathe Strider and his brother with a washcloth.

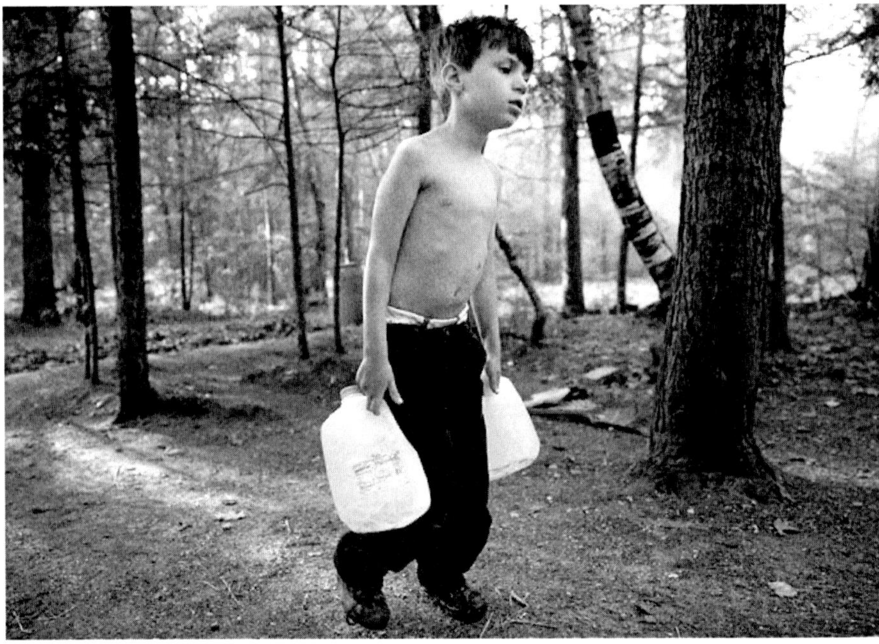

BIRTHDAY PARTY

Photo, published November 8, 2015, shows the first part of Strider's sixth birthday party. While his grandmother drives to Walmart to pick up his cake, Strider is eagerly waiting together with his grandfather that she will return soon so that the party can continue.

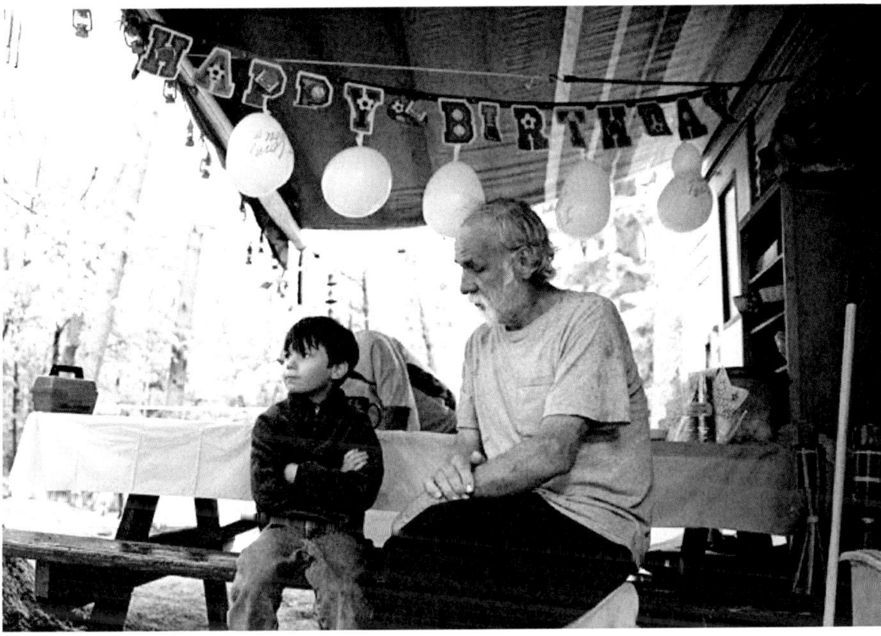

2017 Award

A YOUNG BOY'S PHASES OF RECOVERING AFTER HE SURVIVED A SHOOTING IN CHICAGO IN 2O16

by JASON WAMBSGANS, *Chicago Tribune*

Katie Falkenberg of the *Los Angeles Times* was one of the three 2017 finalist for a photo essay from the front lines of Brazil's war on Zika. „Thousands of women", the jury report of March 2017 states, „were affected by the outbreak of the Zika virus between these women and anyone looking at these pictures will feel the fear, vulnerability, and love between these women and children. It's one thing to show the horrors of the illness, it's another to take photographs that everyone around the world can relate to... These pictures achieve a high level of artis~
try and sophistication."

Jake May of the *Flint Journal*, another finalist, was praised by the jurors „for striking, wonderfully conceived photographs from Flint's contaminated water crisis... This is true community journalism," the jury report adds, „by a dedicated journalist telling a difficult and personal story. The Flint water crisis was initially undercovered. The photographer followed all the twists and turns, telling the personal stories of his community, to following politicians to hold them accountable. Viewers understood what it meant to have to live with a poisoned water supply. These pictures capture both the emotional and physical toll of the crisis."

E. Jason Wambsgans of the *Chicago Tribune*, third among the finalists, was selected „for a portrayal of a 10-year-old boy and his mother striving to put the boy's life back together after he survived a shooting in Chicago ...This ongoing story of Chicago violence is humanized trough its focus on Tavon and his mother... Tavon rediscovers those aspects of his life over time. The story is told from his perspective, a testament to the skill of the photographer at building trust with Tavon. The Pulitzer Prize Board voted in favor of Wambsgans.

E. Jason Wambsgans was born in Detroit, Michigan, and graduated from Central Michigan University. He became a staff photographer of the *Chicago Tribune* in 2002. He spent about four years intensively documenting the problem's gun violence and was honored with the Pulitzer Prize in 2017.

AWAITING SURGERY

Photo, published October 18, 2016, shows Tavon Tanner, who was shot on August on a Chicago Street. He tears up before surgery at Lurie Children's Hospital on Oct. 17 to remove the bullet that ripped through his pancreas, stomach, spleen, a kidney and his left lung before becoming lodged just below his shoulder.

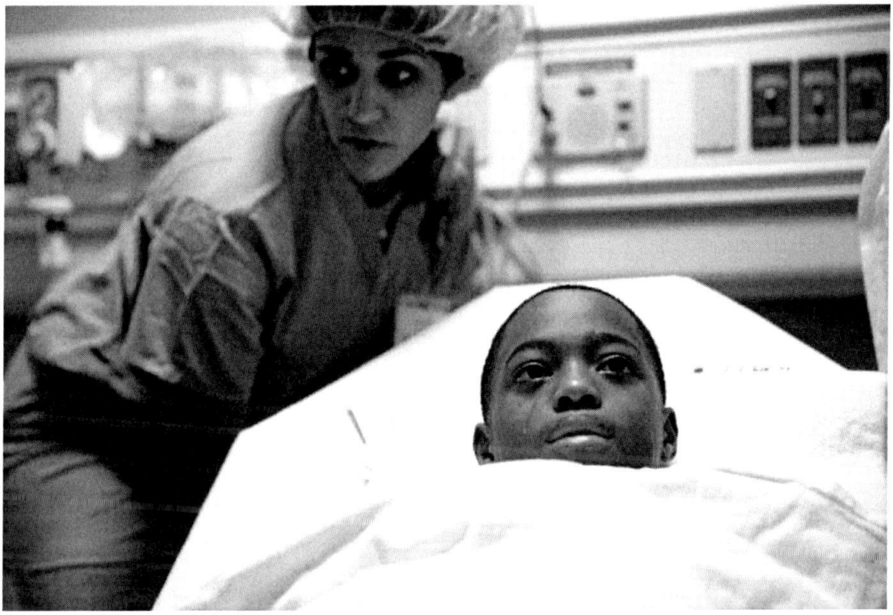

AFTER OPERATION

Photo, published October 20, 2016, shows Tavon Tanner in a wheelchair to recover from the complicated operation. He had to stay in hospital until late October.

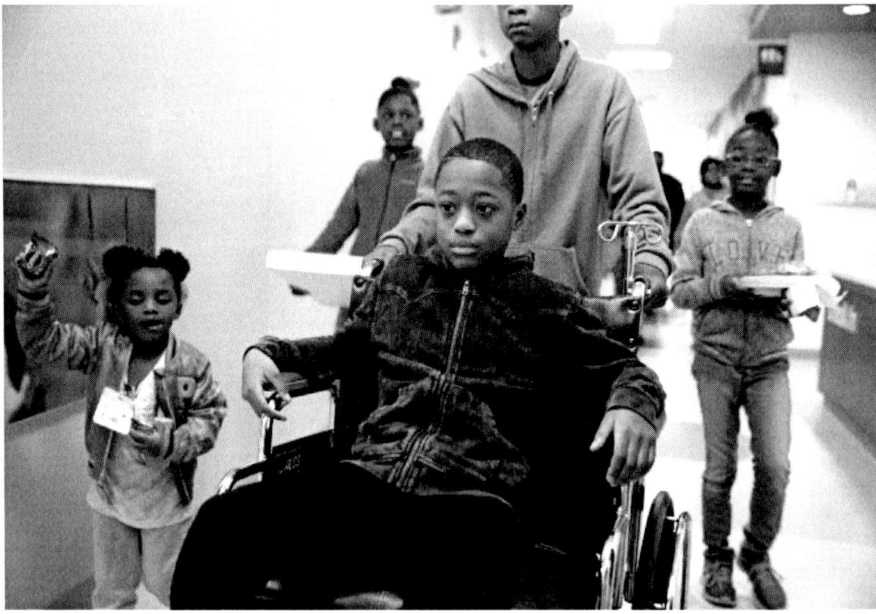

REENTERING SCHOOL

Photo, published November 28, 2016, shows Tavon Tanner returning to school on a part-time basis after the shooting and the operation. He is getting counseling to help him deal with the aftermath.

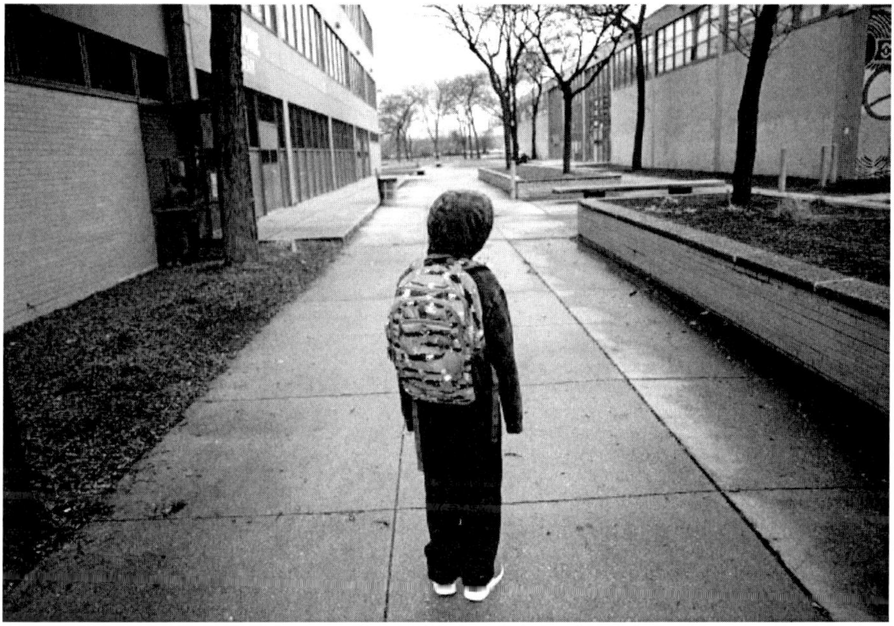

2018 Award

ROHINGYA REFUGEES FACE VIOLENCE IN MYANMAR AND FLEE TO BANGLADESH IN 2017

by ADNAN ABIDI ET AL., *Reuters*

Freelance photographer Kevin Frayer from *Getty Images* was first on the jury's shortlist „for profoundly moving and historic pictures that portrayed Rohingya Muslims with dignity and grace as they fled ethnic cleansing in Myanmar,.. There is a timelessness about them", the jury report of March 2018 adds, „this is a tragedy with a depth of feeling that is almost biblical in its nature. There is a quiet sadness and grace to these images."

Meredith Kohut, freelance photographer of the *New York Times*, was placed second on the jury's list „for wrenching images from the streets, homes and hospitals of Venezuela, where government policies have resulted in widespread malnutrition and starvation of children... It is hard to show hunger," the jury report said, „these photographs are stunning and show the photographer's ability to visually translate the concept. The variety of ways that hunger is depicted, for example the images of women preparing to be sterilized, gives this story power... There is intimacy in many of the images."

Lisa Krantz of *San Antonio Express-News* had made it on the jury's shortlist „for intimate, poetic images that captured the vibrant life of a boy born with an incurable, rare disorder, and his physical, spiritual and emotional journey... The photographer's immersion in this story is striking and it gives a sense of the time and commitment needed to build trust with the family," the jury report explains and then continues: „Documenting the journey of illness is not uncommon in photography, yet this series transcends clichés because of its authen-ticity and without gimmicks."

But the Pulitzer Prize Board members did not think that any of the three finalists on the jury's list of proposals was prizeworthy. So they used their right to find a prizewinner on their own selection. They moved an entry from the Breaking News Photography award category and awarded the Feature Photography Prize to the Photography Staff of *Reuters* „for shocking photographs that exposed the world to the violence Rohingya refugees faced in fleeing Myanmar." The Pulitzer decoration went to the following seven members of the *Reuters* Staff: Adnan Abidi, Danish Siddiqui, Soe Zeya Tun, Mohammad Ponir Hossain, Hannah McKay, Damir Sagolj and Cathal McNaughton.

LEAVING THE COUNTRY

Photo, taken September 11, 2017, shows smoke seen on the Myanmar border as Rohingya refugees walk on the shore after crossing the Bangladesh-Myanmar border through the Bay of Bengal, in Shah Porir Dwip, Bangladesh.

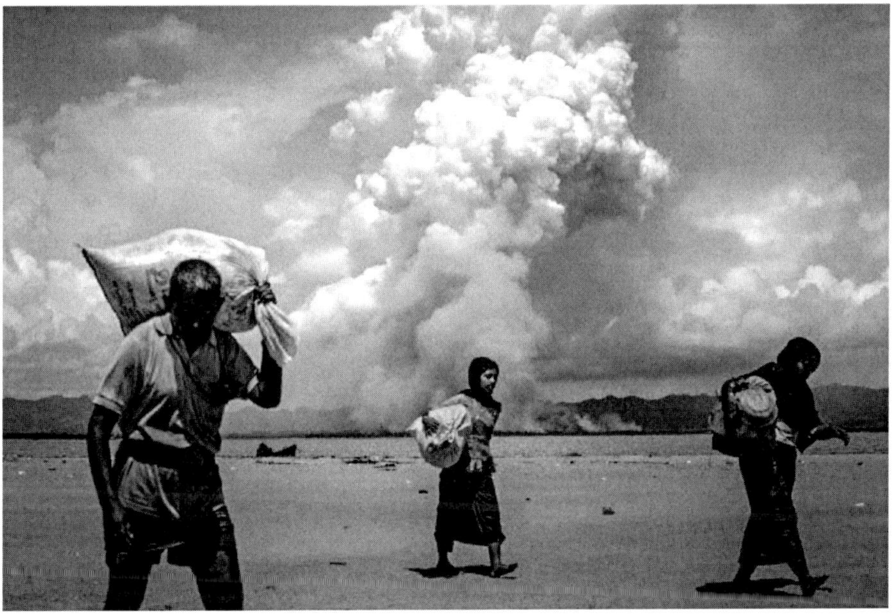

CROSSING A RIVER

Photo, taken November 1, 2017, shows Rohingya siblings fleeing violence hold one another as they cross the Naf River along the Bangladesh-Myanmar border in Palong Khali, near Cox's Bazar, Bangladesh.

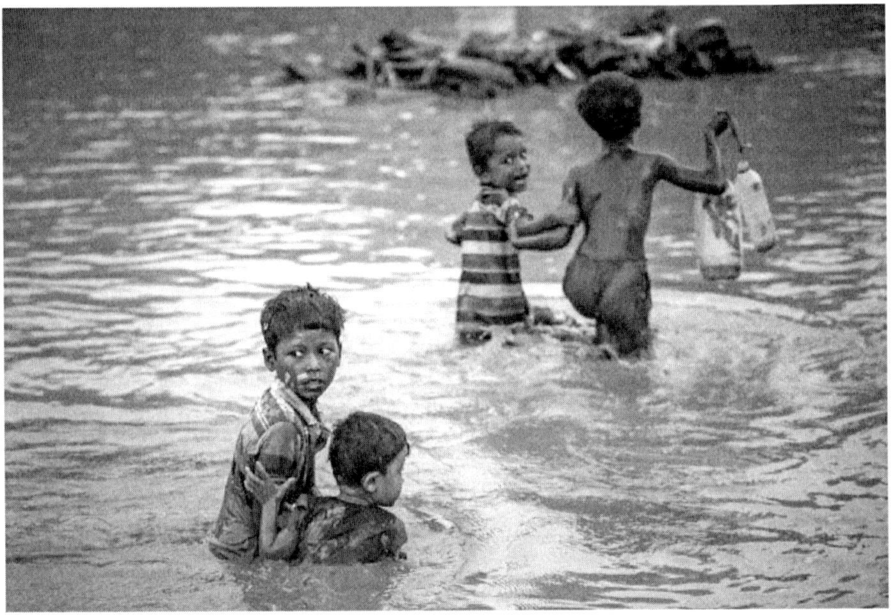

ARRIVING IN BANGLADESH

Photo, taken November 12, 2017, shows Rohingya refugees crossing the Naf River with an improvised raft to reach Bangladesh in Teknaf.

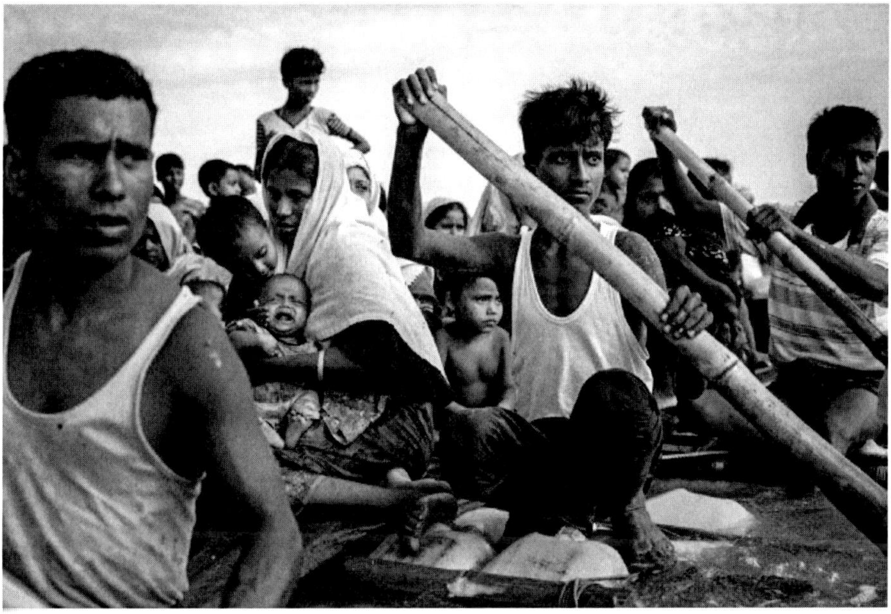

2019 Award

IMPRESSIONS FROM THE BLOODY YEMEN CIVIL WAR AND THE WIDESPREAD FAMINE PROBLEMS IN 2018

by LORENZO TUGNOLI, *Washingtgn Post*

When the 2019 jurors met in March, they put Craig F. Walker of the *Boston Globe* on first rank for his collection of „superb photography and sophisticated visual storytelling with an impeccable narrative edit." Freelance photographers Maggie Steber and Lynn Johnson of *National Geographic* magazine made it on second place for „a dignified photo narrative that detailed a highly unusual organ transplant."Lorenzo Tugnoli of the *Washingpgn Post* was praised for his Yemen famine story „that went byond starving baby photographs to show more depth, complexity, and subtlety without being exploitive... The story had beauty and composure intertwined with devastation. The photographer told a more complete narrative by positioning himself in multiple locations, a move that was a great risk to his personal safety." For the Board members it was clear that Lorenzo Tugnoli deserved the Pulitzer recognition.

Tugnoli had visited Yemen in June and again in November and December 2018, witnessing the harrowing effects of a conflict that had claimed the lives of more than 50,000 people and created one of the worst famines in history. The war started four years ago - four years that had split Yemen in two, with a pro-government coalition supported by Saudi Arabia and United Arab Emirates fighting against a group of rebels, known as the Houthis, for control of the country - in the middle: 28 million Yemenis. In the part of the country most affected by the conflict, malnutrition was so widespread that clinics could only accept the most severe cases. In one such clinic in Hajjah, in northwestern Yemen, a ten-year-old girl came in with her father. „She had big sweet eyes and bone-thin arms, but the clinic could not accept her," Tugnoli said.

Lorenzo Tugnoli was born 1979 in Lugo, Emilia-Romagna, Italy. He worked as a photojournalist in the Middle East before moving to Kabul, Afghanistan, in 2010, where he lived and worked until he moved to Beirut, Lebanon, in 2015. His work was published by the *New York Times*, the *Wall Street Journal, Le Monde, Newsweek* and *Time* magazine. He was a regular contributor of the *Washington Post* where also his Pulitzer Prize-winning photos were published first.

MILITARY HOSPITAL

Photo, published December 31, 2018, shows Militia members and civilians at the entrance of the military hospital in Mokha, Yemen. The city is a few miles south of a front line in the war between northern Shiite rebels and the government of President Abed Rabbo Mansour Hadi. Until last year, the town was ruled by Houthi rebels, but now it was controlled by Saudi-led coalition forces.

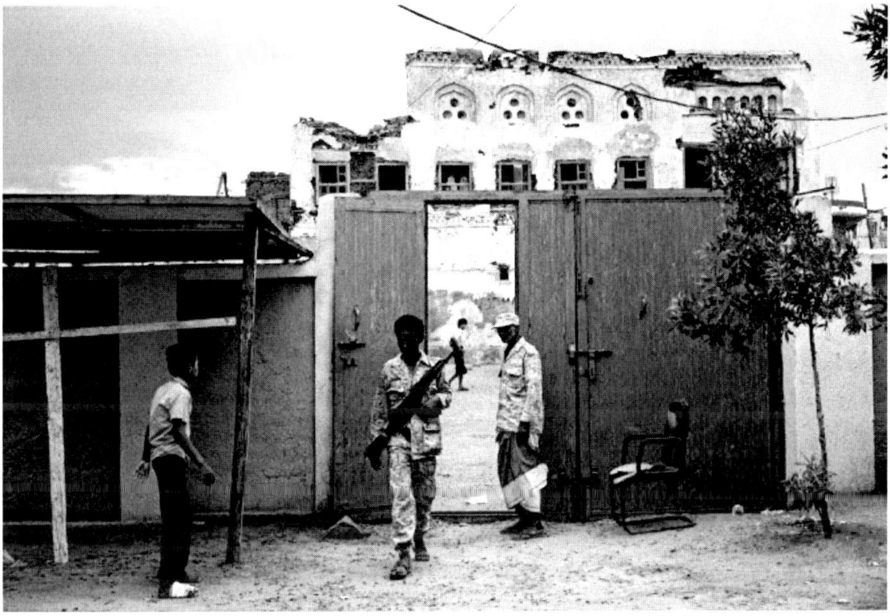

GROCERY STORE

Photo, published December 31, 2018, shows a commander of the Shabwani Elite Forces, walking outside a grocery store in the village of Azzan. The village was under the control of al-Qaeda until a militia liberated the area in December. The militia was aligned with a coalition led by Saudi Arabia and the UAE and was operating in the area in the fight against Al-Qaeda.

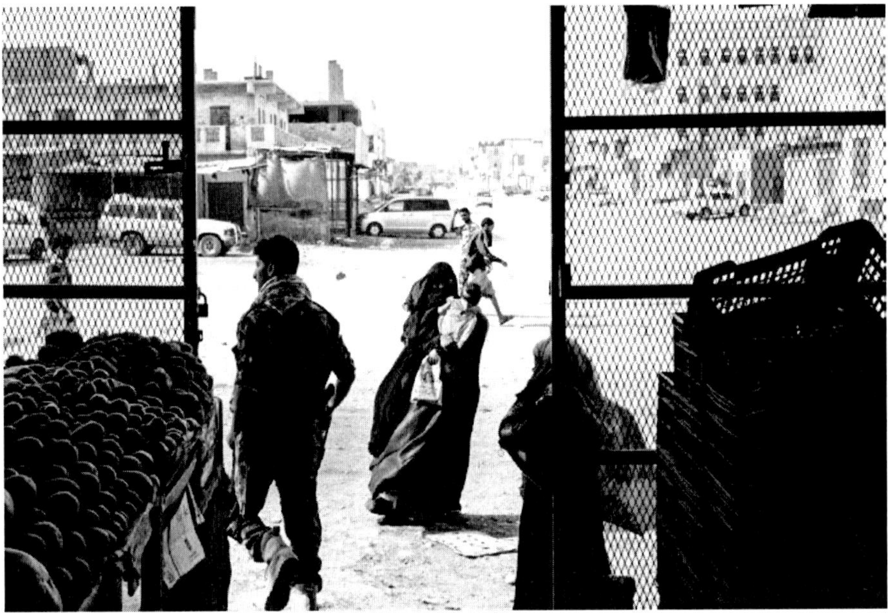

FOOD STANDS

Photo, published December 31, 2018, shows food stands in the Souk al Meleh, in the old city of Sanaa, Yemen. In the capital, Sanaa, as well as in towns across north Yemen, there was no lack of food in the markets. But war and inflation had pushed food costs beyond the reach of many people.

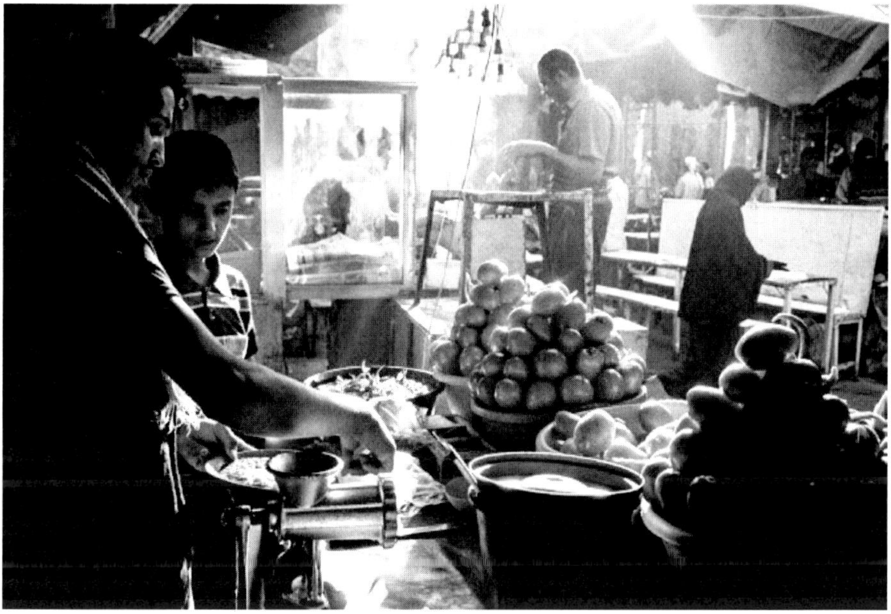

2020 Award

INDIA'S CRACKDOWN ON KASHMIR AND SHUTDOWNS OF PHONE AND INTERNET SERVICE IN 2019

by CHANNI ANAND, MUKTHAR KHAN and DAR YASIN, *Associated Press*

The 2020 jury members made their selections on February 18 and 19 at Columbia University and made these decisions for their shortlist: Eric Clark of the *Boston Globe* was praised „for respectful and compassionate photography of a working Maine family as it falls into homelessness." Mary F. Calvert of the *New York Times* impressed, according to the jury report, „for pictures... that look intimately at male sexual assault survivors in the armed forces." Three photographers of the *Associate Press*, Channi Anand, Mukhtar Khan and Dar Yasin, had shot „striking images captured during a communications blackout in Kashmir depicting life in the contested territory as India stripped it of its semi-autonomy." The Board was so impressed by this entry that it declared the three *AP*-photographers as the Pulitzer Prize winners.

The story of India's crackdown on Kashmir in August 2019 was difficult to show to the world. The unprecedented lockdown included a sweeping curfew and shutdown of phone and internet service. Shaking around roadblocks, sometimes taking cover in strangers' homes and hiding cameras in vegetable bags, the three photographers captured images of protests, police and paramilitary action and daily life. „It was always cat-and-mouse", Dar Yasin recalled, „these things made us more determined than ever to never he silenced." With communications shut down, the journalists had to find out about protests and other news by finding them in person. They took turns roving the streets in and around the regional capital of Srinagar, facing mistrust from both protesters and troops. The journalists were unable to go home for days or even let their families know they were doing okay. It was very hard to file pictures and get them to the *AP* bureau in New Delhi.

Channi Anand, an Indian photographer and resident of Jammu, Kashmir, worked for *AP* since 2000. He had covered India-Pakistan border violence, political developments, stories of displacement after the Earthquake in South Asia. - *Mukhtar Khan* from Jammu and Kashmir had extensively covered the conflict on Kashmir, the Earthquake in South Asia and other stories and earned the 2015 Atlanta Photojournalism award. - *Dar Yasin* from Jammu had studied computer Science and technology in South India and worked for *AP* covering the Kashmir conflict as well as the Afghanistan war and the Rohingya refugee crisis in Myanmar.

SHOUTING WOMEN

Photo, taken August 9, 2019, shows women shouting slogans as Indian policemen fire teargas and live ammunition in the air to stop a protest march in Srinagar, Indian controlled Kashmir.

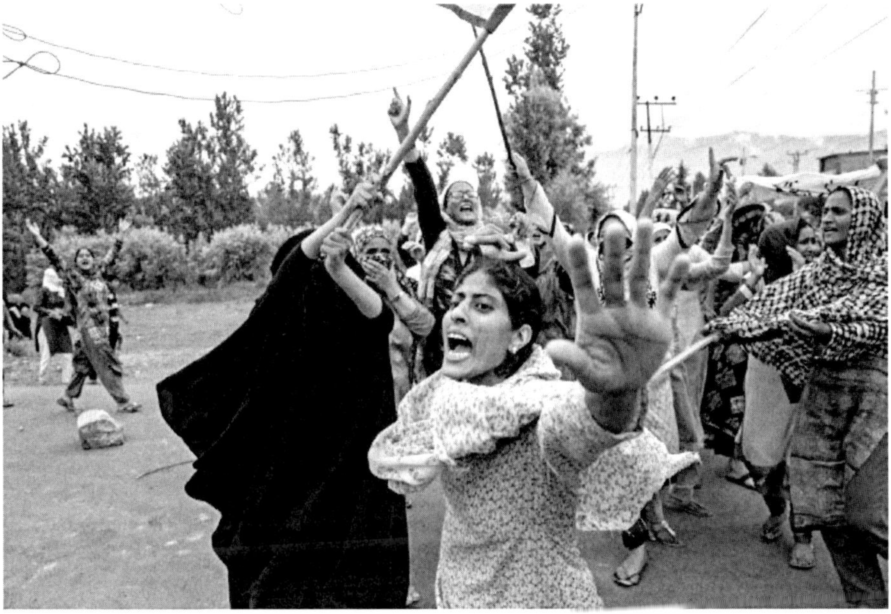

FREEDOM PROTEST

Photo, taken August 23, 2019, shows Kashmiri men shouting freedom slogans during a protest against New Delhi's tightened grip on the disputed region, after Friday prayers on the outskirts of Srinagar, Indian controlled Kashmir.

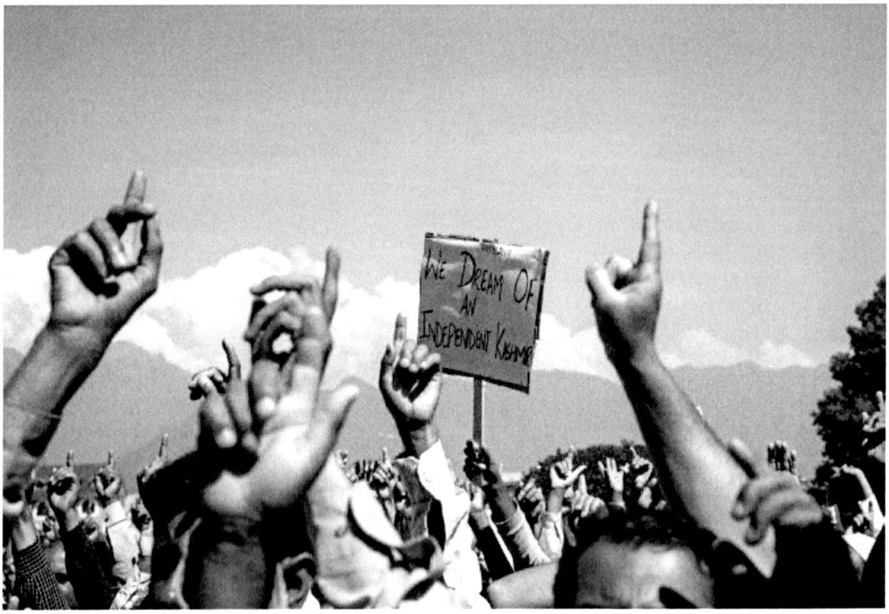

ANGRY KASHMIRIS

Photo, taken October 4, 2019, shows masked Kashmiris shout slogans during a protest after Friday prayers on the outskirts of Srinagar, Indian controlled Kashmir.

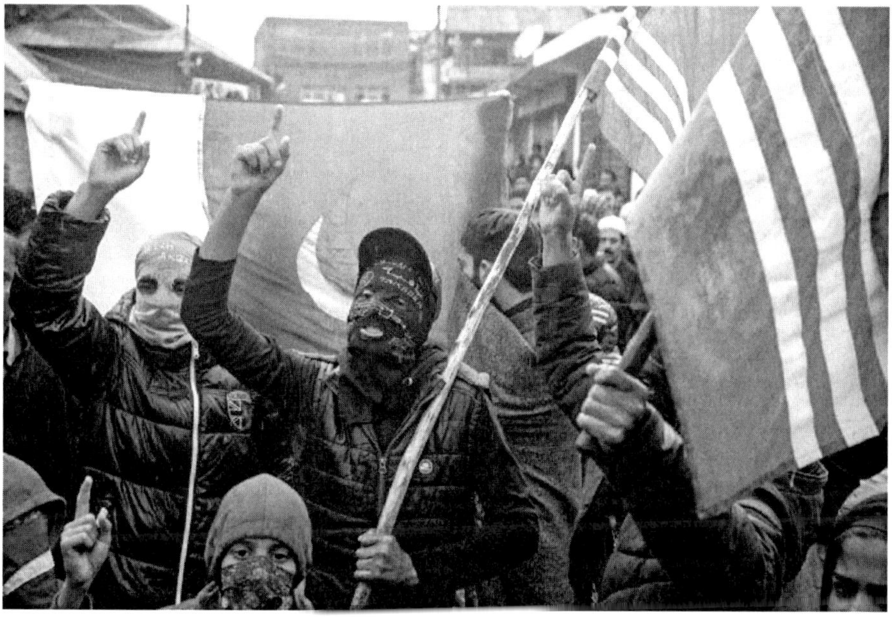

BIBLIOGRAPHY

Unpublished Materials

Media Exhibits

Agence France Press Entry for Javier Manzano, 2013
Âssociated Press Entry for Slava Veder, 1974
Associated Press Entry for J. Ross Baughman, 1978
Associated Press Entry for the Photo Staff, 1993
Associated Press Entry for the Photo Staff, 1995
Associated Press Entry for Alexander Zemlianichenko, 1997
Associated Press Entry for the Photo Staff, 1999
Associated Press Entry for Anand/Khan/Yasin, 2020
Block Newspapers Entry for John Kaplan, 1992
Boston Globe Entry for Stan Grossfeld, 1985
Boston Globe Entry for Jessica Rinaldi, 2016
Boston Herald-American Entry for the Photo Staff, 1979
Chattanooga News-Free Press Entry for Robin Hood, 1977
Chicago Sun-Times Entry for Jack Dykinga, 1971
Chicago Sun-Times Entry for John H. White, 1982
Chicago Tribune Entry for E. Jason Wambsgans, 2017
Concord Monitor Entry for Preston Gannaway, 2008
Dallas Morning News Entry for William Snyder, 1991
Dallas Times-Herald Entry for Erwin H. Hagler, 1980
Dallas Times-Herald Entry for James B. Dickman, 1983
Denver Post Entry for Anthony Suau, 1984
Denver Post Entry for Craig F. Walker, 2010
Denver Post Entry for Craig E. Walker, 2012
Des Moines Register Entry for David Peterson, 1987
Detroit Free Press Entry for Taro M. Yamasaki, 1981
Detroit Free Press Entry for Manny Crisostomo 1989
Detroit Free Press Entry for David C. Turnley, 1990
Ebony Magazine Entry for Moneta Sleet Jr., 1969
Los Angeles Times Entry for Clarence Williams, 1998
Los Angeles Times Entry for Don Bartletti, 2003
Los Angeles Times Entry for Carolyn Cole, 2004
Los Angeles Times Entry for Barbara Davidson, 2011
Louisville Courier-Journal and Times Entry for Staff, 1976
Miami Herald Entry for Michel duCille, 1988
Newark Star-Ledger Entry for Matt Rainey, 2001

Newhouse News Service Entry for Stephanie Welsh, 1996
New York Times Entry for Kevin Carter, 1994
New York Times Entry for Photo Staff, 2002
New York Times Entry for Damon Winter, 2009
New York Times Entry for Josh Haner, 2014
New York Times Entry for Daniel Berehulak, 2015
Palm Beach Post Entry for Dallas Kinney, 1970
Philadelphia Inquirer Entry for Larry C. Price, 1985
Philadelphia Inquirer Entry for Tom Gralish, 1986
Reuters Entry for the Photo Staff, 2018
Rocky Mountain News Entry for Todd Heisler, 2006
Sacramento Bee Entry for Renée C. Byer, 2007
San Francisco Chronicle Entry for Deanne Fitzmaurice, 2005
Topeka Capital-Journal Entry for Brian Lanker, 1973
United Press International Entry for Toshio Sakai, 1968
United Press International Entry for Dave Kennerly, 1972
Washington Post Entry for Matthew Lewis, 1975
Washington Post Entry for Guzy/Williamson/Perkins, 2000
Washington Post Entry for Lorenso Tugnoli, 2019

Jury Statements

Feature Photography Jury Report, March 7, 1968, 2 pp.
Feature Photography Jury Report, March 7, 1969, 2 pp.
Feature Photography Jury Report, March 5, 1970, 3 pp.
Feature Photography Jury Report, March 4, 1971, 2 pp.
Feature Photography Jury Report, March 9, 1972, 1 p.
Feature Photography Jury Report, March 8, 1973, 1 p.
Feature Photography Jury Report, March 7, 1974, 4 pp.
Feature Photography Jury Report, March 7, 1975, 1 p.
Feature Photography Jury Report, March 5, 1976, 1 p.
Feature Photography Jury Report, March 4, 1977, 2 pp.
Feature Photography Jury Report, March 6, 1978, 1 p.
Feature Photography Jury Report, March 6, 1979, 1 p.
Feature Photography Jury Report, March 4, 1980, 2 pp.
Feature Photography Jury Report, March 3, 1981, 2 pp.
Feature Photography Jury Report, March 2, 1982, 1 p.
Feature Photography Jury Report, March 8, 1983, 1 p.
Feature Photography Jury Report, March 7, 1984, 1 p.
Feature Photography Jury Report, March 5, 1985, 1 p.

Feature Photography Jury Report, March 4, 1986, 1 p.
Feature Photography Jury Report, March 4, 1987, 1 p.
Feature Photography Jury Report, March 1, 1988, 1 p.
Feature Photography Jury Report, Febr. 28, 1989, 1 p.
Feature Photography Jury Report, March 6, 1990, 1 p.
Feature Photography Jury Report, March 5, 1991, 1 p.
Feature Photography Jury Report, March 4, 1992, 1 p.
Feature Photography Jury Report, March 2, 1993, 1 p.
Feature Photography Jury Report, March 1, 1994, 1 p.
Feature Photography Jury Report, March 7, 1995, 3 pp.
Feature Photography Jury Report, March 5, 1996, 3 pp.
Feature Photography Jury Report, March 5, 1997, 3 pp.
Feature Photography Jury Report, March 8, 1998, 3 pp.
Feature Photography Jury Report, March 3, 1999, 3 pp.
Feature Photography Jury Report, March 1, 2000, 3 pp.
Feature Photography Jury Report, March 7, 2001, 3 pp.
Feature Photography Jury Report, March 6, 2002, 3 pp.
Feature Photography Jury Report, March 5, 2003, 3 pp.
Feature Photography Jury Report, March 3, 2004, 3 pp.
Feature Photography Jury Report, March 2, 2005, 3 pp.
Feature Photography Jury Report, March 8, 2006, 3 pp.
Feature Photography Jury Report, March 7, 2007, 3 pp.
Feature Photography Jury Report, March 4, 2008, 3 pp.
Feature Photography Jury Report, March 3, 2009, 3 pp.
Feature Photography Jury Report, March 3, 2010, 3 pp.
Feature Photography Jury Report, March 9, 2011, 3 pp.
Feature Photography Jury Report, March 2012, 1 p.
Feature Photography Jury Report, March 2013, 1 p.
Feature Photography Jury Report, March 2014, 1 p.
Feature Photography Jury Report, March 2015, 2 pp.
Feature Photography Jury Report, March 2016, 1 p.
Feature Photography Jury Report, March 2017, 1 p.
Feature Photography Jury Report, March 2018, 1 p.
Feature Photography Jury Report, March 2019, 2 pp.
Feature Photography Jury Report, March 2020, 2 pp.

Published Materials

Bates, J. Douglas, The Pulitzer Prize - The Inside Story of America's Most Prestigious Award, New York 1991.

Blumenfeld, Harold, The 1980 Pulitzer Prize Pictures - An Insider's Look, in: Popular Photography, July 1980.

Brennan, Elizabeth A./Elizabeth C. Clarage, Who's Who of Pulitzer Prize Winners, Phoenix, Az. 1999.

Brian, Denis, Joseph Pulitzer - A Life, New York 2001.

Chapnick, Howard, Behind the Pulitzer Prize Controversy, in: Popular Photography, June 1979.

Columbia University, The Pulitzer Prizes - Winners, 1917 to the Present, including nominated finalists, 1980 to the Present, New York 2019.

Durniak, John, The Pulitzer Puzzle, in: Popular Photography, October 1984.

Fischer, Heinz-Dietrich: Acclaimed Press Coverage of Latin American Countries - Pulitzer Prize winning Articles, Cartoons and Photos, Vienna - Zurich 2018.

Fischer, Heinz-Dietrich: Ambitious Newspaper Sports Journalism - Pulitzer Prize winning Articles, Cartoons and Photos, Vienna - Zurich 2020.

Fischer, Heinz-Dietrich: Coverage of Political Occurrences in Asia - Pulitzer Prize Winning Articles, Cartoons and Photos, Berlin - Zurich 2015.

Fischer, Heinz-Dietrich: Facets of the Vietnam War in American Media - Pulitzer Prize winning Articles, Books, Cartoons and Photos, Vienna - Zurich 2019.

Fischer, Heinz-Dietrich: Key Images of American Life - Pulitzer Prize winning Pictures, Berlin - Zurich 2015.

Fischer, Heinz-Dietrich: Medical and Health-Related Coverage in Print-Media - Pulitzer Prize winning Articles, Books, Cartoons and Photos, Vienna - Zurich 2020.

Fischer, Heinz-Dietrich: Picture Coverage of the World. Pulitzer Prize winning Photos, Berlin 2011.

Fischer, Heinz-Dietrich: Sports Journalism at its Best - Pulitzer Prize Winning Articles, Cartoons and Photographs, Chicago 1995.

Fischer, Heinz-Dietrich: The Pulitzer Prize Century - All Winners and their Merits 1917-2016, Vienna - Zurich 2017.

Fischer, Heinz-D./Erika J. Fischer: Complete Biographical Encyclopedia of Pulitzer Prize Winners 1917-2000, Munich 2002.

Fischer, Heinz-D./Erika J. Fischer, Complete Historical Handbook of the Pulitzer Prize System, 1917-2000 - Decision-Making Processes in all Award Categories based on unpublished Sources, Munich 2003.

Fischer, Heinz-D./Erika J. Fischer, Der Pulitzer-Preis - Konkurrenten, Kämpfe, Kontroversen, Berlin 2007.

Fischer, Heinz-D./Erika J. Fischer: The Pulitzer Prize Archive - Press-Photography Awards 1942-1998, Munich 2000.

Hohenberg, John, The Pulitzer Diaries - Inside America's Greatest Prize, Syracuse, N.Y., 1997.

Hohenberg, John, The Pulitzer Prizes - A History of the Awards in Books, Drama, Music, and Journalism, New York - London 1974.

Hohenberg, John, The Pulitzer Prize Story - News Stories, Editorials, Cartoons, and Pictures, New York - London 1959.

Hohenberg, John, The Pulitzer Prize Story II - Award Winning News Stories, Columns, Editorials, Cartoons, and News Pictures, 1959-1980, New York 1980.

Klyman, Julius H., Photography Awards, in: Columbia Library Columns (New York), Vol. VI/No. 3, May 1957.

Laub, Gerhard J., Joseph Pulitzer - Schöpfer der modernen amerikanischen Tagespresse, PhD dissertation, University of Vienna, Austria, 1960.

Leekley, Sheryl/John Leekley, Moments - The Pulitzer Prize Photographs, New York 1982.

Morrison, Mary E., The Pulitzer Prizes in Journalism, 1917-1985 - A Guide to the Microfilm Edition, Ann Arbor, Mi., 1986.

Rothmyer, Karen, Winning Pulitzers - The Stories Behind Some of the Best News Coverage of Our Time, New York 1991.

Rubin, Cyma/Eric Newton, Capture the Moment - The Pulitzer Prize Photographs, New York 2007.

Seitz, Don C., Joseph Pulitzer - His Life and Letters, New York 1924.

Siebert, Horst, Pulitzer als Journalist und Verleger, PhD dissertation, University of Munich, Germany, 1956.

Swanberg, William A., Pulitzer, New York 1967.

Topping, Seymour, Joseph Pulitzer and the Pulitzer Prizes, in: Brennan/Clarage: Who's Who of Pulitzer Prize Winners, Phoenix, Az., 1999, pp. VII-XIV.

Heinz-Dietrich Fischer

KEY IMAGES OF AMERICAN LIFE

Pulitzer Prize Winning Pictures

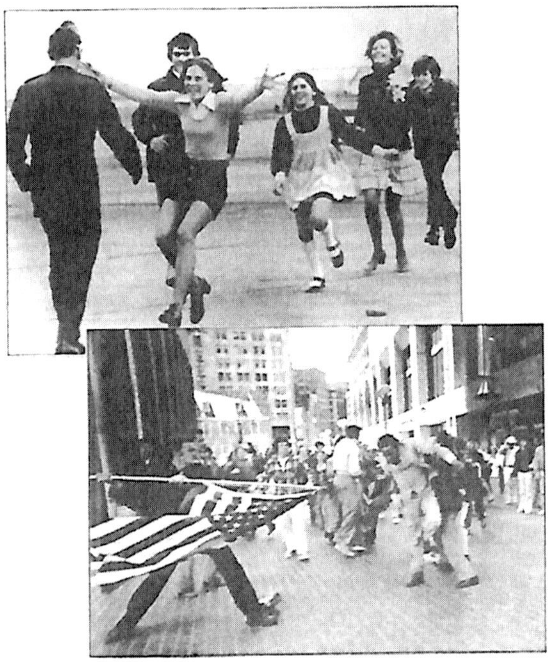

Pulitzer Prize Panorama No. 9

LIT